Windows NT and UNIX Integration

Gene Henriksen

MACMILLAN
TECHNICAL
PUBLISHING
U·S·A

Windows NT and UNIX Integration

By Gene Henriksen

Published by:
Macmillan Technical Publishing
201 West 103rd Street
Indianapolis, IN 46290 USA

Composed in SABon and MCPdigital by Macmillan Computer Publishing

Printed in the United States of America
2001 00 99 98   4 3 2 1

Interpretation of the printing code: The rightmost double-digit number is the year of the book's printing; the rightmost single-digit, the number of the book's printing. For example, the printing code 98-1 shows that the first printing of the book occurred in 1998.

Library of Congress Cataloging-in-Publication Number 97-80989

ISBN: 1-57870-048-5

Warning and Disclaimer

This book is designed to provide information about integrating Windows NT and UNIX. Every effort has been made to make this book as complete and as accurate as possible, but no warranty or fitness is implied.

The information is provided on an as-is basis. The authors and Macmillan Technical Publishing shall have neither liability nor responsibility to any person or entity with respect to any loss or damages arising from the information contained in this book or from the use of the discs or programs that may accompany it.

Publisher   *Jim LeValley*

Executive Editor   *Linda Ratts Engelman*

Managing Editor   *Caroline Roop*

Acquisitions Editors
Jane Brownlow
Karen Wachs

Development Editors
Lisa M. Gebken
Kitty Wilson Jarrett

Project Editor
Brian Sweany

Copy Editor
Susan Hobbs

Indexer
Sandra Henselmeier

Technical Editors
David Blank-Edelman
Brian D. Keegan

Market Reviewer
David W. Egan

Team Coordinator
Amy Lewis

Manufacturing Coordinator
Brook Farling

Book Designer
Gary Adair

Cover Designer
Aren Howell

Production Team Supervisor
Tricia Flodder

Production Team
Betsy Deeter, Joelynn Gifford, Kelly Maish, Gina Rexrode

About the Author

Gene Henriksen is a private consultant and software developer who teaches courses on Windows NT at Microsoft Training Centers and UNIX at SCO Training Centers. With more than 15 years of experience with the UNIX operating system, he has been using Windows NT since the first version was introduced. Gene is a Microsoft Certified Systems Engineer (MCSE), Microsoft Certified Trainer, SCO UNIX Advanced Certified Engineer (ACE), SCO UNIX Instructor, and is also certified to teach Solaris. Gene contributes to both *Windows NT Magazine* and *Windows Magazine*.

With more than 20 years in the field of computers, Gene has worked with a wide variety of systems, ranging from electronic posting machines using paper tape and ledger cards to mainframes. His work experience includes two years in Germany developing UNIX-based software for the U.S. Army and occasional trips to Europe, Honduras, and the Dominican Republic. He was educated at North Carolina State University before computer science was a degree option, with additional work at Old Dominion University and Christopher Newport University in computer science.

Gene speaks at conferences across the country, including SCO's 1996 Worldwide Systems Engineering conference on UNIX/Windows integration and SCO's 1997 Forum in Santa Cruz on Advanced File and Print Server. Gene is also part of the SCO beta test group for UnixWare 7. In his private consulting business, several companies use Gene as their emergency support person. His customer base ranges from very small companies to Fortune 500 and U.S. Government installations and networks, who need help primarily with UNIX and Windows. He also writes for one of his client's quarterly publications on the subjects of UNIX and NT.

About our technical reviewers...

These reviewers contributed their considerable practical, hands-on expertise to the entire development process for **Windows NT and UNIX Integration.** *As the book was being written, these folks reviewed all of the material for technical content, organization, and flow. Their feedback was critical to ensuring that* **Windows NT and UNIX Integration** *fits our reader's need for the highest quality technical information.*

David W. Egan is an engineer and a Microsoft Certified Trainer with 20 years of programming and operating system experience. After receiving a BASc in engineering in 1978 from the University of Toronto, David started his career working in the oilfield industry performing computerized geological downhole formation testing in North and South America. After this David was programming in Assembler and C for several years, providing worldwide support for the CP/M operating system on a proprietary Z80 PC. David then attained a two-year lecturing position at a college in southeast Asia in the Department of Communications and Electrical Engineering, teaching programming and hardware design. This led to four years as Digital Equipment Corporation's VMS and UNIX instructor of system management, internals programming, programming languages, CASE tools, and PC connectivity, as well as security and performance tuning of these operating systems. David has since been writing course material and technical books, as well as consulting and teaching VMS, UNIX, and NT for the past six years.

David lives with his wife and two children in the Vancouver, British Columbia area where they enjoy hiking, camping, biking, roller blading, hockey, squash and running in between frequent trips abroad.

Brian D. Keegan has 18 years of technical support and product development experience in the computer industry. Upon receiving a BSc in Physics from the University of Birmingham, England, Brian went to work as a programmer on IBM 3780 and 3270 terminal emulation products. After one year, Brian transferred to a technical support role, a career path that he followed for the next 14 years. While working in technical support, Brian developed an in-depth knowledge of computer networking solutions across a broad range of networking technologies. He has recently returned to the product development environment as a software engineer and technical lead on Windows networking products.

Currently, Brian is a Senior Software Engineer at Santa Cruz Operation, Inc. where he and his group are focused on providing Windows remote file and print services for SCO UNIX systems. He lives in Santa Cruz, California, with his wife and baby daughter. In his free time, he enjoys cycling, skiing, and hiking.

Trademark Acknowledgments

Dedication

This book is dedicated to my parents.

To my mother who is technologically challenged and refers to the mouse as "the rodent." Her love of good books was passed on to me, and I thank her for that.

In memory of my father who always encouraged me to do what I loved. I wish he were alive to see this book. I have sorely missed him and his advice.

Acknowledgments

Before attempting to write this book, I wondered why authors always thanked the editors. Now I know. I would like to thank Linda Engleman for having the faith that I could write this book. I would like to thank Jane Brownlow for suffering through getting me to finish chapters on time and juggling the table of contents as we found new directions. Thanks to Karen Wachs who took Jane's place when Jane was transferred to a new arena within Macmillan. Thanks to Kitty Jarrett and Lisa Gebken for the editing of this work. If a book was compared to a ship with the author as the engine, the editors would be the rudder. As the book finishes the long journey, they are the tugboats that nudge it into place.

I would also like to thank the technical reviewers David Egan, Brian Keegan, and David Blank-Edelman. They provided a fresh viewpoint when all I could see were the details.

To all the software vendors who provided copies of their software and technical support—without your support there would have been no book. In particular, I would like to thank Dave Trowbridge and Peter Auditore at Hummingbird. Peter gave of his time freely in discussing the future of UNIX to NT file and printer sharing. Dave made sure the software went out overnight to help keep me on schedule.

Brian Keegan at SCO has been a constant source of information on SCO's Advanced File and Print Server. Dave Ewart at SCO has kept me up to date on VisionFS and took the time in Santa Cruz to cover the details of application rejuvenation. David Wight of SCO in Leeds, England provided help with TermVision.

Jenell Kheriaty at Syntax sent whatever I requested in spite of her boss' question about my email being one of those "crazy Internet relationships." Writing a book becomes a series of crazy Internet relationships. Her tech support people provided several hours explaining the intricacies of TotalNet.

Thanks go out to Nick Wells at Caldera for the copy of Linux, the good people at Sun for a copy of Solaris, and all the other vendors mentioned in this book.

Thanks also to Jim Nichols of Hampton Roads Computer in Newport News for loaner computers and other hardware help.

One note of discord: For all companies that write software for Windows NT and do not include good uninstall utilities, a pox upon you. How many hours are we supposed to spend searching the Registry and the disk drive to find some renegade program that refuses to uninstall?

Most important, I want to thank my wife, Susie, for putting up with the hours I spent at my computer network writing, installing software, writing, sending email, writing, writing, and writing. She helped eliminate those small automatic "correction" features of Word that would occasionally drive me to distraction. (Has anyone found a cure for the aggravating animated paperclip?) Especially, I want to thank her for tolerating the dining room table at the ski condo being covered with my 3-computer network over the holidays while she vacationed and I wrote.

Would I be remiss in not mentioning the two who often provided companionship during those keyboard hours? Lizzie and Hacker, the sibling feral cats that Susie brought home, who love to walk across the keyboard at inopportune times to check out a blinking cursor or moving mouse pointer. They often forced breaks in my writing by butting my "mouse" hand until I gave up and rubbed them.

Thanks to you the reader for taking time to read the book.

Gene

Gene@henriksens.com

Feedback Information

At Macmillan Technical Publishing, our goal is to create in-depth technical books of the highest quality and value. Each book is crafted with care and precision, undergoing rigorous development that involves the unique expertise of members from the professional technical community.

Readers' feedback is a natural continuation of this process. If you have any comments regarding how we could improve the quality of this book, or otherwise alter it to better suit your needs, you can contact us at networktech@mcp.com. Please make sure to include the book title and ISBN in your message.

We greatly appreciate your assistance.

Contents at a Glance

Table of Contents

Introduction

NT and UNIX in Heterogeneous Networks

As an instructor certified to teach both NT and UNIX, I have students continually ask me about connectivity options for UNIX and NT. To the administrator faced with both operating systems and the limited connectivity each provides in its native form to the other, this problem can seem insurmountable. Without an understanding of the issues involved, the administrator may choose a product that is unsuited to the task.

Picking through the many products available may lead to confusion and analysis paralysis. The administrator needs a guide to categories of products, the services offered, and ease of installation and maintenance.

The result of the constant questions from students and clients is this guide to the methods that can be used to share files and printing services on a heterogeneous network. Products in each category are covered to provide the reader with an overview of the scope of connectivity tools available.

Contents of the Book

UNIX and Windows NT are both present in enterprise networks. Each has specific strengths and weaknesses. All estimates of future operating system growth show both UNIX and NT continuing to grow through the end of the forecast period, usually around 2005. Interoperability—file and print sharing—is not a problem that will disappear quickly.

Windows NT is a proprietary product of Microsoft and maintains a common interface across Workstation, Server, Enterprise Server, and Small Business Server. UNIX is an open system specification and different versions are sold by Sun, Santa Cruz Operation (SCO), Silicon Graphics, IBM, ICL, Digital, and so on. Companies like Auspex have created specialized UNIX versions that are tuned to be high-speed file servers. Because of its low price, Linux has a wide following with many Web servers running on Linux.

This book contains many tools for internetworking between UNIX and Windows NT. Why so many different tools? If the only tool you have is a hammer, every problem looks like a nail. Operating systems, programming languages and internetworking products are all tools in the computer professional's toolbox. Picking the appropriate tool and making it work well is what the computer professional does for a living. This book is intended to help with the process.

Part I: Windows NT and UNIX Fundamentals

For the reader whose background is UNIX systems, Chapter 1, "An Introduction to Windows NT," covers the major components of Windows NT and how those components correlate to their UNIX counterparts. User administration, domains and trusts, services and scheduling, disk management and the boot-up and shutdown sequences are detailed.

The Windows NT administrator will want to read Chapter 2, "An Introduction to UNIX," to get a look at three major UNIX variants: Solaris, SCO OpenServer, and Linux. Learn how to manage users and how system services (daemons) are started. Examine the UNIX file system and how its layout varies from Windows NT. Learn how to boot and shut down UNIX.

For the UNIX administrator, Chapter 3, "Microsoft TCP/IP on Windows NT 4.0," covers Windows NT TCP/IP. The chapter takes you through setting up TCP/IP and show you how Microsoft implements common TCP/IP utilities. You learn about DHCP and WINS. The Server Message Block (SMB) file sharing protocol is discussed. In addition, learn about the Browser service: what it does and how to work with it.

UNIX TCP/IP is covered in Chapter 4, "UNIX TCP/IP," for the Windows NT administrator. The files and commands that are used to set up TCP/IP are covered with the common TCP/IP utilities. You learn how NFS file sharing is configured.

Part II: File Sharing Between UNIX and Windows NT

To share files between UNIX and Windows NT, NFS connectivity software can be installed on Windows NT. Chapter 5, "Windows NT-Based Solutions," steps through installation and use of NFS for clients, servers, and gateways.

UNIX products that provide SMB file sharing are available from several vendors and for free by downloading from the Web. Chapter 6, "UNIX-Based Solutions," examines the installation and management of SAMBA, Advanced Server for UNIX, TotalNet, Fusion, and VisionFS, as well as the advantages, and disadvantages of all.

One category of tools that is just becoming available is the thin server, as discussed in Chapter 7, "Thin Server Technologies." Thin servers have a real-time operating system that provides file access to both UNIX and NT but is neither UNIX nor NT. A major advantage of thin servers is price; they are inexpensive. Are they the future? A spokesman for one company said server operating systems are obsolete.

Part III: Printing Between UNIX and NT

Printing between UNIX and Windows NT can be implemented with no additional software. The TCP/IP LPR/LPD protocol is available on UNIX and Windows NT. Learn the setup and use of LPR printing in Chapter 8, "LPR/LPD."

The NFS products covered in the chapter on file sharing also provide printing through PCNFS. In Chapter 9, "Windows NT-Based NFS Print Providers," learn what is necessary to configure, share, and use printers with NFS.

UNIX SMB products provide printing between UNIX and Windows NT. The printing from Windows NT to UNIX is generally straightforward. The details of printing from UNIX to Windows NT printers are not always simple. Learn how to configure each of these in Chapter 10, "UNIX-Based SMB Print Providers."

Part IV: Application Integration

Another new tool is the application broker (discussed in Chapter 11, "Application Brokers"). Application brokers are systems that sit between the client computer and the server computer. The broker hides the application's source. The broker makes the server operating system invisible to the client/user, reducing the need for the user to understand operating system differences.

Telnet and X Windows have been around the TCP/IP and UNIX community for quite a while. In Chapter 12, "Telnet and Application Enhancement," see how to configure two X Windows servers. The telnet dumb terminal emulation looks antiquated running on top of a graphical display. Learn how to rejuvenate your applications from adding color and boxes through a complete Windows front end without changing the original application.

Part V: Windows NT and UNIX Tools

The Windows NT Resource Kit and TechNet are two Microsoft products that you should have if you are working with NT. Learn about the utilities included in the Resource Kit, and the differences between the Server and Workstation Resource Kit in Chapter 13, "Microsoft Tools: The Resource Kit and TechNet."

For UNIX administrators working in a Windows NT environment, there is a sudden loss of the familiar tools available at the command line in UNIX. The MKS toolkit will provide a UNIX shell and over two hundred UNIX command line utilities. OpenNT provides a replacement for Windows NT's POSIX environment and provides a UNIX environment acepted by the U.S. Government. This topic is discussed in Chapter 14, "UNIX Tools for Windows NT."

Part VI: Appendixes

Finally, the appendixes—Appendix A, "Products for File and Print Sharing," and Appendix B, "References"—list products, books, and Web sites. Download your own copies and try them yourself.

Conventions Used in this Book

The following conventions are used in this book:

Tip

Tips provide you with helpful ways of completing a task.

Troubleshooting Tip

Troubleshooting tips provide resolutions of some problems you may encounter during deployment.

Warning

Warnings provide you with information you need to know to avoid damage to data, hardware, or software, or to avoid error messages that tell you that you are unable to complete a task.

Author's Note

In these areas, I relate to you personal experiences I've encountered that give you a real-life understanding of a topic.

Part I

Windows NT and UNIX
Fundamentals

Chapter 1

An Introduction to Windows NT

- **Windows NT User Administration**
  Learn how to create and control user accounts, restrict logon hours and workstations, and create user profiles and policies.

- **Using Groups in a Domain**
  Learn how to use groups in domains to reduce administration. Distinguish between local and global groups. Assign resource permissions to groups. Learn how permissions work.

- **Domains and Trusts**
  Learn how to create a domain and use Server Manager to manage the NT computers in the domain. See how trust relationships between domains extend the range of a domain's access to resources.

- **Services**
  See how NT services are started and monitored. Learn how to use the AT command. Monitor tasks and system performance.

- **Disk Drives**
  Learn about the two file systems available on NT. Span multiple disks with a single file system. Learn how to create RAID 1 and RAID 5 for crash recovery.

- **Booting and Shutdown**
  Explore the files that are required to boot on RISC or Intel. Build emergency diskettes to recovery from failure of a mirrored root drive. Learn how to shut down NT properly.

The Windows NT Operating System Overview

At first glance, NT would appear to be an easily managed operating system with an interface that looks like Windows 95 (NT Version 4) or Windows 3.*x* (NT Version 3.51 and earlier). This graphical interface similarity should not be mistaken for proof of management simplicity. Beneath the interface lies a world of complexity, much of which is configured using the graphical interface, but there are still command line requirements and the database known as the Registry.

From the origin of NT, the operating system was single-user and multitasking in nature. Citrix developed a multi-user version to work with thin clients. *Thin clients* are diskless PCs or even old 286-based PCs that perform local display of data while the computing occurs on a server. Popular demand led Microsoft to license the Citrix technology to provide multi-user capabilities in a product named *Terminal Server* that is being released for Version 4 and will be part of Version 5. Terminal Server will provide thin clients the capability to run programs on an NT server, allowing true multi-user capabilities on NT.

The primary method of administering NT is with the Administrative Tools, available through a single point on the Start menu as shown in Figure 1.1.

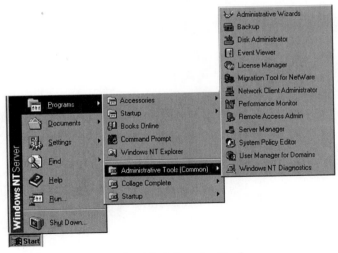

Figure 1.1. *The path on NT 4.0 to the Administrative Tools.*

Where possible, NT utilities are equated to their UNIX equivalents to help the UNIX administrator find similarities in the operating systems.

The UNIX root account has a counterpart in the NT world known as the *Administrator account*. Like root, the Administrator account is the all-powerful login.

An association of computers sharing a single accounts database in NT is known as a *domain*. NT domains are not the same as domains in the Domain Name System (DNS) sense of the word. NT does support DNS, but the domains are not necessarily the same group of computers. The NT domain is somewhat analogous to Network Information Services (NIS). Both have a master computer containing the accounts database and both may replicate that database to other computers.

NT Server can be installed as a domain controller or as a member server. A *member server*, such as NT Workstation, may be part of a domain but plays no role in domain control. Member servers generally fall into two roles: file and print server and application server. Application servers host database applications such as Microsoft SQL Server.

NT uses the *group* concept to manage the large number of users and the rights of these users. Users are assigned to *groups* and groups are assigned *rights* to access resources. There are two types of groups: local and global. Rights can be assigned to users. Microsoft recommends against assigning rights to users in favor of assigning rights to groups to simplify administration.

In the DOS and early Windows operating systems, much of the configuration was controlled by .ini files. These files were initialization files similar in some respects to the .profile or .login files. The system and most applications had .ini files. With NT, Microsoft built a database called the *Registry*. The Registry, in part, consists of information determined at boot time about available hardware as well as tuning and administrative parameters set through the graphical administration tools.

Some settings that may need to be adjusted are only available through the Registry. When editing the Registry, no online help warns of illegal values. The Registry help file is only available on the Resource Kit.

Warning

References to editing the Registry are usually preceded by a warning. Editing the Registry may result in an unbootable system and Microsoft does not guarantee that the system can be rescued.

Remote access, via Point-to-Point Protocol (PPP), is a standard part of NT. With Microsoft Remote Access Service (RAS), it is possible to configure required dialback for security, use multilink to combine multiple telephone lines to a server as a single link, and to implement PPTP, Point-to-Point

Tunneling Protocol. PPTP provides a Virtual Private Network (VPN) over the Internet.

Microsoft has produced a network operating system that includes much more than file and print services. New additions to the operating system are being released regularly.

Windows NT User Administration

User administration on Windows NT is accomplished through the User Manager for Domains on NT Server and User Manager on NT Workstation and member servers. User Manager for Domains updates the domain database and is available on the Primary Domain Controller (PDC) and Backup Domain Controller (BDC), while User Manager updates the local database for member servers and NT workstation.

The Accounts database includes both user and computer accounts. All NT computers that are members of the domain must have a computer account. This is true for the PDC, BDC, member servers, and workstations. The collection of login and security information is referred to as the *SAM (Security Accounts Manager)*. The SAM database is maintained on domain controllers, not on local servers. Each computer that is not a domain controller has a local SAM database.

The role of the PDC is to maintain the master copy of the SAM and periodically replicate the SAM to the BDCs. Both PDC and BDC may authenticate user logins.

The User Manager for Domains is located in the Administrative Tools (Common) submenu of the Start button, as shown in Figure 1.1.

All user accounts are displayed in the window shown in Figure 1.2, even if the domain contains 20,000 accounts. To locate an account, use the scroll bar on the right side of the Username listing.

The Administrator account is created at installation. This account cannot be deleted but it can be renamed for security purposes, and is equivalent to the UNIX root account.

At installation, one of the default user accounts created is Guest. This account is for connections from users who do not have a domain account and who are perhaps members of another domain. Details of the Guest account can be seen by double-clicking the name, which displays the information shown in Figure 1.3.

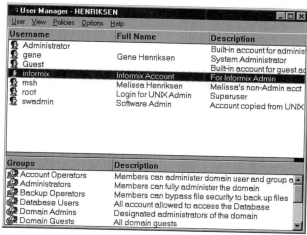

Figure 1.2. *The User Manager for Domains main window.*

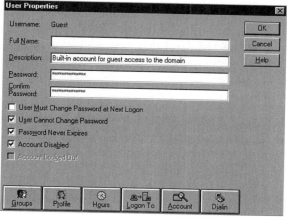

Figure 1.3. *The User Manager for Domains User Properties dialog box.*

Note the capabilities of the User Manager. The administrator may change the username, full name, description, or the password of the account.

User Properties

When a user account is created, a *SID (Security Identifier)* is assigned to the account. The SID, not the username, is the critical component for security. Compared to the UNIX UID, the SID is a long number. Microsoft doesn't give out the formula for SID creation. If a user account is deleted, the SID is retired.

If the user account is re-created, a new SID is assigned. The new username has no relationship to the old username and does not inherit any of the rights, privileges or files of the old username.

The administrator may require the user to change passwords at the next logon, a useful option on initial account creation or when resetting a forgotten password. The administrator can disallow password changes and set the Password Never Expires option. The administrator has the power to disable an account from this screen.

The final option is Account Locked Out. This is not an administrator function, but one used by the security system on login failure. The administrator may unlock the account.

Tip

When installing Arcada Backup Exec and other software that runs as a service (the equivalent of a UNIX daemon process), an account name must be provided for the software to use for login. Do not use the Administrator's account. When the Administrator's account is used, the service will work properly until the password is changed for the Administrator. The service will then not be able to log in at the next system boot. Instead, create a new user and provide a password that would be exceptionally difficult to break. Set the account for Password Never Expires.

A line of additional function buttons at the bottom of the screen provides access to the user controls: Groups, Profile, Hours, Logon To, Account, and Dialin. The discussion on groups is postponed until later in this chapter in the "Using Groups in a Domain" section.

Controlling Users with Account Profiles

Account profiles are used to set standards for account usage. Profiles may be mandatory and may prevent changes in the account setup. Account profiles provide the administrator with a degree of control over users that can simplify the administrator's work, make the user more efficient, and prevent down time.

For accounts used by temporary help, a mandatory profile can prevent the user from changing network connections and screen colors, running unauthorized programs, or making other changes that would alter the environment. By not being able to effect permanent changes, the users will always have the same setup.

Windows NT and Windows 95 use different profile methods, and the profiles must be created on the operating system with which they will be used. Older operating systems, such as Windows 3.1 or Windows for Workgroups, do not support profiles and must use a logon script. Logon scripts may also be used for Windows 95 and NT users.

Figure 1.4 illustrates setting the home directory to the Z drive on a remote server. The home directory may be on the local machine or on a network share. The Home directory does not have the same significance as in UNIX. The NT Home directory is the default location for the File Open and Save As dialog boxes and for applications that do not have a defined working directory.

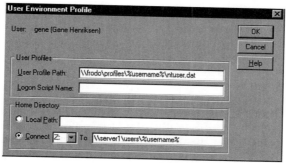

Figure 1.4. *The User Environment Profile dialog box.*

In UNIX, the home directory would store the startup files; the equivalents of .profile and .login are the user profile and the logon script.

Tip

In providing the Home directory path, it is convenient to name home directories for the users that use them. In the path name, use %USERNAME% *to represent the current user, the equivalent of the UNIX* LOGNAME *environment variable.*

Logon Hours Restrictions

The logon hours for individual users may be restricted. In Figure 1.5, the user is limited to logging on from 7 a.m. through 6 p.m. Monday through Friday. This setting prevents users from logging on to the computer during the disallowed hours. Restrictions can be used to keep users off the system during backup. As a security precaution, it keeps users off at unauthorized times.

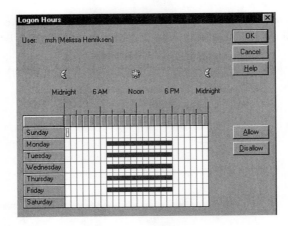

Figure 1.5. *Limiting logon hours.*

The user attempting to log on during disallowed hours receives the message

```
Your account has time restrictions that prevent you from logging on at this
time. Please try again later.
```

This restriction applies to any attempted logon from any computer in the domain. Users logged on at the time logon hours expire receive a message stating the network resource is not available when attempting to connect to a network resource.

Restricting Logons to Specific Workstations

Users can be restricted to specific workstations for logon. The procedure for restricting users is shown in Figure 1.6. By default, a user may log on to all workstations. If restricted, the maximum number of possible workstations is eight.

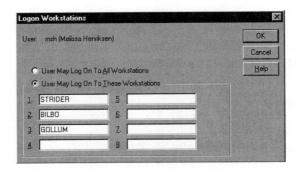

Figure 1.6. *User can log on to all workstations or only the workstations listed.*

Account Information

The Account Information options allow the administrator to select an expiration date for an account. The default is Never. Accounts for users who have been hired for a specific period may be set to expire at the completion of the hire period, as shown in Figure 1.7. Using this option, the administrator does not have to remember to disable the account or change the password when the user's date of completion arrives.

The second option on this screen allows the creation of a Global or Local account. Global accounts are the default. Microsoft's explanation of the Local Account feature is to create a local account for a user who needs access to a specific server and is not a member of the domain to which the server belongs.

Tip

> *When installing software, you may be required to create an account for the software itself. For instance, Informix NewEra requires a local account. Creating a normal, global account for Informix will yield an* Unknown user *error when attempting to use the software.*

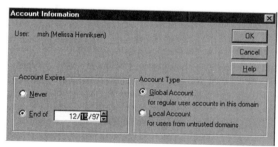

Figure 1.7. *The Account Information dialog box.*

Dialin Permissions

Dialin permissions may be assigned to allow the user access to the domain over RAS, also known as *Dialin*.

Tip

> *If the computer is a domain controller, then the setting is domain wide when setting this option. If the computer is an NT server installed as a member server or an NT workstation, the setting is for the local machine.*

The Call Back option is primarily used for billing purposes (see Figure 1.8). The default is No Call Back. When the option Set by Caller is selected, the server prompts for a telephone number, disconnects the line, and dials the user. Use Call Back to have the billing paid by the server rather than the caller.

Selecting the Preset To option fixes the callback number. This is a nice security feature if the remote user is always at the same location, but would not work well for a mobile user. This feature also limits the use of multilink capabilities because the system can dial only one number. Multilink requires multiple numbers to be dialed. There is one exception to this rule—if the link is a two-channel ISDN line using a single phone number.

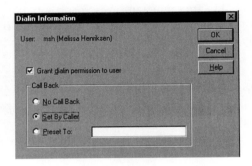

Figure 1.8. *Dialin permissions for a user.*

Policies

The User Manager for Domains menu has a Policies option, which includes four options: Account Policy, User Rights Policy, Audit Policy and a fourth, separated from the first three, Trust Relationships.

Account Policies

Account policies are domain wide. The administrator can override account policies for certain individuals with account settings where the two conflict. The Account Policies dialog box is illustrated in Figure 1.9.

Most of the features in the Account Policy dialog box should be familiar to the UNIX administrator:

- Maximum Password Age ranging from Password Never Expires or Expires in 1 to 999 Days.

- Minimum Password Length ranging from blank passwords to 14 characters in length.

- Minimum Password Age to restrict how often a user can change passwords.

- Uniqueness allows a password history to be maintained. Passwords in the history may not be repeated. The maximum history is 24.

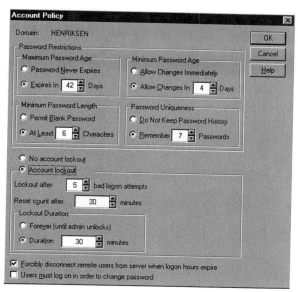

Figure 1.9. *Account policy settings.*

Accounts can be locked out automatically after a set number of failed login attempts. The maximum failed attempts is 999 before lockout, in which case the No Account Lockout option may be a better choice. After failures occur, the count can be reset after a fixed period of time. This time ranges from 1 to 99,999 minutes, which computes to about 69.5 days.

Once an account is locked out, the lockout can remain Forever or until the administrator unlocks the account (remember the Account Locked Out box on the Account main dialog box in Figure 1.2). The lock can be set to automatically clear after a duration of a set period. The maximum duration is 99,999 minutes.

At the bottom of the Account Policy dialog box is one option that should not be overlooked. If accounts are set to limit the logon hours (see Figure 1.5), the system will not forcibly disconnect them at the completion of the logon period. Checking the Forcibly Disconnect Remote Users from Server When Logon Hours Expire option disconnects the shared resources. The affected user receives a notice stating the logon time has expired and to please log off.

User Rights Policy

NT makes the assignment of rights to users or groups a simple process. Select Policies, User Rights from the User Manager window. Like the Account policy discussed previously, the User Rights policy is domain-wide and not for the specific account highlighted when selecting this option.

Rather than selecting a group or user and applying a set of rights, the procedure works the other way around. Select a right and then add or remove users and groups. Currently, there is no easy way to list the rights associated with users and groups except to view them through this utility.

> **Tip**
>
> *Some UNIX systems offer similar functions. SCO UNIX allows assignment of privileges and authorizations to individual users, but not to groups. Solaris offers no comparable facility.*

Figure 1.10 illustrates the User Rights Policy dialog box.

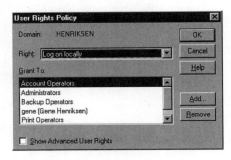

Figure 1.10. *The User Rights Policy dialog box.*

Figure 1.11 illustrates adding groups to a specific right. When a user or group is selected by single-clicking the name, the Add button becomes active. Click the Add button to add the right. Alternatively, double-click the name and it will be added. By default, only groups are shown. To show users, click the Show Users button.

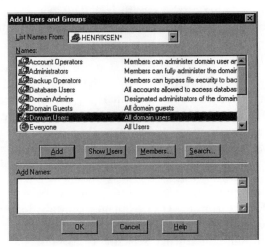

Figure 1.11. *Adding a group to a right.*

Notice that the default is to add rights to groups, not users. Assignment of rights to groups reduces the administrative load compared to assigning rights to users.

Audit Policy

The final option on the Options group is Audit. Auditing can be configured for Success or Failure on seven major areas. Auditing is generally used to comply with security requirements and is similar to the UNIX auditing. Windows NT does meet the Orange Book C2 level of security.

Using Groups in a Domain

Windows NT uses groups to ease the administrative burden of assigning permissions. Two types of groups exist: local and global. Groups have different scopes of existence on domain controllers and servers. Domain controllers have both local and global groups. A local group on a domain controller is local to the domain. A domain local group can be used anywhere in the domain from any domain controller. A local group on a member server is local to the member server computer. Global groups may not be created on member servers.

Local groups:

- Provide users with permissions or rights to resources

- Include user accounts or global groups from any domain

- Do not include other local groups

- Have permissions and rights assigned in the local domain

- Can be assigned resources anywhere in the domain on a domain controller

- Can be assigned resources only on the local machine on an NT workstation or member server

On the other hand, global groups:

- Cannot be created on a workstation or member server

- Can include only users from the local domain

- Cannot contain local groups or global groups

- Cannot be assigned to local resources
- Must be created on the domain controller where the accounts reside
- Are used to organize users into groups
- Are assigned to local groups

The order of progression for assigning permission and rights to a user for a resource is

1. Accounts get included into global groups.
2. Global groups get included into local groups.
3. Local groups are assigned permissions or rights to resources.

Tip

Global groups should not be assigned permissions to a resource. To sum this up, remember the slogan, "Think Globally, Act Locally."

Microsoft provided built-in groups to cover the most common requirements. The built-in groups should be used whenever possible to prevent an explosion of groups. Too many groups could create the same problem as no groups requiring administration of a large number of entities.

Groups are displayed at the bottom of the User Manager window. The User Manager screen lists the groups at the bottom (refer to Figure 1.2 earlier in the chapter). In the list of groups, try to spot the difference between local and global groups. Default global groups have Domain as the first part of the name, a standard that might be wise to follow in creating new global groups.

The global group icon has a small globe that appears to the left of the two heads, whereas the local groups have a computer in place of the globe.

Creating Groups

When laying out the requirements for user administration, try to use the built-in groups. To create a global group, from the User Manager for Domains select User, New Global Group. This option is grayed out on a member server. Figure 1.12 illustrates creating a global group. To add members to the group, click on the user's name in the right-hand column labeled Not Members. As users are selected, the names disappear from the Not Members column and appear in the Members column.

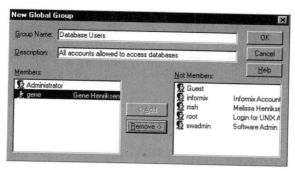

Figure 1.12. *Creating a new global group.*

To allow specific users to have access to a database on an NT server:

1. Create a global group (for instance, **Domain Database User**).

2. Add user accounts to the global group.

3. Create a local group (local to the domain or server) named **Database Users**.

4. Assign the global group to the local group.

5. Assign privileges for the database folders and files to the local group.

Assigning Permissions

In Windows NT, two file systems can be used on the computer. The *FAT (File Allocation Table) file system* has been around since the early days of DOS. Permissions may not be assigned to files or folders. Anyone logged in at the console "owns" all the files on a FAT file system. Anyone with a DOS bootable disk who has access to an NT computer can reboot from disk and "own" all the files on the computer if FAT is the file system. The only security for a FAT system is over the network through permissions on FAT shares.

The other file system is *NTFS or NT File System*. NTFS supports assignment of permissions. NTFS is not readable if the machine is booted on a DOS disk. NTFS carries more overhead than FAT, but is more crash-resilient. Use FAT for small partitions (under 400 MB) where security is not required. Use NTFS for large partitions or where security is an issue.

With NTFS shares, local permissions and share permissions may be assigned. On shared NTFS resources, the more restrictive of the share and local permissions is used to determine access.

Permissions are different from the usual UNIX rwxrwxrwx permissions that only allow for a single owner, single group, and anyone else logged in. When a user attempts access to a file, the actions are controlled by the permissions granted to the user. Table 1.1 shows permissions and the corresponding action that can be taken on a file or folder.

Table 1.1. Permissions and their actions.

Permission	File Action	Folder Action
Read (R)	Display data, file, permissions, and owner.	Display names, attributes, permissions, and owner.
Delete (D)	Delete the file.	Delete the folder.
Write (W)	Display owner and permissions, change file attributes, create data, and append to the file.	Display owner and permissions, add files and folders to the folder, change attributes.
Execute (X)	Display attributes, owner, and permissions. Run if the file is executable.	Display attributes, owner, and permissions. Make changes to folders with the folder.
Change Permissions (P)	Change a file's permissions.	Change folder's permissions.
Take Ownership (O)	Take ownership of the file.	Take ownership of the folder.

In addition, the permissions are grouped into standard permissions. Standard permissions are not listed in the preceding table, but consist of one or more of the permissions above. The standard permissions are listed in Table 1.2.

Table 1.2. Standard permissions.

Permission	File Action	Folder Action	Files in the Folder
Full	All permissions	All permissions	All permissions
No Access	No permissions	No permissions	No permissions
List	Not a choice	RX	Not specified
Read	RX	RX	RX
Add	Not a choice	WX	Not specified
Add & Read	Not a choice	RWX	RX
Change	RWXD	RWXD	RWXD

To assign permissions to an NTFS resource, right-click the resource and select Properties, Security, Permissions. Figure 1.13 illustrates changing the permissions for group with access to a file. Note the available permissions displayed in the Type of Access drop-down list.

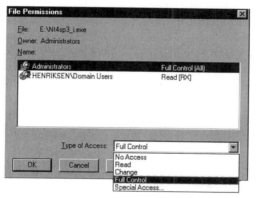

Figure 1.13. *Changing permissions of the Everyone group on the file Nt4sp3_i.exe.*

To add permissions for a group that does not have permissions on a resource, click the Add button. The Add Users and Groups dialog box appears. Click the user or group to be added, then click on the Add button. Select the permissions from the Type of Access drop-down box. The Add User and Groups dialog box (refer to Figure 1.11) is used, although for a different purpose.

How Permissions Work

When a user logs on to an NT domain, a token is created that consists of the sum of the rights and privileges of the user. Each resource or object in the domain has an Access Control List (ACL) that contains requirements to obtain access to the resource. The token is associated with every process the user creates. When a user's process requests access to a resource, the token is compared to the ACL. If the token passes inspection, access is granted.

If a user belongs to any group that is specifically denied access to a resource, then regardless of other memberships and access rights, the user is denied access. Access denial takes precedence over access.

Troubleshooting Tip

Bob belongs to the Domain Users, Programmers, and Testers global groups. As a member of the Programmers group, he has full control of the folder C:\Program_Notes. The Testers group has No Access to C:\Program_Notes; therefore, Bob is denied access. Bob calls an administrator and asks to be removed from the Testers group because he no longer works in that department. The administrator removes Bob from the Testers group. Bob again attempts to access the resource with the same result. What is the problem? Bob needs to log out and log on to get a new token that does not include the Testers group.

Figure 1.14 illustrates modifying an account's group memberships. To add a user to a group, click on the group name in the Not Member Of column and click the Add button. To remove a group, click the group under the Member Of column and click the Remove button.

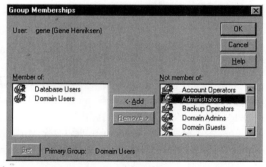

Figure 1.14. *Modifying a user's group memberships.*

Creating NT Domains and Trusts

Prior to Windows NT, Microsoft's networking model consisted of the peer-to-peer workgroup as implemented in Windows for Workgroups. For Windows NT to be accepted as a server in the larger business networking scheme, Microsoft had to create a client/server network model with centralized administration and control.

Microsoft's goal was to create a network operating system in which the user had a single logon and password to access all authorized resources. To fill the requirement of a client/server model network, Microsoft created the NT Domain.

The replication of the domain SAM to the BDCs allows the user to log on and be authenticated by the PDC or any BDC. This logon authentication is incorporated into Microsoft's BackOffice suite of applications including SQL Server, Exchange Server, SNA Server, and Systems Management Server.

In a small network environment (less than 2,000 users), a PDC could handle logon authentication without a BDC; however, there would be no backup to the PDC, and failure of the PDC would prevent users from logging on to the domain. It is recommended that at least one BDC be present for backup. In a very small environment, the PDC may also be the only application server, in which case, if the PDC is down, so is the application. Only an NT server, not an NT workstation, can become a domain controller. The decision to make a server into a domain controller is made at installation time and cannot be reversed without reinstalling.

The SAM has to exist in its entirety on each domain controller and will reside in memory in the domain controller; therefore, the domain controllers must have enough memory to support this load. Memory is the most important resource on a domain controller.

To figure out the amount of space required for the SAM, estimate 1K for each user account and .5K for each Windows NT computer account. Microsoft's maximum recommended size for the SAM database is 40 MB. This limits the domain to approximately 25,000 user accounts (25 MB) and 25,000 computer accounts (12.5 MB). Keep in mind that Windows 95 computers do not need to have computer accounts in a domain. The domain controllers should have roughly three times the SAM size in total RAM, the maximum 40 MB SAM requiring about 120 MB of RAM.

Creating a Domain

When starting the domain creation process, the first Windows NT computer installed has to be the PDC. At installation, the user is asked if the computer is a PDC, BDC, or member server. If the computer is a BDC, it must be able to contact the PDC during installation. You cannot install a BDC off the network that's not in communication with the PDC, and later have it join the domain.

Once installed as a PDC or BDC, a computer must be reinstalled to become a member server. Likewise, a member server cannot be promoted to a BDC or PDC without reinstallation. In large networks, domain controllers should not be configured to handle application loads. The overhead of the domain is sufficient load for the domain controller.

Server Manager

The primary tool for working with the NT computers in the domain is *Server Manager*, which is located in the Administrative Tools (Common) menu option. Figure 1.15 illustrates Server Manager.

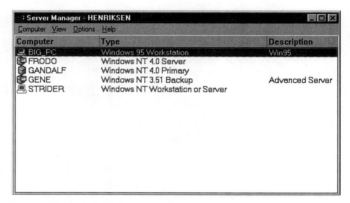

Figure 1.15. *Server Manager's main screen.*

Server Manager lists all computers that have been made a member of the domain.

> *Tip*
>
> *The computer name is preceded by an icon. Note there are three icon styles. The domain controller, GANDALF, has a small box with no computer monitor or display. The BDC, GENE, has the same small box with a small display screen in front. Servers have the same icon as the BDC. The workstations, only one Windows 95 computer in this case, have a desktop computer icon. Icons for computers that are not running will be grayed out. The grayed out symbol is a desktop computer, representative of a workstation.*

Tip

When a computer first starts up, it may not appear to be "up" in Server Manager. This problem can also appear in the Browse list when browsing for resources. Browsing is a network-intensive service with each computer announcing itself upon startup and every 12 minutes thereafter. If you must connect to a shared resource on a computer that just booted and is not in the browse list, connect via the Universal Naming Convention (UNC) name, such as \\Frodo\Public.

The main options of Server Manager can be reached by clicking on the Computer option.

Properties

The first item on the drop-down menu is Properties. Figure 1.16 illustrates the properties for a domain controller named GENE. The properties for GENE indicate there are six current network sessions with one open named pipe and no open files or file locks.

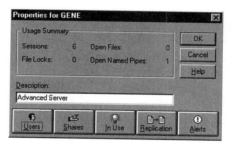

Figure 1.16. *Server Manager Properties for a computer named GENE.*

Users

Clicking the Users button lists the users connected to the computer. Any specific user or all users may be disconnected by selecting the Disconnect (for a highlighted user) or Disconnect All.

Shares

The Shares button on the Properties displays shared resources. The options at the bottom of the screen allow disconnect of one or all connected users.

In Use

To examine the open resources on a computer, select the In Use button on the Properties window.

Replication

Directory replication provides a method of duplicating information onto servers. The most frequent use of directory replication is to duplicate the login batch scripts and user profiles to BDCs. It could be used for other reasons, perhaps to duplicate some information that many computers need to access on a regular basis, thereby reducing congestion at the computer that has the master copy.

> **Tip**
>
> *Directory replication is not a substitute for backups. It should not be used for large databases because it will replicate after changes are made which could overload a network with traffic.*

Alerts

Many servers are locked out of sight in closets or other secure areas. Administrative alerts appearing on the console of the server will not be observed. Alerts can be sent to other computers. For these alerts to be sent, the Alerter and Messenger services must be running on the computer originating the alerts, and the Messenger service must be running on the receiving computer. Administrative alerts are generated by the NT operating system concerning printer problems, server shutdown, user session problems, security, and access problems.

Shared Directories

Shared directories on any NT computer in the domain can be managed from the Computer, Shared Directories option in Server Manager. Shares ending with the $ character are usually administrative shares and are always hidden from browsing. Select a share by highlighting (single click) the directory to be shared, and click the Properties button; the Properties window appears providing access to the name of the share and the comment. A button on the share window provides access to the Permissions window.

To create a new share on the computer, whether local or remote, click New Share in the Shared Directories window. Figure 1.17 demonstrates adding a new share named Reskit, a popular name for the Windows NT Resource Kit. Clicking the Permissions button enables you to set the permissions on the new share. The Everyone group is given Full Control unless otherwise modified.

On the local computer, shares can be controlled by right-clicking the resource, C:\NTRESKIT in the example, and selecting Sharing from the drop-down menu.

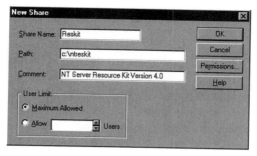

Figure 1.17. *Creating a new share on FRODO.*

Services

Services on a remote computer can be controlled through the Services option. Figure 1.18 illustrates the Services on FRODO. Depending on the service and the current state of the service, the Start, Stop, Pause, and Continue buttons may or may not be active. The Pause function operates differently for different services. Check the documentation to be sure that Pause provides the functionality you want. For instance, pausing the Netlogon service on the PDC stops the service from authenticating logins but does not hinder its ability to synchronize the SAM database to BDCs.

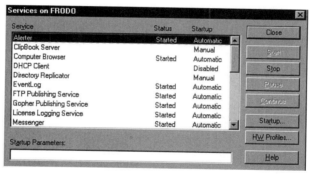

Figure 1.18. *Services on FRODO.*

Server Manager has an Add to Domain and a Remove from Domain option. Only Windows NT computers should be added to the domain; Windows 95 or prior versions should not. To remove a computer from a domain, highlight the computer and select the Remove from Domain option. The purpose for domain computer accounts is to allow centralized administration. Only NT computers may be administered in this manner.

When a new Windows NT computer is installed, it must have a computer account in the domain. Two methods are provided:

- Click the Server Manager Add to Domain option.

- The person installing the computer is asked to enter an account name and password with administrative rights during the install procedure to create the computer account. If a non-administrator is installing the computer, the administrator should create the computer account from Server Manager to avoid giving away the administrator password.

Interdomain Trusts Relationships

Trusts allow accounts in one domain to access resources in a trusting domain. Microsoft created the trust relationship between domains to overcome limitations on the scalability of domains. Without trust relationships, domains would not be practical in an organization with more than 20,000 to 25,000 users.

Trust relationships enable users in a trusted domain to access resources in a trusting domain. The terms *trusted* and *trusting* may get confusing so be careful in setting up these relationships. If the trust relationship does not yield the expected results, check the trust relationship to make sure it is set up with the trust in the correct direction. Figure 1.19 explains the essence of trust relationships.

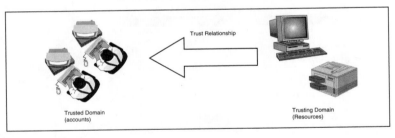

Figure 1.19. *Trust relationships.*

Setting Up Trusts

To add a domain as a trusting domain:

1. Select Start, Administrative Tools, User Manager for Domains, Policies, Trust Relationships.

2. Click the Add button beside the Trusting Domains box. The result is illustrated in Figure 1.20.

3. Enter the domain name and an optional password. The password does not have to be entered; a blank password will work. To prevent the slight

possibility that another Windows NT PDC could spoof one of the two systems setting up the trust relationship, use a password.

Figure 1.20. *Adding a trusting domain.*

The trusting domain's administrator follows the same procedure above and clicks Add on the Trusted Domains box (see Figure 1.21). The administrator then enters the domain name and the password, if one was entered by the trusted domain. If the sequence of events is followed as outlined here, the administrator should receive a message indicating the trust has been established. If the sequence is accidentally reversed, the relationship can take up to 15 minutes to become established.

Figure 1.21. *Adding a trusted domain.*

> **Tip**
>
> *If any logical connection exists between the PDCs of the two domains starting a trust relationship, the trust will fail. Rebooting will ensure there is no relationship in use. A logical relationship can occur if one domain PDC has connected to a resource on the other domain's PDC. The two PDCs must be able to establish contact on the network. If one PDC uses TCP/IP and the other uses only IPX, the trust will fail.*

The domain trust account passwords will be changed by the two domain's PDCs on a weekly basis. This provides a secure channel between them and no one can break the trust by masquerading as a trusted domain because the passwords will not match. A trust works by logging in to a hidden account.

Once the trust relationship has been established, the administrator of the trusting (resource) domain can add trusted (accounts) domain global groups to the trusting domain. Adding the trusted global Domain Users group to the trusting domain's Users local groups allows users with accounts in the trusted domain to access resources in the trusting domain. The addition of the trusted

Administrators group allows the trusted domain administrators to administer resources on the trusting domain.

Trust Models
Microsoft defines three models:

- Single master

- Multiple master

- Complete trust

The *single master domain* has one domain that maintains all accounts. The other domains are resource domains. The single master works well for up to 25,000 accounts or so. The administrators in the master domain handle the accounts while the resources are managed by the administrators of the resource domains. All domains trust the master domain. All users log in to the master domain.

The *multiple master domain* has multiple account domains and resource domains. The reason for multiple account domains may be that the number of accounts exceeds the limits of a single domain, the geographical distribution of accounts (U.S. and Europe, for instance), or the accounts may be divided by function (Admin, Sales, Manufacturing). The other domains in the model are resource domains. This domain model is very similar to the single master except there are multiple accounts domains. The accounts (master) domains should trust each other.

The *complete trust model* is useful in an organization that needs local control of resources and accounts, but needs to share resource between localities. Every domain is both trusted and trusting with every other domain. The number of trust relations ships grows rapidly. To compute the number of trust relationships, use the formula:

number of trusts = $(n \times n\text{-}1)$

where n is the number of domains. A five-domain complete trust would have $(5 \times 5\text{-}1)$, or 20 trusts.

NT Background Services

An operating system depends heavily on programs that handle specific tasks. Windows NT refers to these programs as *services*. NT Services are the equivalent of UNIX daemons. Monitoring, stopping, starting, and troubleshooting services is an important part of Windows NT administration.

Many services are set up at installation. Other services are installed as new programs are installed. To view services, click Start, Settings, Control Panel and double-click the Services icon. There are three logs available for viewing by clicking on the Log menu:

- System

- Security

- Application

By default, the System log is viewed. Figure 1.22 illustrates the Services window.

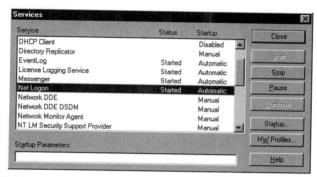

Figure 1.22. *The Services applet in the Control Panel.*

The major services that should be running on a Windows NT Server are described below. These services vary with the network setup installed and other applications that can run as a service.

- *Alerter.* Sends alerts to specified users and computers

- *Computer Browser.* Maintains up-to-date lists of other computers on the network

- *Directory Replicator.* Replicates directories and files from one computer to another

- *Event Log.* Maintains the logs viewed with Event Viewer

- *Messenger.* Serves as a transport for the Alerter service

- *Net Logon.* Authenticates logins, services pass-through authentication to another domain, and synchronizes the domain SAM between controllers

- *Schedule.* Schedules commands to be run, similar to the UNIX cron utility

- *Server.* Provides services to the network such as file and print sharing

- *Spooler.* Spools print jobs

- *TCP/IP NetBIOS Helper.* Provides support for NetBIOS over TCP/IP

- *Workstation.* Sends requests to the Server service on a remote computer for access to shared files and printers

The Event Viewer

As the system boots, entries are made in event logs concerning the success or failure of services. These logs can be viewed through the Event Viewer.

Whenever trouble occurs on an NT computer, check the System log in the Event Viewer. To start the Event Viewer, click Start, Programs, Administrative Tools, Event Viewer. Look for services that failed to start. The log provides a colored symbol on the left that indicates the severity of the problem. A blue circle with a letter i is informational, a yellow circle with an ! is a warning. For serious problems, a red octagon with the word stop is displayed.

In Figure 1.23, the Event Viewer shows a series of stop signs. The source of the errors is NETLOGON. Double-clicking the error produces a window with more detail.

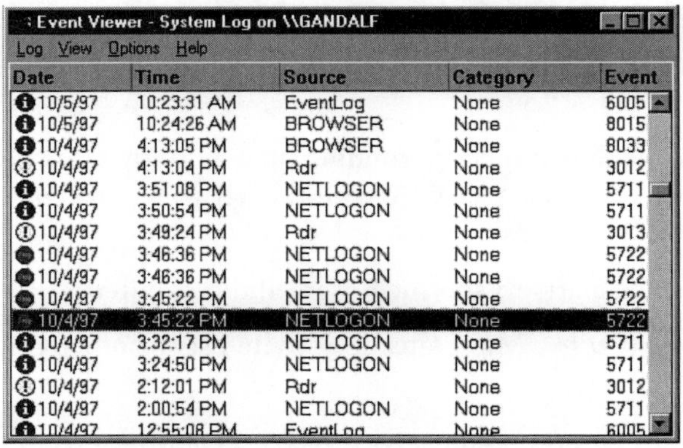

Date	Time	Source	Category	Event
10/5/97	10:23:31 AM	EventLog	None	6005
10/5/97	10:24:26 AM	BROWSER	None	8015
10/4/97	4:13:05 PM	BROWSER	None	8033
10/4/97	4:13:04 PM	Rdr	None	3012
10/4/97	3:51:08 PM	NETLOGON	None	5711
10/4/97	3:50:54 PM	NETLOGON	None	5711
10/4/97	3:49:24 PM	Rdr	None	3013
10/4/97	3:46:36 PM	NETLOGON	None	5722
10/4/97	3:46:36 PM	NETLOGON	None	5722
10/4/97	3:45:22 PM	NETLOGON	None	5722
10/4/97	3:45:22 PM	NETLOGON	None	5722
10/4/97	3:32:17 PM	NETLOGON	None	5711
10/4/97	3:24:50 PM	NETLOGON	None	5711
10/4/97	2:12:01 PM	Rdr	None	3012
10/4/97	2:00:54 PM	NETLOGON	None	5711
10/4/97	12:55:08 PM	EventLog	None	6005

Figure 1.23. *The Event Viewer Log with problems occurring in the NETLOGON service.*

The AT Command

The method of scheduling batch jobs for future execution is the AT command. AT is a command line, not a window, function. The syntax for AT is shown below. The Schedule service must be running to use the AT command.

```
AT [\\computername] [ [id] [/DELETE] ¦ /DELETE [/YES]]

AT [\\computername] time [/INTERACTIVE][ /EVERY:date[,...] ¦ /NEXT:date[,...]]
"command"
```

- *computername*. Specifies a remote computer. Commands are scheduled on the local computer if this parameter is omitted.

- *id*. An identification number assigned to a scheduled command.

- /delete. Cancels a scheduled command. If *id* is omitted, all the scheduled commands on the computer are canceled.

- /yes. Used with cancel all jobs command when no further confirmation is desired.

- *time*. Specifies the time when command is to run.

- /interactive. Allows the job to interact with the desktop of the user who is logged on at the time the job runs.

- /EVERY:*date*[,...]. Runs the command on each specified day of the week or month. If *date* is omitted, the current day of the month is assumed.

- /NEXT:*date*[,...]. Runs the specified command on the next occurrence of the day (for example, next Thursday). If *date* is omitted, the current day of the month is assumed.

- "*command*". The Windows NT command or batch program to be run.

The Windows NT Resource Kit includes a Windows version of the AT command. The Windows version can be found at Start, Programs, Resource Kit 4.0, Configuration, Command Scheduler. While the Windows version is considerably more intuitive, there are no more options. Figure 1.24 illustrates the Windows version of AT, actually an executable named WINAT.EXE.

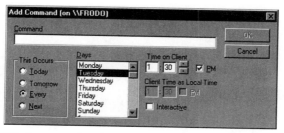

Figure 1.24. *The Windows graphical version of AT.*

While WINAT.EXE is considerably friendlier than the UNIX cron table, there are limitations to AT's underlying capability. The UNIX administrator may quickly notice there is no option to schedule an event to occur on a particular date, the way the UNIX AT command does. Nor is there a capability to specify months for execution. In order to specify multiple days for a single command, such as Monday through Friday, click on each day in succession. Scrolling down the days of the week will reveal the numbered days of the month.

Program Status and Monitoring Utilities

With the tools provided in the Windows NT operating system and the additional tools included in the Server Resource Kit, analyzing the performance of a Windows NT computer is relatively easy. UNIX administrators should be familiar with the sar (system activity reporter) command on UNIX. There are also graphical programs indicating CPU usage on Solaris and SCO.

In addition, UNIX provides a number of command-line utilities for analysis of the state of the operating system. Windows NT is also blessed with a number of utilities.

Task Manager

Task Manager is a useful and easily executed program. To execute Task Manager, right-click on the taskbar at the bottom of the screen, and a menu containing Task Manager appears. Figure 1.25 illustrates Task Manager in its performance monitoring mode.

Note there are four graphs: CPU Usage, MEM Usage, and a historical version of both. Important information on this window includes Commit Charge Total and Physical Memory Total. If Commit Charge Total is greater than Physical Memory Total, then more memory may be needed. Commit Charge Limit indicates how much virtual memory can be used before expanding the paging file. At the bottom of the window appears the number of Processes, CPU Usage, and Memory Usage regardless of the tab selected for display.

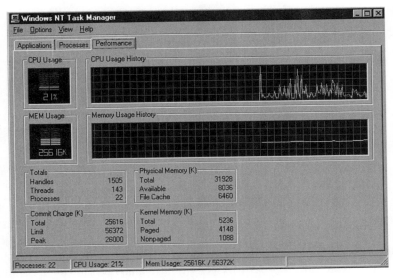

Figure 1.25. *The Performance tab of Task Manager.*

Rather than looking at a static ps listing in UNIX, Windows NT offers a dynamic view with Task Manager's Processes view. Selecting the View menu option displays Select Columns, which enables the administrator to customize the column listing.

Performance Monitor

Performance Monitor is a powerful tool for the system administrator. Run Performance Monitor from Start, Programs, Administrative Tools, Performance Monitor. A large number of counters exist within the operating system that can be monitored. Counters are available for most of the NT's component subsystems such as memory, cpu, disk, and so on. Once Performance Monitor is running, select Edit, Add to Chart, and an Add to Chart window appears. Select the computer you want to monitor. You can monitor multiple computers simultaneously.

Where multiple instances of an object exist, the Instance can be chosen. The instances can be multiple disk drives, network cards, or processors. Click the Explain button to have a short explanation displayed as you highlight counters.

After all counters have been selected, click Done, and the chart comes into full view. The chart will run continuously. When a counter is highlighted on the bottom of the chart, the numbers in the line starting with Last reflect the highlighted counter. Figure 1.26 illustrates the Performance Monitor Chart view. Note the computer name to the right of the counters.

Performance Monitor provides four different views:

- *Chart view* is appropriate for watching current activity. The chart can be converted to a histogram in the Chart Options.

- Administrators use *Alert view* to set alerts on specific resource conditions. An example would be to generate an alert when disk space drops below a certain percentage or number of megabytes. Alerts can be set on a number of different conditions on different computers with alerts sent to the administrator elsewhere.

- Setting up *Log view* to log performance over time provides information for baseline performance measurement or checking for specific problems. Logs can be played back as a chart or a report.

- *Report view* is used to generate reports from logs with averages of the selected counters.

The Windows NT Workstation Resource Kit provides an in-depth discussion of Performance Monitor. Performance Monitor settings can be saved to a file once the setup has been made. Double-clicking this file will start Performance

Monitor with those settings enabled. Batch logging can be configured with the Monitor.exe program; see the Resource Kit for details.

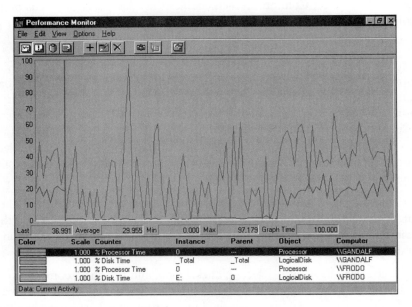

Figure 1.26. *The Chart view of Performance Monitor.*

> ### Tip
>
> *To monitor disk performance, the disk counters must be enabled. The default condition is disk counters off. To enable disk counters, run*
>
>   Diskperf -y
>
> *For enhanced disk reporting with software RAID, run*
>
>   Diskperf -ye
>
> *When monitoring TCP/IP, there may be very few counters available. Install the Microsoft SNMP agent on the monitored system to have the full suite of TCP/IP counters available to Performance Monitor.*

Other Monitoring Tools

Process Explode or *Pview.exe* provides the internal details on a specific process. Pview displays detailed information for troubleshooting specific procedures rather than looking at overall system performance.

PMON.EXE provides a character-based output similar to the UNIX ps command. PMON refreshes the data on screen every second or two. PMON can be run from the Start, Run menu. Enter **PMON** and press Enter. PMON is part of the NT Resource Kit.

Pstat (pstat.exe) is a command-line utility that provides more that a window full of data. It should be run through the `More` command or redirected to a file or printer. Pstat provides a static view of the system, unlike Pmon. Pstat's listing is similar to Pmon at the start, but Pstat breaks down additional information by process ID (PID). Pstat also provides a list of loaded modules with data for troubleshooting, such as load address and the link date, which is helpful to Microsoft in debugging.

Perf Meter (wperf.exe) is another of the NT Resource Kit programs. Execute Wperf.exe from the NT Resource Kit's Perftool\Meastool folder. By default, Perf Meter displays CPU usage. Click the Select option to have additional choices shown. Perf Meter can be minimized to the taskbar and maximized onto the display as required.

Quick Slice (qslice.exe) is the final variation on the performance theme that we will discuss. Quick Slice is another of the NT Resource Kit utilities. Quick Slice constantly updates the window providing a quick, real-time look at the percent of CPU usage by various processes.

The number and variety of utility programs available on Windows NT, most available with the Resource Kit, should provide even the most hardened UNIX administrator with enough tools to analyze the performance on Windows NT.

Windows NT and Disk Drives

Unlike UNIX, Windows NT does not have an extensible file system allowing a file system on one drive to be mounted onto a directory or folder on a mounted file system. The file system is not presented as one contiguous structure starting at the root directory.

Disk Drive Organization

Each file system in Windows NT, like its DOS predecessors, has a drive letter. Full pathname references to file systems on any partition are listed by drive letter such as C:\Winnt\System32. Note also that the separators are backslashes, not the UNIX forward slash. As additional partitions or disks are added, more drive letters are used as the root of each file system. These drive letters are also assigned to network-accessible file resources. The A and B drive letters are reserved for the floppy drives.

With the Intel-based computer limit of four partitions on a disk drive, four primary partitions can be created on a Windows NT disk. On the primary disk drive, these drives would be C, D, E, and F. All disk space must be included in one of the four partitions or it will not be accessible. If the user wants more drive letters in order to subdivide the disk further, a partition may be created as an extended partition. *Extended partitions* are special case partitions allowing logical drives to be created within the extended partition. Unfortunately, drive letters may shift as extended partitions are created or removable drives are used on the NT system.

Windows NT has no equivalent to the UNIX mount command. On the good side of this, floppy disks are automatically recognized upon insertion. CD-ROMs are likewise auto-recognized. The autorun feature will automatically start up the software on a CD-ROM unless disabled. Autorun is either a nice feature or a nuisance depending on your point of view. Inserting a CD to explore it rather than to install it will result in the install screen appearing if auto-run is enabled.

Author's Note

On computers configured to attempt booting from the CD-ROM, the BIOS will attempt to boot from the CD-ROM if available, therefore do not leave the Windows NT installation CD in the drive or it will start the install sequence upon reboot.

The lack of a mount command is not necessarily a positive feature, though. Removable hard drives, such as the Jaz drive from Iomega, can be used with Windows NT. When formatted with NTFS, a removable drive is only removable when the system is not running. The drive cartridge must be inserted before booting and removed after shutdown.

NTFS and FAT

When you decide to format a drive, you must select the filesystem type. FAT is more advantageous on small partitions with its lower overhead. In fact, floppy disks cannot be formatted with NTFS because the disk space overhead is greater than the size of the floppy disk.

Let's examine the specifics of file systems on Windows NT. FAT has been available in various forms since the beginning of DOS. It is a low overhead file system with no advanced features such as file permissions. NTFS was developed for Windows NT. NTFS provides for security (file permissions) and is more efficient on large file systems. NTFS is capable of handling a file system of 16 exabytes; however, the functional limit is 2 terabytes due to industry standard limitations on the number and size of disk sectors.

The following table provides some comparison between NTFS and FAT file systems.

Function	NTFS	FAT
Filesystem overhead	1-5 MB	1 MB
Built-in security	Yes	No
Accessible through	NT only	NT, DOS, Windows
Transaction-based recoverability	Yes	No
Compression on file-by-file basis	Yes	No
Optimal partition size	>400MB	<400MB

Any computer that will be dual-booted between Windows NT and Windows 95 or other Windows version must use a FAT filesystem for commonly accessible data and programs. The compatibility issue is of no concern over the network. A Windows NT computer can share data on an NTFS file system that will be readable by Windows 95 or other DOS systems. The network translation takes care of the problem.

When sharing FAT-based data, the only permissions that can be assigned are on the share itself and those permissions will apply to all files and folders within the share when accessed over the network.

NTFS data can have individual permissions on files and folders and also be protected by share permissions. When accessing NTFS data over the network, the most restrictive permissions apply. For instance, if a user is a member of group Accounting and the permissions are Full Control for local access and Read Only for network access by members of group Accounting, then network access yields Read Only access.

Using Disk Administrator

Disk Administrator is the tool that provides a graphical combination of the DOS utilities FDISK, FORMAT and LABEL (see Figure 1.27). When run for the first time or after adding new disk drives, Disk Administrator will comment that there is no signature on the disk and one should be added. Click OK. Without a signature, Disk Administrator will not operate on the disk.

Disk Administrator color-codes partition types, making identification graphical and easy. Note that partitions are not scaled to size, though. The 8 MB Compaq EISA utilities partition takes as much space on the graph as the 596 MB D drive. In the Disk 0 pictured in Figure 1.27, the D drive is a Logical drive. The C drive is a primary partition. The EISA Utilities segment is only booted and addressable if the Compaq F10 option is selected at boot time.

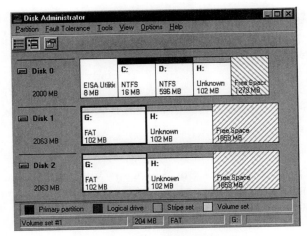

Figure 1.27. *Disk Administrator for a three-disk system.*

Volume Sets

In addition to primary and extended partitions, NT can create *volume sets*, collections of free space combined into a single drive letter. Two or more areas of various sizes may be combined. Volume sets do not offer data redundancy for fault tolerance or enhanced rates of access. If any portion of a volume set crashes, it must be completely rebuilt and the data restored. Volume sets are more susceptible to crashes because any disk that crashes with a part of a volume set on it causes the loss of the entire volume set and any other volume sets with space on that disk.

To create a volume set, select two areas of free space on disk. To select two areas, click on the first area and hold down the Ctrl key while clicking the additional areas. From the Partition menu select Create Volume Set. Since you clicked on free space, Windows NT assumes you want to use it all but allows you to set the size. The volume set needs to be formatted before use. In Figure 1.27, the G drive is a volume set. The part of G on the second drive would be filled before data were written to the G drive on the third disk.

Stripe Sets

Stripe sets provide another method of combining disk areas into one drive letter. In Figure 1.27, three disk areas have been combined into a stripe set. Areas used to create a stripe set must be the same size. Stripe sets provide faster access to data in large files because the data is spread across multiple drives. Spreading the data improves the chances that multiple access will occur on different drives thereby reducing the queuing of requests for a single drive. Stripe sets do not offer data redundancy for fault tolerance if the drive crashes.

In Figure 1.27, the H drive would have data written to the H portion of Disk 1 and then to Disk 2 and then to Disk 3 in a 64KB stripe and return to Disk 1 for the next stripe.

Saving Disk Information

When changes have been made with Disk Administrator and you choose to exit, Disk Administrator will ask to save the changes. Since disk layout will not be recognizable to a new copy of the operating system, be sure to run the RDISK utility described later. Without saved disk information, loss of the operating system will result in loss of the stripe set.

While using Disk Administrator, you can choose a free area, create a partition, and format. The Format option will be grayed out until the new disk information is saved. To save the information, click on Partition and then click Commit Changes Now.

Another method of saving disk information is the Configuration option of the Partition menu. Under Configuration are both a Save and Restore option. The Save option writes the data to a floppy disk. This data can be used to recover stripe sets, volume sets and mirrored partitions. The Restore option will read the data from the floppy disk and restore the configuration to the settings stored on the floppy disk.

A second method of restoration requires a second copy of NT installed on the computer. The Search option will find the configuration in another NT installations file and restore it. If the two installations did not have the same configuration, then the original configuration will not be recovered.

The disk configuration restore could be used if the Emergency Recovery Disk is lost, the data on the Emergency Recovery Disk is out of date, or Windows NT was reinstalled and you want to set the disk configuration to the previous settings.

Formatting New Areas

Figure 1.28 illustrates the options available when the Format option is selected from the Tools menu. The file system may be either FAT or NTFS. The allocation unit size is calculated based on the size of the area. A FAT partition can be converted to NTFS using the command line CONVERT.EXE utility. While CONVERT is designed to keep the data intact, backing up data before any conversion is a wise precaution. The partition is marked for conversion at reboot. The syntax of the command is

```
CONVERT drive /fs:ntfs
```

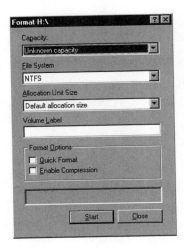

Figure 1.28. *Formatting drive H as NTFS.*

There is no conversion from NTFS to FAT. Using Disk Administrator to format an NTFS partition as FAT does not convert the partition with data intact, rather it reformats the partition with all data being destroyed.

The Capacity drop-down list box provides the capability to control the formatted capacity. This option does nothing for fixed disks and works only with removable disks.

The File System option defaults to FAT. Selecting FAT will gray out or disable the Enable Compression check box.

The Help screen for Allocation Unit Size strongly recommends accepting the default. This determines the cluster size for disk organization.

Volume labels are optional descriptions of a disk.

The format options are Quick Format for a previously formatted area and Enable Compression for NTFS to allow selective compression of files and folders.

Stripe Sets with Parity

One of the two fault tolerant methods supported by Windows NT within the operating system is *RAID 5* or *stripe sets with parity*. To create a stripe set with parity requires 3 to 32 areas of disk on different physical disks. Only one area can be selected from each physical disk. Select the areas to be included and then select Create Stripe Set with Parity from the Fault Tolerance menu.

To compute the usable amount of space in the stripe set, the parity stripe is not included. The formula for available disk space is number of areas minus one times disk space per area (area -1 * megabytes). The loss of disk space is proportional to the number of disk drives in the stripe set since one drive contains parity information. With three disks, one-third of the space is used for parity while with eight disks only one-eighth is lost to parity.

Stripe sets with parity provide fault tolerance by storing parity information so that the loss of a single drive does not destroy the data. The operating system can retrieve data after the loss of a drive by computing the lost information. A new area can be selected to replace the damaged area and the stripe set rebuilt through the Regenerate option on the Fault Tolerance menu.

Stripe sets with parity have excellent read performance and moderate write performance. The read performance is enhanced by spreading data across multiple drives. The write performance requires updating a minimum of two drives, one for data and the other for parity on each write. More memory is required for writes than a normal write due to parity information computation. A stripe set may not contain either the boot or system information for Windows NT.

Mirroring

RAID 1, *mirroring*, is supported by Windows NT as a Disk Administrator option. To create a mirrored set requires two disks with the areas being of equal size. Select the areas and select Establish Mirror from the Fault Tolerance menu.

Mirrored partitions are expensive compared to stripe sets with parity because 50% of the disk space is lost to the mirrored partner. The advantage of mirroring is that the system and boot partitions can be mirrored. Mirrors require less memory than stripes with parity and have good read and write performance.

If the boot partition is to be mirrored, special precautions have to be taken in order to boot after a failure of the primary drive. While hardware implementations will boot regardless of which drive fails, with software implementations the computer BIOS still attempts to boot from the primary drive. If the primary has failed, the boot attempt will fail.

To overcome the boot problem, a fault tolerance boot diskette must be created. The fault tolerance boot diskette must have a modified Boot.ini file that points to the boot partition on the mirrored drive. The creation of the recovery diskette is discussed in the section "Emergency Recovery from a Mirrored Drive Failure."

Disk Utilities

In addition to controlling the disk layout through Disk Administrator, there are disk utilities for checking the disk. To find these utilities, right-click on a drive and select Properties. Three selections are available Error Checking, Backup, and Defragmentation. Error checking is the same as running CHKDSK from the command prompt.

Error Checking

To run the Error Checking, exclusive access must be available on the drive. In cases where this is impossible, such as the boot partition which is busy running the computer, an option will appear to allow running the disk check at reboot.

Defragmentation

The Defragmentation option will state No Defragmentation tool is currently installed unless a third-party tool has been installed. Microsoft does not include defragmentation as a part of the operating system.

On the computer pictured in Figure 1.29, a Defragmentation tool has been installed. Diskkeeper Lite is available as a free download from Executive Software.

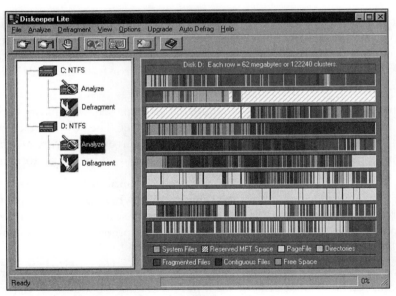

Figure 1.29. *Diskkeeper Lite's analysis of the D drive.*

NTFS and FAT partitions become badly fragmented with use. In this disk, the pagefile is fragmented, which is a cause of slower performance. Defragmenting a disk drive can improve performance considerably. The actual display in color provides a nice graphical interpretation of the fragmentation and the progress as the drive is defragmented.

> **Warning**
>
> *Do not use third-party disk utilities not specifically designed for Windows NT, NTFS, or long filenames. Damage to filenames or the directory structure may occur.*

Performance Issues

Performance is important on any operating system. NT has some features that can adversely affect system and network performance.

To tune some aspects of Windows NT requires directly editing the Registry. The Registry is indirectly edited when using configuration tools in the Control Panel. The most dangerous of all NT system administration tools is the *Registry Editor*. There are two versions, REGEDIT.EXE and REGEDT32.EXE. The REGEDIT.EXE version provides better search capabilities. Neither provides protection for the user administering the system.

NT uses a swap file called the *pagefile*. Fragmentation of the pagefile can occur as the pagefile grows. When the pagefile is fragmented, move it to another disk and then defragment the drive.

To move the pagefile:

1. Go to the Control Panel, System.

2. Select the Performance tab and click on the Change box in the Virtual Memory area.

3. Select another drive and create the pagefile file.

4. Delete the pagefile from the current drive.

5. Reboot to complete the procedure.

For performance reasons, the pagefile should be on a drive other than the one with the operating system.

For more performance enhancements, set the initial and maximum size of the pagefile to the same value. This reduces fragmentation and system resources required to expand the pagefile when more virtual memory is required. Spread the pagefile across as many disks as possible to emulate a stripe set.

> **Author's Note**
>
> *The experts seem to split on whether to put the pagefile on FAT or NTFS. They also do not agree on whether to put the pagefile on a stripe set (without parity). Try it both ways and see what works for you.*

Windows NT can maintain file names with lengths of 255 characters. For backward compatibility with DOS, names are generated to meet the 8.3 naming convention of DOS. If no machine on the network uses DOS or Windows 3.*x*, disable 8.3 filename generation to save processor time and directory space. This setting is made through the Registry. All standard warnings about editing the Registry apply. To disable filename generation, locate the Registry key:

```
HkeyLocalMachine\SYSTEM\CurrentControlSet\Control\FileSystem
```

Set `NtfsDisable8dot3NameCreation` to 1 to stop generation of the 8.3 names. This does not work retroactively. To clear out 8.3 names, move files to a different volume and back.

Tip

Microsoft supplies several screen savers, and the Windows NT Resource Kit supplies even more. Be wary of using screen savers on a server. The 3D screen savers, usually labeled OpenGL, can use up all available processor cycles. The faster the processor, the better the screen saver will work. Several cases have been documented of extensive troubleshooting to resolve performance problems that were caused by the screen saver. The best screen saver is the blank screen.

Booting Windows NT on RISC-Based Computers

The RISC architecture simplifies the boot process for Windows NT as compared to the Intel platform. The ROM firmware reads the non-volatile ROM with system information, goes to the primary hard disk, finds the active partition and runs the osloader.exe program. Osloader.exe is given control of the boot process and passed hardware configuration information from ROM. Osloader.exe loads and runs the Windows NT kernel (Ntoskrnl.exe), the Hardware Abstraction layer (Hal.dll), and loads the System hive of the Registry.

From the System hive, Osloader.exe determines the device drivers that are configured to run at boot time and loads them. After the device drivers are loaded, Osloader.exe turns control over to the Ntoskrnl.exe.

The files required to boot are

File	Folder
Osloader.exe	os\nt40
Hal.dll	os\nt40
*.pal (Alpha only)	os\nt40

File	Folder
Ntoskrnl.exe	WINNT\System32
System	WINNT\System32\Config
Device Drivers	WINNT\System32\Drivers

The designation WINNT is the folder in which Windows NT was installed.

Booting Windows NT on Intel-Based Computers

On the Intel architecture, the initial stages of the boot process are similar to other Intel-based operating systems. After the POSTs run, the BIOS looks for a bootable disk or diskette, or in the case of Compaq, a bootable CD-ROM. If hard disks are installed, the Master Boot Record on the primary disk is read to find the active partition. Once the active partition is located, the operating system specific information at the beginning of the active partition begins to load the operating system.

The Windows NT–specific operating system code in the active partition loads and executes the Ntldr program. Ntldr switches from the DOS memory mode to a flat 32-bit memory model, loads file system drivers, and loads the Boot.ini file. Boot.ini has the information to locate the operating system. Ntldr displays the boot options and waits until the preset timeout period for user intervention. If the user does not specify an option, the default operating system is loaded.

Boot Files

The files required to boot are divided into two groups: *system* and *boot*. Normally the boot partition is thought of in terms of booting the computer. System files are the operating system itself. With NT, the system partition is where the files that initially boot the computer are located. The *boot partition* is where the operating system is located. The system and boot partitions can be the same partition or different partitions. The system partition must be marked as the active partition for the BIOS to locate the correct files.

The files required for booting are

File	Partition
Ntldr	System
Boot.ini	System
Ntdetect.com	System

File	Partition
Bootsect.dos	System
Ntbootdd.sys	System
Ntoskrnl.exe	Boot
Hal.dll	Boot
System	Boot\System32\Config
Device Drivers	Boot\System32\Drivers

The Bootsect.dos is required only for a system that is dual bootable between DOS and NT. Bootsect.dos is a copy of the DOS boot code from the active partition. When NT is loaded this code is copied to Bootsect.dos for execution when a DOS boot is required.

Ntbootdd.sys is only found on systems that have the boot drive on a SCSI controller with no BIOS. Ntbootdd.sys is a copy of the actual SCSI driver.

The Boot.ini File

Since the System partition is determined by being marked as the active partition, how does the Ntldr know where the Boot partition is located? That information is in the Boot.ini file. The Boot.ini file below comes from a computer with two copies of NT loaded.

```
[boot loader]
timeout=30
default=multi(0)disk(0)rdisk(1)partition(1)\WINNT
[operating systems]
multi(0)disk(0)rdisk(1)partition(1)\WINNT="Windows NT Server Version 4.00"
multi(0)disk(0)rdisk(1)partition(1)\WINNT="Windows NT Server Version 4.00 [VGA
mode]" /basevideo /sos
multi(0)disk(0)rdisk(0)partition(3)\WINNT="Windows NT Server Version 4.00
(SP3)"
multi(0)disk(0)rdisk(0)partition(3)\WINNT="Windows NT Server Version 4.00
(SP3)[VGA mode]" /basevideo   /sos
C:\="MS-DOS"
```

There are two sections to the Boot.ini file: Boot loader and operating systems. *Boot loader* determines the default boot and the time for user intervention to change the default boot. The Boot.ini file is a hidden, read only file. The easy way to change this file is through Settings, Control Panel, System and select the Startup/Shutdown tab. Figure 1.32 illustrates System Properties dialog box that appears.

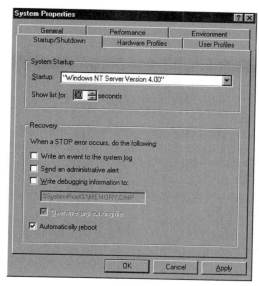

Figure 1.30. *Boot options set for Windows NT Server Version 4.0 with a 30 second timeout.*

The operating systems section reveals that there is a DOS-based boot capability. The DOS operating system may be DOS or it may be a Windows version. The DOS product must be installed first.

The boot file location is determined by the Advanced RISC Computing (ARC) path in the operating system. The ARC path is composed of four components: controller, disk, rdisk and partition (see Table 1.3).

Table 1.3. ARC path components.

Components	Description
Controller	Multi designates an IDE or SCSI with BIOS. SCSI designates a SCSI with no BIOS. Controllers are zero relative, the first is 0.
Disk	Designates the physical disk for a SCSI controller. Always zero for a Multi controller. Disks are zero relative, the first disk is 0.
Rdisk	Designates the physical disk for a Multi controller. Always zero for a SCSI controller. Rdisks are zero relative, the first rdisk is 0.
Partition	Indicates the boot partition. Partitions are one relative, the first partition is 1 (actually partition zero refers to the whole disk but is not used by Microsoft).

The example below will look for the first controller of the Multi variety—
multi (0). Disk (0) will be ignored for multi. Rdisk (0) is the physical disk that
was listed as Disk 0 on the Disk Administrator window. Partition (3) is the
third partition on the drive. Recall our primary disk (rdisk 0) has an EISA
Utilities area (partition 1), a C drive (partition 2), and a D drive (partition 3).
The boot partition is the D drive. The actual files required are in the WINNT
folder of partition 3.

```
multi(0)disk(0)rdisk(0)partition(3)\WINNT="Windows NT Server Version 4.00 (SP3)"
multi(0)disk(0)rdisk(0)partition(3)\WINNT="Windows NT Server Version 4.00
(SP3)[VGA mode]" /basevideo /sos
```

Both lines contain a user added note, (SP3), to indicate that this version had
Service Pack 3 applied. The second boot line ends with [VGA Mode] /basevideo
/sos. This line is a recovery boot that will put the video into a standard VGA
mode to recover from incorrect video drivers. The /sos option will provide a
display of the individual files as they are loaded which can help troubleshoot a
faulty boot.

Emergency Recovery from a Mirrored Drive Failure

The purpose of mirroring the boot drive is to recover from a crash on the primary disk. If the boot partition and possibly the system partition of the primary drive are not working, how will the BIOS locate the mirrored partition?

The administrator must create a fault tolerant recovery diskette. This diskette
must be bootable into Windows NT, therefore it must be formatted on
Windows NT. A DOS formatted diskette will only look for DOS boot programs and will not work.

Once formatted, the files for the system partition must be copied to the
diskette. At a minimum these will be Boot.ini, Ntldr and Ntdetect.com. The
ARC path on the Boot.ini must be modified to address the shadow partition.

Warning

*Be very careful to make this diskette and test it. Changes in partitions
may affect the diskette. Keep it up to date. Be aware of what happens
when the primary drive is no longer recognized by the computer. When
adding or deleting partitions that affect the boot path, NT will display a
warning; it does not update the path in the Boot.ini. Heed warnings
about boot path changes.*

Examine the following scenario.

Initial configuration:

- Drive 0: system and boot are in one partition, the C drive
- Drive 1: the first partition is the shadowed member of a mirror set for C on drive 0

The ARC path to boot in the Boot.ini is

```
multi(0)disk(0)rdisk(0)partition(1)
```

The ARC path to boot in the emergency diskette is:

```
multi(0)disk(0)rdisk(1)partition(1)
```

Problem: Drive 0 completely fails and is no longer recognized by the SCSI BIOS.

Attempted Recovery: The administrator boots from the fault tolerant recovery diskette and gets an error message. Windows NT will not load. An error message appears indicating a corrupt or missing NTOSKRNL.EXE.

Solution: With the failure and disappearance of Disk 0, disks are renumbered. Disk 1 becomes Disk 0. The correct ARC path is the same as the original Boot.ini.

Tip

Keep alternate ARC paths in the Boot.ini of the recovery diskette to handle different kinds of failure. If the Boot partition of Drive 0 becomes unreadable but data is still accessible elsewhere, then the ARC path should refer to Disk 1.

For the administrator unfamiliar with Windows NT recovery, it would be wise to spend time experimenting with recovery procedures. It's far better to learn on a spare machine than in the heat of battle when the corporate server is down.

There is no way to completely boot Windows NT from a floppy disk. If your emergency recovery procedures fail, install a second copy of Windows NT into a non-system partition to allow getting the computer up so that repairs to the boot system can be made. Some NT experts recommend installing a minimal second copy of Windows NT for recovery purposes.

The RDISK Utility

Critical operating system information can be saved to floppy disk and to the WINNT\repair folder. The RDISK.EXE program creates these files. RDISK is not well documented and you should always remember to used the /s option to get the security files in the repair directory and onto the floppy disk. RDISK should be run whenever there are changes to the configuration of the computer.

> **Warning**
>
> *If the Accounts database security files become too large to fit on a floppy diskette, the RDISK utility does not ask for a second diskette. In this case, RDISK cannot be run with the /s option. The administrator will have to rely on tape backups and the repair folder.*

RDISK creates a set of files in the repair folder during installation. Subsequent executions without the /s option update all information except security which includes user accounts. Failure to use the /s option could mean a repair operation would restore the default accounts available after an install. On a domain controller, this is not a crucial concern since the security and user information is updated from the PDC, therefore a reinstall of a BDC would result in a fresh download. With Windows NT Workstations or Windows NT Servers that are member servers, not controllers, loss of the security information would force the administrator to manually re-create the accounts and other security information.

To use the repair information, boot from the original setup diskettes or compact disk. When prompted to install Windows NT or repair files, enter **r** to start the repair process. Follow directions to repair the information. Four options appear in the repair process: Inspect Registry Files, Inspect Startup Environment, Verify Windows NT System Files, and Inspect Boot Sector.

With the serious nature of repairs, practicing the procedure on a spare computer will provide the administrator with the confidence to use the procedure in an emergency.

> **Author's Note**
>
> *System administrators who do not maintain control of an emergency lose data and jeopardize their employers.*
>
> *When it comes to losing data, I have never had to tell a client that I lost all of his data. However, I am reminded of the old Air Force proverb: There are two kinds of pilots—those that have landed gear up and those that are about to.*
>
> *Hewlett-Packard revealed in a Microsoft briefing the startling consequences of losing a company's data. Only 6% of companies that irretrievably lose their data survive for more than two years.*

Shutting Down Windows NT

Shut down is far simpler than startup. From the Start button, select Shutdown. Click the Shutdown the Computer option and click Yes. Wait until the It is now safe to turn off your computer message appears before turning off the power.

In addition to shutting down, two other options are available:

- You can shut down and restart the computer.

- You can close all programs, log off, and log back on as a different user.

In the Windows NT Resource Kit a useful program, Shutgui.exe, can be used by the administrator to shut down a remote computer. Figure 1.31 shows the Shutgui set to shut down Gandalf and reboot the computer. A message will be sent to the computer. After 30 seconds the computer will shut down. The user on the local system has no defense against this shutdown.

Figure 1.31. *The Shutgui.exe command from the Windows NT Resource Kit.*

The Windows NT startup process is complicated, but an understanding of the files involved can hasten the recovery of an unbootable system. It is in the best interest of every system administrator to understand all the recovery options available.

Chapter 2

An Introduction to UNIX

- **The UNIX Operating System Overview**
  Learn the origin of UNIX and its variants. Discover the purpose of shells and select the one that best meets your needs. Understand UNIX permissions.

- **UNIX User Administration**
  Explore the /etc/password, /etc/group and /etc/shadow files. Learn how the UNIX home directory differs from the NT home folder. Find out about UNIX startup scripts: what they are and what they do. Administer users from a GUI.

- **Using Groups in UNIX**
  Learn how groups are used in UNIX.

- **Performance Monitoring**
  How is your system running? Do you need more RAM, faster disks, faster CPU? The UNIX Performance Monitoring tools provide answers.

- **Daemons, Processes and Log Files**
  Learn about UNIX background jobs and their functions. Where are the log files? Observe processes and kill them.

- **UNIX and Disk Drives**
  Learn how to add new file systems to a UNIX environment and mount filesystems.

- **Booting and Shutting Down UNIX**
  Learn how to shut down UNIX with the `shutdown`, `init`, `haltsys` and `reboot` commands.

The UNIX Operating System Overview

UNIX was written in the late 1960s at AT&T's Bell Labs. It was designed to be a programmer's development platform. At the time, AT&T was under a federal order restraining them from entering the computer market. The AT&T version is referred to as *System V UNIX*. Copies of UNIX source code were freely distributed to universities, such as the University of California at Berkeley; thus, the Berkeley additions and development to UNIX came to be known as the *Berkeley Systems Division (BSD)* version. Later, AT&T began selling source code to various hardware manufacturers who developed their own versions, or *flavors*, of UNIX.

From the open origins of UNIX, the operating system developed into a number of versions. Digital Equipment Corporation (DEC) developed Ultrix for the VAX line. Data General came out with DG-UX while Hewlett-Packard has HP-UX. IBM's RS6000 series computers run AIX, Silicon Graphics has Irix. Sun is a major vendor of RISC computers running Solaris. The Santa Cruz Operation (SCO) has grown from XENIX to UNIX, acquiring Novell's UnixWare along the way. Novell had acquired UNIX from AT&T. SCO has released UnixWare 7, a merging of their OpenServer product with UnixWare 2. In addition to these, there is the UNIX lookalike called *Linux*, which is essentially a freeware product distributed by several companies for very low prices.

Versions of UNIX

To limit the size of the book, only three UNIX flavors are covered. Solaris is the leader in big UNIX systems. SCO is the leader in Intel-based UNIX and sells 40 percent of all UNIX operating systems. Solaris and SCO combined make up the major part of the UNIX market. Several smaller players have agreed to drop their proprietary versions and adopt either Solaris or SCO UNIX, consolidating a part of the UNIX marketplace.

To round out these two commercial UNIX offerings, Caldera's Linux represents the UNIX look-alikes.

Solaris

Solaris offers two graphical interfaces:

- Sun's Open Windows (OpenWin) has been around for some time.

- At login, you may choose the *Common Desktop Environment (CDE)*, a new cross-vendor UNIX standard.

In this book, I am using Solaris version 2.6 for the Intel platform.

SCO

SCO began as a value added reseller of XENIX. XENIX was originally written by Microsoft, under license from AT&T. XENIX was a scaled-down UNIX designed to run on the Intel 8086 chip. As the Intel chip power grew, XENIX was replaced by UNIX. In this book, I am using SCO's OpenServer 5, version 5.0.4, with the SCO GUI.

Linux

Linux was created as an alternative to commercial UNIX. Not based on the official UNIX source code, Linux is available as freeware for those who want to build their own UNIX-like operating system. I show Caldera's Linux and the Looking Glass GUI.

Putting Them Together

Some UNIX functions are shown in two formats:

- command line

- GUI

Author's Note

For the Windows NT administrator reading this book, I do not expect you to become a command-line oriented UNIX guru. You are accustomed to a GUI for the majority of your administrative work and I will try to keep you on that path. Command line syntax is shown for generic UNIX purposes. In some cases, file syntax is shown, just in case you need to troubleshoot. Often, UNIX flavors warn about hand editing a file. In cases where the vendor recommends against hand editing, it is noted.

Operating System Shells

UNIX was designed by programmers for programmers. When operating at the command line, programmers need a rich set of commands and environment settings to search, edit, compile and generally make themselves more productive. UNIX shells and the UNIX command set serve that purpose well. Operating system shells serve as an interface between the user and the operating system. *Shells* interpret commands, handle file manipulation, display data and generally make the operating system responsive to a user. UNIX shells have different capabilities in command line editing, history recall and shell programming functionality.

There are several shells from which to choose for your work environment. Pick the shell that suits your needs.

The Bourne Shell (sh)

The first shell released with UNIX was the *Bourne shell*. Dating back to 1970, it is the most limited of the shells. When you log in to a command line environment, the Bourne shell will provide a $ prompt for a user and a # prompt for the root user, the equivalent of the NT administrator. Most avid UNIX users will move on to a more advanced shell. The Bourne shell runs as a process named sh. Most system startup scripts in UNIX use the Bourne shell as their interpreter.

The C Shell (csh)

The *C shell* was created to provide a shell with a feel like the C programming language. The C shell displays a % for the prompt, except in Linux which displays a tilde, ~, by default. The C shell is a program named csh. The C shell maintains a history of commands executed and permits command recall and editing.

> ### Warning
>
> *C shell and Bourne shell scripts are not compatible. For example, to set an environment variable in Bourne shell:*
>
> ```
> VARIABLE=123 ; export VARIABLE
> ```
>
> *The* export *statement makes the variable available to new programs or shells run from the current shell. To set the same variable in C shell:*
>
> ```
> setenv VARIABLE 123
> ```

The Korn Shell (ksh)

The *Korn shell* is an extension of the Bourne shell. Borrowing capabilities of C shell and vi, but sticking with the syntax of Bourne, Korn shell adds command line editing, command line history, expansion of variable types, data arrays and other advanced features. Korn is an efficient command line environment for many small programming tasks. The Korn shell is the ksh program. Because ksh is an extension of sh, it uses the same command prompts.

The move appears to be away from C shell for general use and toward Korn shell. If you do not need the C shell syntax, use Korn shell.

The Born Again Shell (bash)

Bash is a Bourne-compatible shell with extensions from both C and Korn shells. It was written to be Portable Operating System Interface (POSIX)–compliant. Bash is licensed by the Free Software Foundation, not a UNIX vendor. Bash uses the # and $ prompts like sh and ksh. Bash is the default on Caldera Linux.

Permissions

UNIX permissions are handled differently from Windows NT. A file will have one set of permissions divided into three groups: user (owner), group and other (everyone). A listing of a UNIX file with its permissions follows:

```
-rwxr-xr-x   1 gene     sales      382 Aug  3  1997 hosts
```

The permissions are the nine characters following the dash at the beginning of the line. That initial dash indicates that this is a regular file. The dash could be replaced by a d for a directory, p for a pipe, c for a character device, b for a block device, and so on.

The permissions are composed of three groups of three attributes. The first three, rwx, indicate that the user who created the file has read, write and execute permissions. Note on the line that gene is the user. The second group of three permissions apply to the group, sales, that has group permissions of read and execute. The third set apply to other, essentially the same as the NT EVERYONE group.

Looking further at the information from this listing, generated with the ls -l command—list file with long option—the number 1 to the left of gene is the number of links to the file; *links* are additional named references to the file. The number 382 is the file size in bytes. The file was last updated on Aug 3 1997 and the file name is hosts.

The Change Permissions Command

Permissions are changed with the change mode or chmod command. The most common usage of chmod is with octal arguments. Think of the read, write and execute attributes as having the values 4, 2, and 1, respectively. The value of rwx is, therefore, 7. The value of read and execute, r-x, is 5. To change permissions, compute the three octal numbers representing the desired permissions. If hosts should have read and write for the user, read only for group, and no access for everyone, the command would be:

```
chmod 640 hosts
```

Alternatively, the user can use the symbolic mode for setting permissions. The letters u, g and o represent user, group and other. The letters r, w and x are used instead of octal. The advantage of this method is changing a permission without reference to the others. For example, to add write permissions to group for hosts:

```
chmod g+w hosts
```

The g+w translates to "for group, add write." Similarly, g-w would be "for group, subtract write."

The Change Owner and Group Commands

You know from the `ls -l` command output that `gene` is the user owner and the `sales` is the group owner of the file `hosts`. We can change the user to `mina` with the `chown` command:

```
chown mina hosts
```

You can change the group ownership to `admin` with the `chgrp` command:

```
chgrp admin hosts
```

User names and group names must exist to be used in the commands. To reduce the amount of work for the administrator, the `chown` command can also change the owner and the group in a single operation.

```
chown mina:newgroup hosts
```

If you have to change an entire directory and its subdirectory components, use the `-R` option for recursive changes.

```
chmod -R mina:newgroup /usr/mina
```

setUID and setGID Permissions

UNIX has extended permissions called *setUID* and *setGID*. When an executable with these permissions is run, it sets the user's effective user ID or group ID to that of the owner of the program file. A setUID program will be able to update files on behalf of the user who does not have permission to update.

A good example is the password updating process. While SCO, Solaris and Linux differ slightly on the `passwd` file permissions, the effect is the same.

```
---x--s--x   1 bin       auth       63100 May 13  1997 /bin/passwd
-rw-rw-r--   1 bin       auth        1483 Dec 15 14:15 /etc/passwd
```

The /etc/password file contains the accounts information. On SCO, it is readable and writable by user `bin`, group `sys`. As a user, you do not have permission to update your account password. The /bin/passwd program has an s in the group permissions in place of the x. This causes your effective group membership to be set to the `auth` group when you execute the /bin/passwd program. Since the `auth` group has write permission on /etc/passwd, you can change your password. When you exit /bin/passwd, you return to your normal group membership. Since the passwd program controls the nature of the edits to the passwd file, there is no danger of the user making unauthorized changes.

Programs written for these permissions are very tightly written to prevent breaking out with powerful effective owner or group IDs.

Another possible permission is the *sticky bit* that can be set on directories. The name goes back to the days of non-virtual memory when the sticky bit on an executable caused the text (the executable part of the program) to stick in memory as the user finished execution. This allowed faster startup of the program when the program was next invoked.

The sticky bit is used to provide special protection for files in publicly writable directories. Here you see unanimous agreement with the three UNIX vendors. Next is listed the `ls -l` showing the /tmp directory.

```
drwxrwxrwt 9 root root 1024 Feb 17 07:04 /tmp
```

The trailing t on the permissions shows the sticky bit has been set. Only the owner of a file or root can delete the file in a directory with a sticky bit. For example, if user1 creates /tmp/work and user2 attempts to create /tmp/work, user2 will get an error indicating they could not create the file.

Setting the setUID/GID permissions involves another 421 combination. The 4 is for setUID, the 2 for setGID and the 1 is for the sticky bit on directories. Changing the permissions on a directory to set the stick bit would look like this:

```
chmod 1777 /tmp
```

Setting the setUID on an executable would look like this:

```
chmod 4555 /bin/newprog
```

UNIX User Administration

Basically, all UNIX systems use the same files to contain a user account's database: /etc/passwd and /etc/group. Command line programs for maintaining user varied from one version to another. With the introduction of GUIs, each flavor of UNIX moved out further in its own direction.

One piece of information in the /etc/passwd file is the user's home directory. The UNIX home directory serves a different purpose from the Windows NT home directory. This section looks at home directories and the login files that reside there.

The /etc/passwd File

The /etc/passwd file is the basis of the UNIX accounts database. The file has a standard syntax with colon-separated fields:

```
Username:password:UID:GID:comment:homedir:program
```

- *Username* is the user's login name.

Tip

UNIX uses lower case names and is case sensitive. UNIX will allow upper case logins, but the password is case sensitive, so a user with Caps Lock turned on will probably not get logged in.

- *password* is the user's encrypted password, except when an /etc/shadow file is used. A lower case *x* appears as a placeholder for the shadowed password when a shadow file is in use. The *shadow file* was introduced as a security feature to hide encrypted passwords in a file that is not readable by users.

- *UID* is the user's ID. root is 0. User IDs generally range from 100 to 60,000. Solaris offers higher numbers but recommends keeping it below 60,000 for compatibility with other UNIX flavors.

- *GID* is the user's group ID.

- *comment* is anything you want—user name, phone, and so on.

- *homedir* is the user's home directory.

- *program* is the shell or program that will be executed at login.

An example of a passwd entry is:

```
lisa:x:1003:10:Lisa Gebken x 3777:/exports/home/lisa:/bin/sh
```

The passwd entry is for Lisa Gebken at extension 3777 who logs in as lisa, has a home directory in /exports/home/lisa and uses the Bourne shell. The x in the password file indicates the password is stored in the /etc/shadow file.

The /etc/shadow File

The exact format of /etc/shadow depends on the version of UNIX. It is used to store the password and additional information about the user. UNIX was written at a time when network security was not a concern and the shadow file is in response to added security. The shadow file is not readable by users. The Solaris format for the shadow file is:

```
username:password:lastchg:min:max:warn:inactive:expire:flag
```

- *username* is the same as in the passwd file.

- *password* is an encrypted password.

- *lastchg* is the date of last password change as the number of days since Jan 1, 1970 (the beginning of time, as far as UNIX is concerned).

- *min* is the minimum number of days between password changes.

- *max* is the maximum number of days between changes.

- *warn* is the number of days prior to password expiration that the user is warned.

- *inactive* represents the number of days of inactivity before the account is locked.

- *expire* is the date on which the account expires.

- *flag* is currently an unused field for future expansion.

An example of a Solaris shadow file entry would be:

```
lisa:wrcJIqoGWsoWC:10274:20:60:100:10:12053:
```

SCO OpenServer does not store the *warn*, *inactive*, or *expire* data here. SCO maintains a security database in the /tcb/files/auth/[a-z] directories. The trusted computing base (tcb) database maintains information on last successful login, last unsuccessful login, maximum login attempts before lockout and other security information. The entry for gene is:

```
gene:u_name=gene:u_id#31001:\
    :u_pwd=oN.C5cWgNGp9MqVCgpc0ZDfE:\
    :u_type=general:u_succhg#881886109:u_pswduser=gene:u_suclog#887482491:\
    :u_suctty=ttyp0:u_unsuclog#886770352:u_unsuctty=ttyp0:u_lock@:\
    :chkent:
```

Warning

Use the administrative tools provided with the operating system to manipulate these files. Editing security files could badly damage a system and prevent further logins. At least one UNIX version would not allow further logins if the passwd file was edited.

The /etc/group File

The /etc/group file is a text list of the groups, their group ID and the members. Windows NT and UNIX both allow users to belong to multiple groups. /etc/group is where UNIX keeps the records.

The format is:

```
groupname:password:gid:user list
```

- *groupname* is the name of the group.

- *password* is an optional group password, not used in SCO.

- *gid* is the group ID, generally below 60,000.

- *user list* is a list of the users that belong to the group.

An example group entry might be:

```
stooges::100:larry,moe,curly
```

The UNIX Home Directory

The UNIX home directory is specified in the /etc/passwd file. When a user logs in, her process changes directory to her home directory. If the user is a command line user, she will be presented with a command line prompt, depending on the shell specified in the passwd file.

The home directory does not have any effect on the preferred place to open or save files as it does in NT.

The home directory of the root login is usually the root directory, identified as /. Caldera Linux uses a /root directory as home for the root user.

> **Tip**
>
> *Normal users have the current directory, ".", included as part of their* PATH *variable. When logged in, they can easily execute anything in their current directory without an explicit entry for that directory in their* PATH. *When logged in as root, the current directory is not included.*
>
> *As root, to execute a file in the current directory, if the specific directory is not in your* PATH, *specify the current directory as:./program or use the full path name. The absence of the current directory is for security. It prevents root from accidentally executing a current directory program with the same name as a system command. This prevents hackers from creating Trojan horses by naming programs after system commands in directories the hacker can access.*

The Login Files

When a user logs in to UNIX, the login process looks in the /etc directory for a system-wide initialization file, login for C shell, or profile for Bourne, Korn, and Bash. After executing the system wide command file, the process looks in the user's home directory for login files based on the selected shell. Bourne, Korn, and Bash shells all use a .profile script. The Korn shell also uses a .kshrc script. C shell users have a .login and optionally a .cshrc script. Bash users optionally may have a .bashrc.

These script files set the PATH, environment variables, the terminal type, and command aliases, and possibly execute programs. A user whose UNIX function was to run an accounts payable program and nothing more could have the program executed by the login script and be logged out upon exiting the program. That user would never encounter a shell prompt.

The following is a .login file:

```
set ignoreeof             # don't let control-d logout
set path = (/bin /usr/bin /u/informix/bin /etc /u/wpbin /u/shbin .)    #
execution search path
set noclobber             # don't allow '>' to overwrite
setenv INFORMIXDIR /u/informix
setenv DBPATH /u/pfms:/u:/u/pm
set noglob
```

```
set term = (`tset -S `)
if ( $status == 0 ) then
    setenv  TERM      $term[1]
setenv  TERMCAP  /u/informix/etc/termcap
endif
unset term noglob
umask 022
```

The .profile for a Solaris user is shown next. This script will set the PATH variable, set the TERM variable, run OpenWindows if it is on the system, and logout after exiting OpenWindows.

```
#
# @(#)local.profile 1.4     93/09/15 SMI
#
stty istrip
PATH=/usr/bin:/usr/ucb:/etc:.
export PATH
#
# If possible, start the windows system
#
if [ `tty` = "/dev/console" ] ; then
  if [ "$TERM" = "sun" -o "$TERM" = "AT386" ] ; then
    if [ ${OPENWINHOME:-""} = "" ] ; then
        OPENWINHOME=/usr/openwin
        export OPENWINHOME
    fi
    echo ""
    echo "Starting OpenWindows in 5 seconds (type Control-C to interrupt)"
    sleep 5
    echo ""
    $OPENWINHOME/bin/openwin
    clear         # get rid of annoying cursor rectangle
    exit          # logout after leaving windows system
  fi
fi
```

The .cshrc, .kshrc, and .bashrc are for users to customize their environment by creating aliases and other shortcuts. For instance, a C shell alias could be created to change directory to /u/pm, and set the DBPATH environment variable to /u/pm, all to be performed when the user types **pm**. This can be achieved with the following line:

```
alias pm 'cd /u/pm; setenv DBPATH /u/pm'
```

To become good at reading and writing login scripts, the administrator must learn the shell languages.

Administering Users

All three of the operating systems have a GUI. Here we look at how to administer users with each. Finding the GUI is different among all operating systems.

On Linux, the startx command will start X Windows. As shown in the .profile script from Solaris, the GUI will start up automatically on login. SCO OpenServer offers 12 login screens on the console. Pressing the Alt key and a function key switches to a login screen with the number of the function key. For instance, Alt+F6 will switch to screen 6, designated as terminal tty06. An automatic GUI login is brought up on screen 2. On SCO OpenServer, startx will bring up a GUI on any screen.

Solaris Admintool

The Solaris tool for managing users and groups is *Admintool*. To start this from the GUI:

1. Right-click the background.

2. Move the cursor to the arrowhead to the right of Programs and then highlight Shell Tool on the drop down list.

3. From the shell tool, type **admintool&**. The Admintool appears.

To edit a user, highlight the user, and select Edit, Modify. To add a user, select Edit, Add. Figure 2.1 illustrates adding a user to Solaris. The data fields below the Account Security heading are all included in the shadow file.

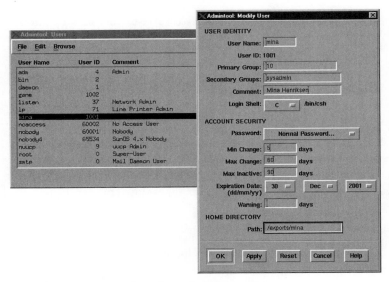

Figure 2.1. *Adding a user to Solaris through Admintool.*

SCO SCOadmin

SCO has more user controls than most UNIX versions. Figure 2.2 illustrates modifying an account to change the home directory. Note that SCO will move the users files from the old home directory if requested.

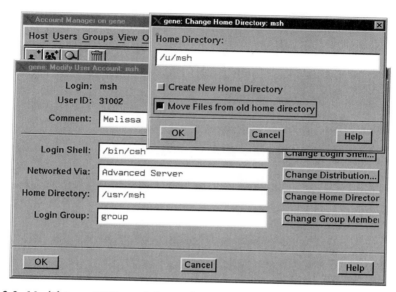

Figure 2.2. *Modifying a SCO user's home directory through the GUI.*

SCO has implemented *user authorizations*, which provide users capabilities similar to Windows NT's built-in groups such as account operator, print operator, and backup operator. Denying a user authorization for mem, for example, denies them the right to obtain a list of all processes running on the system. Providing a user with all authorizations creates a power user but leaves him a bit less powerful than root.

These authorizations, like NT's, allow an administrator to hand out specific jobs to subadministrators without providing the root password. Figure 2.3 illustrates adding authorizations.

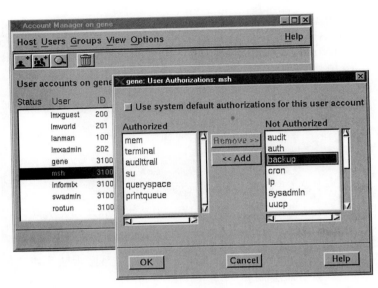

Figure 2.3. *Adding user authorizations to a user's account.*

Caldera Linux

The Looking Glass GUI on Caldera Linux is very attractive and easy to use. The user administration window is shown in Figure 2.4. Unlike most UNIX systems, it displays the encrypted password on the user setup window. The Quotas button is grayed out because it is used with Novell NDS volumes. Figure 2.4 illustrates the user window on Caldera Linux.

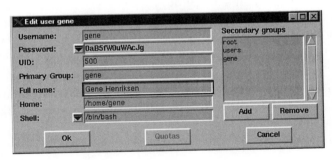

Figure 2.4. *Caldera Linux user administration window.*

Using Groups in UNIX

Groups in UNIX are used in a manner similar to Windows NT. Permissions are not assigned the same way NT assigns permissions, that is multiple groups may not be assigned rights to a file or folder. Users in UNIX must be assigned to multiple groups to access files owned by groups other than their primary group. The primary group is determined when the user is created.

> **Tip**
>
> *A user logs in as* rick, *and he belongs to group* research. *He wants to access a file named sales.rpt. The permissions on sales.rpt are:*
>
> ```
> rw-r----- 1 harold sales 1024 22 Feb sales.rpt
> ```
>
> *Rick is denied access. If an administrator attempts to give Rick permissions through the* chmod, chgrp, *or* chown *command, permissions will be removed from some existing user or users. To grant Rick access, the administrator makes* rick *a member of group* sales. *Rick then must log out and back in to get his new group membership.*

Getting Help

UNIX manual pages are available online through the man command. Two programs help with the man pages: whatis and apropos. In addition, graphical help is available on the GUI.

The man Command

To learn how to use the man command, execute man man which will run the manual page for the man command. Man pages are arranged by section, so you may see references such as man(1) or man(c). The parentheses refer to the section. Man pages provide syntax, such as file formats and other pertinent data. The man pages are not a guide to how to perform functions such as setting up a printer. These will be found in other documentation.

Executing the man command for the man page, man man, displays the following:

```
man(C)
   ******


man -- display reference manual pages
Syntax
======
man [ -a ¦ -f ] [ -bcw ] [ -d dir ] [ -p pager ] [ -t proc ] [ -T term ] [
```

```
section ] title
man -e command ...
man -k keyword ...

Description
===========
man locates and prints the entry named title from the designated reference
section. For historical reasons, ''page'' is often used as a synonym for
''entry'' in this context.
```

The previous listing has thirteen more pages of detail not shown here. Solaris stores the help pages in the /usr/share/man directory. These may not be installed and you may need to access them from another Sun system on the network. Sun uses an environment variable to set the man configuration. A configuration file, man.cf, is located in the /usr/share/man directory and specifies the manual sections available and the order in which they are searched.

SCO stores the man pages in the /usr/man directory. The configuration file is /etc/default/man. The contents of this file specify the directory for man pages, the search order, the pager used to display the pages on the screen and other options.

Caldera Linux stores the man pages in /usr/man and uses a configuration file: /etc/man_db.config.

When man is executed, it searches for the first occurrence of the title, displays the information, and quits. To search for repeated entries, the -a option will search all sections for the entry displaying each in order by section searched.

The apropos Command

If you do not know the exact command you need to use, the man pages do not help. The command apropos, which is the same as man -k, provides information on the commands that reference a subject. For example, to determine the commands that reference login:

```
apropos login
Sdsk (HW)               - SCSI hard disk driver
acct: acctdisk, acctdusg, accton, acctwtmp (ADM)      - overview of
accounting and miscellaneous accounting commands
acctdisk (ADM)          - gather user disk block data
acctdusg (ADM)          - calculate disk consumption for accounting records
acctsh: chargefee, ckpacct, dodisk, lastlogin, monacct, nulladm, prctmp,
prdaily, prtacct, shutacct, startup, turnacct (ADM)      - shell procedures for
accounting
aio (HW)                - pseudo-device driver for asynchronous disk I/O on raw
disk partitions
badtrk (ADM)            - scan fixed disk for flaws and create a bad
track/block table
```

The list for login was considerably longer. The commands are listed on the left with their purpose on the right. On Linux, executing apropos without any arguments results in Linux posing the question: apropos what? On SCO, if nothing is found, the system responds with: nothing appropriate.

The whatis Command

The whatis command searches all man books and reports on the entries by heading.

```
# whatis passwd
passwd          passwd (1)      - change login password and password attributes
passwd          passwd (4)      - password file
```

The above list is from Solaris. To display the man page for the password file, execute man -s 4 passwd. SCO and Linux do not require the -s designation. The -s specifies the section to search.

Graphical Help

In addition to the man command, graphical help is available. Figure 2.5 is the Caldera Linux help and 2.6 is the SCO help.

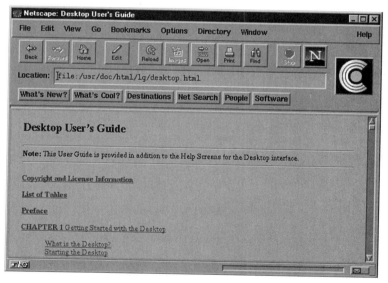

Figure 2.5. *The Caldera Linux help system.*

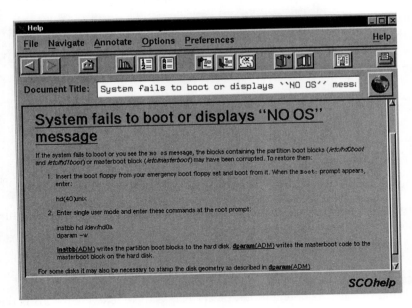

Figure 2.6. *The SCO graphical help system.*

Performance Monitoring with sar

UNIX has had performance monitoring built into the system for years. The *System Activity Reporter* (sar) is the primary tool for performance monitoring. sar is a command line tool and has many options, just as NT's Perfmon tool has. Both Solaris and SCO support sar. The syntax for sar is:

```
/usr/bin/sar [ -abBcdghLmnOpqrRSuvwy ] [ -A ] [ -o file ] t [ n ]
/usr/bin/sar [ -abBcdghLmnOpqrRSuvwy ] [ -A ] [ -s time ] [ -e time ] [ -i
sec ] [ -f file]
```

The options for sar are:

- -A. Runs all options

- -a. File access operations

- -b. Buffer cache activity

- -B. Copy Buffer activity

- -c. System calls

- -d. Disk or block device activity (CD-ROM, tape, disk)

- -g. Serial I/O

- -h. Physical I/O, DMA and scatter/gather disk activity
- -L. Latching operations
- -m. IPC and semaphore activity
- -n. namei cache, tracks cache of file name to inode cache
- -o. Asynchronous I/O
- -p. Paging activity
- -q. Queue lengths for run and swap queues
- -r. Unused memory and free swap space
- -R. Process scheduling
- -s. SCSI block request statistics
- -u. CPU activity (default if no option is specified)
- -v. Kernel tables
- -w. Swapping and switching
- -y. Terminal (tty) activity

More information on sar is available in the manual pages. A quick check option uses the

```
sar [options] interval_in_seconds number_of_intervals
```

syntax to collect information.

Tip

The main items to watch on any operating system are the CPU, disks, and memory usage. Look for a CPU running at a low idle time, disks with long queues of requests and for memory, low available RAM and swap usage.

Examples Using sar

Author's Note

The following figures are from a 486/50 with 32 MB of RAM running SCO OpenServer 5 with the GUI in use. While reading this section, ask yourself the following questions: What is the limiting factor on the system? Can we make an inexpensive upgrade or do we need to replace expensive components?

Three sar collections were run simultaneously with five-second and ten-second repetitions. The commands were:

```
sar -r 5 10

sar -u 5 10

sar -d 5 10
```

The data (see Figure 2.7) was collected with one user logged into a GUI and another user starting up a GUI session. The first data is for CPU activity. Idle time has dropped to unacceptably low levels for several intervals. The Waiting I/O time is not bad, indicating that the disk drive is probably not the problem. If %wio was higher than 10 or 15, then the disk drive could be suspected as the bottleneck.

```
SCO_SV gene 3.2v5.0.4 80486    02/18/98

09:38:00    %usr    %sys    %wio    %idle (-u)
09:38:05     16      33      5       45
09:38:10     31      59      3       7
09:38:15     50      27      2       21
09:38:20     88      10      1       0
09:38:25     89      10      0       1
09:38:30     72      27      0       1
09:38:35     69      23      3       5
09:38:40     49      26      4       21
09:38:45     0       4       2       94
09:38:50     1       4       0       95

Average      47      22      2       29
```

Figure 2.7. *CPU utilization.*

The second data set (see Figure 2.8) is for the disk drive. The average queue length and average wait times are very reasonable. Disk activity was as high as 39% busy without long disk queues. This is a result of a caching disk controller.

The third data set (see Figure 2.9) is the free memory pages (4K per page) and free swap space. Swap space declined by approximately 4600 blocks. Each disk block is one-half K in size. If you divide 4600 blocks by 2000 disk blocks per MB, you can see that swap space usage went up by more than 2 MB. Actual swap space is 98,000 blocks. At this point, 10,000 blocks of swap space or 5 MB are in use. The computer needs more memory.

```
SCO_SV gene 3.2v5.0.4 80486    02/18/98

09:38:00  device   %busy   avque   r+w/s   blks/s   avwait   avserv (-d)
09:38:05 Sdsk-0    19.12    1.00   14.14   139.44     0.00    13.52

09:38:10 Sdsk-0    39.17    1.84   37.80   200.39     8.70    10.36

09:38:15 Sdsk-0    37.25    1.00   24.50   249.80     0.00    15.20

09:38:20 Sdsk-0    13.35    1.00    5.38   304.38     0.00    24.81

09:38:25 Sdsk-0     2.78    1.00    3.98    64.41     0.00     7.00

09:38:30 Sdsk-0     5.38    1.00    2.39    97.21     0.00    22.50

09:38:35 Sdsk-0    19.12    1.00   14.14   286.85     0.00    13.52

09:38:41 Sdsk-0    34.26    7.26   37.45   296.81    57.29     9.15

09:38:46 Sdsk-0     5.38    1.00    4.58    66.93     0.00    11.74

09:38:51 Sdsk-0     2.19    1.00    2.19    16.33     0.00    10.00


Average  Sdsk-0    17.82    2.39   14.68   172.27    16.86    12.14
```

Figure 2.8. *Disk utilization.*

```
SCO_SV gene 3.2v5.0.4 80486    02/18/98

09:38:00 freemem freeswp (-r)
09:38:05    143    92648
09:38:10    123    92368
09:38:15     79    92104
09:38:20     41    90672
09:38:25     52    90408
09:38:30     38    89896
09:38:35     95    88872
09:38:40     45    88232
09:38:45     51    88056
09:38:51     65    88056

Average      73    90131
```

Figure 2.9. *Free memory and swap space utilization.*

sar can be configured to collect data automatically at periodic intervals. The data is saved in daily files named s*add*, where the *dd* is the day of the month.

The configuration for automatic collection requires adding information to the crontab file. The manual pages spell out the syntax for sar. Once data collection is enabled, sar may be run to specify a file from which to collect data for reporting. SCO provides a shortcut for enabling the automated collection. Run `/usr/lib/sa/sar_enable -y` and the `sar_enable` command will update the crontab file and start data collection.

Performance Monitoring Tools

While not delivered with the operating system, SCO provides graphical performance monitoring tools from their FTP site and on their Skunkware CD of tools and games.

Solaris has a graphical performance meter with several options. Figure 2.10 illustrates the Solaris Performance Meter.

Figure 2.10. *The Solaris Performance Meter.*

Daemons and Log Files

UNIX runs processes in the background. A process' function is to watch over specific operations. Windows NT refers to these as *services*, UNIX calls them *daemons*.

> **Author's Note**
>
> Daemon *is derived from the Greek meaning "guardian angel" or "guiding spirit." It has no relationship to the Germanic meaning of* demon, *meaning evil spirit. In one instance, a system administrator removed all programs referred to as daemons from his system in an attempt to exorcise the demons from his computer. He then called tech support to ask why processes such as printing no longer worked. Another company had a potential employee who refused to work on UNIX because it contained "demonic" code.*

Daemons are generally brought up at boot time. They manage operating system functionality behind the scenes. Examples of these are printer daemons; the inet daemon that intercepts all initial requests for network service and routes them to the appropriate process; and the cron daemon that runs processes at scheduled times.

Unlike NT, there is no central control panel to start, stop, pause, or change configurations for these system processes. Each daemon is started by a script file in the startup process. What you can do with UNIX daemons varies by process. In some cases, you may change the configuration file used by a daemon and send it a signal that causes it to re-read its configuration file. The sar command's data collection programs, discussed earlier, can be run as background processes.

Log Files

UNIX stores information in several log files. From the character-based interface to UNIX, there is no central point to view log files. Various methods for logging information evolved as the developers of UNIX addressed the need for logging in different environments; therefore, there is no single tool such as NT's Event Viewer to consolidate the viewing of log files. Log files need to be watched, not only for errors, but to keep them at a manageable size. Some will grow forever, like unanswered email.

Depending on the version of UNIX used, log files may appear in different directories and have different formats.

On both SCO and Solaris, the /usr/adm or /var/adm directory contains several log files. One of those log files is messages. The format is very different between the two, but the purpose is the same—to record startup messages including hardware configuration. The sulog is a list of users who have used the su, switch user, command to switch to another user's ID.

SCO has a graphical tool for managing and reading logs. Figure 2.11 shows the GUI log tool in use. In the bottom half of the display labeled Contents of /var/adm/syslog, note that in the last line, sendmail is starting a daemon.

While UNIX does not offer the ease of the Event Viewer for looking at logged messages, Automated UNIX shell scripts provide a method for searching logs for errors and email them to the administrator.

cron

The cron daemon is the equivalent of the NT at command. UNIX has an at command in addition to cron. The UNIX at command is used for one-time executions of programs at a specified date and time. The cron daemon is started at boot time. It reads a series of configuration files called *crontabs*. For example, Linux includes /etc/crontab. The Linux crontab entries trim logfiles, clean old files out of the /tmp and /var/tmp directories, and perform other system functions.

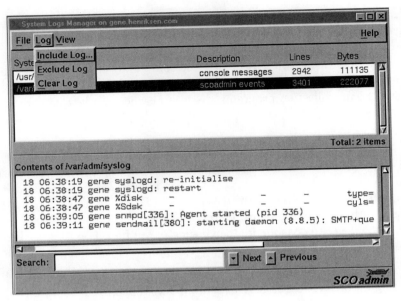

Figure 2.11. *The Log Manager on SCO UNIX.*

Both SCO and Solaris have their crontab files stored in /var/spool/cron/
crontabs. SCO provides four crontabs:

- root

- adm

- sys

- uucp

Solaris adds one for lp. Each of these crontab files is the name of a user in the
/etc/passwd file.

The crontab File

The Solaris sys crontab file is shown below. All of the jobs are comments. In
UNIX, lines for remarks or comments have a pound sign, #, at the beginning of
the line. Any place a pound sign occurs in the line starts a comment. Removing
the leading # from the last three lines would turn on the automated collection
of system activity data for sar.

```
#ident    "@(#)sys    1.5    92/07/14 SMI"    /* SVr4.0 1.2    */
#
# The sys crontab should be used to do performance collection. See cron
# and performance manual pages for details on startup.
#
# 0 * * * 0-6 /usr/lib/sa/sa1
```

```
# 20,40 8-17 * * 1-5 /usr/lib/sa/sa1
# 5 18 * * 1-5 /usr/lib/sa/sa2 -s 8:00 -e 18:01 -i 1200 -A
```

The crontab Syntax

The syntax of a cron line is:

```
minutes hours day_of_month month day_of_week program
```

Numbers can be comma separated to make a list. For example, `0,15,30,45` could be used to run a program at 15 minute intervals. Ranges can be created with a dash. For example, `1-5` in the day_of_week column would represent Monday through Friday. An asterisk is a wild card meaning any legal value.

The lines in the sys crontab would be interpreted as follows:

```
# 0 * * * 0-6 /usr/lib/sa/sa1
```

On the hour, every hour, every day, every month, from Sunday through Saturday, run /usr/lib/sa/sa1

```
# 20,40 8-17 * * 1-5 /usr/lib/sa/sa1
```

At 20 and 40 minutes after the hour, from 8 am to 5 pm, every day, every month, from Monday through Friday, run /usr/lib/sa/sa1.

The combined effect of the two lines is data collection hourly, except for weekdays, when data is collected at 20 minute intervals.

Using crontabs

Any authorized user may have a crontab file. Administrators may deny use of crontabs to users with an entry in the cron.deny file. To specify a small number of users allowed to use crontabs, place their names in the cron.allow; all other users will be denied.

To change a crontab file, the best technique is to make a copy of the current file that is running. Use the following command to create a copy of the current crontab for your effective user (how you are logged in):

```
crontab -l > mycronfile
```

Edit the mycronfile and submit it to cron with:

```
crontab mycronfile
```

Editing the existing files in the crontab directory will not cause cron to recognize the change until the system is rebooted.

Two other options to the crontab command are `-r` to remove a user's crontab and `-e` to edit the current crontab. While the edit option sounds easy, if you make a mistake while editing, it is difficult to quit without wiping out the existing crontab file.

> **Warning**
>
> *Executing crontab with no arguments will provide a help message in Linux. In both Solaris and SCO OpenServer, you will be telling crontab that you want to construct a new crontab file from scratch and will input the entire file at the keyboard. If you try to get out and use a Control-D to escape, crontab submits what you typed in as your replacement.*

One benefit that crontab offers over the NT AT command is the ability to specify months. Commands can be created that will be executed on the first day of a quarter or year by specifying the months for execution.

The at Command

The UNIX at command is for single executions. It is a command line program illustrated below:

```
# at 5 pm Friday
echo "Time for kayaking!!" > /dev/tty01
job 888012000.a-1243:0 at Fri Feb 20 17:00:00 1998
```

The at entry is terminated by entering a Control-D on a blank line. Type the command you want, press Enter, then press Control-D. The job identification is displayed when the job is accepted.

Both at submissions and crontabs are stored in directories under /var/spool/cron named atjobs and crontabs under SCO and Solaris. Linux stores them in /var/spool/cron and /var/spool/atjobs.

> **Warning**
>
> *When disgruntled employees leave, check for crontabs and atjobs after disabling their accounts. If a user had root privileges, check all crontabs and atjobs for potentially damaging commands to be run in the future. I heard of one person who put in a "time bomb" because of upcoming layoffs. He did not get laid off and forgot to undo the bomb. It went off and he was fired.*

Process Status

A *process* is defined as an instance of a program that is running in memory. In UNIX, processes spawned by one process become child processes of the process that spawned them, their parent process. Each process is given a *process ID (PID)*. The parentage of a process can be tracked by the *parent process ID (PPID)* to the process that created it.

Working back up the ladder, the original process in the lineage can be discovered. Managing processes is a part of the administrator's functions. To manage processes, it is necessary to be able to list the processes and diagnose them. We begin with the process status or ps command.

The ps Command

The ps command provides a listing of processes. The verbosity of output is based on the options used to execute the command.

Below is the partial output of the ps -ef command on SCO. The entries with a question mark under the TTY column are not associated with a terminal, therefore they are daemon processes.

```
UID    PID  PPID  C    STIME     TTY       TIME CMD
root     0     0  0  09:27:04     ?      00:00:00 sched
root     1     0  0  09:27:04     ?      00:00:02 /etc/init -a
root     2     0  0  09:27:04     ?      00:00:01 vhand
root     3     0  0  09:27:04     ?      00:00:01 bdflush
root     4     0  0  09:27:04     ?      00:00:00 kmdaemon
root     5     1  0  09:27:04     ?      00:00:05 htepi_daemon /
root     6     0  0  09:27:04     ?      00:00:00 strd
root   693   541  0  09:32:43     ?      00:00:06 lmx.srv -s 1
root    47     1  0  09:29:38     ?      00:00:00 /etc/ifor_pmd
root    48    47  0  09:29:38     ?      00:00:03 /etc/ifor_pmd
root    43     1  0  09:29:34     ?      00:00:00 /etc/syslogd
root    36     1  0  09:29:33     ?      00:00:00 htepi_daemon /stand
root    74     1  0  09:29:46     ?      00:00:00 strerr
root    51    48  0  09:29:39     ?      00:00:00 /etc/sco_cp
root    53    48  0  09:29:39     ?      00:00:03 /etc/ifor_sld
root   285     1  0  09:30:47     ?      00:00:00 /etc/cron
susie  658     1  0  09:32:03  tty01     00:00:01 /bin/login susie
susie  718   658  0  09:33:59  tty01     00:00:01 -sh
root   268     1  0  09:30:46     ?      00:00:00 dllink /dev/net0
susie  823   718  0  09:39:23  tty01     00:22:17 ap
```

The ps listing provides information on who is logged on, what they are doing and how long they have been doing it. The last line indicates user susie started a process named ap at 9:39:23 on tty01. The process has accumulated 22:17 minutes of CPU time, which is quite a bit. If the time the listing was made was 10:00, then the ap process is possibly locked in a loop.

The parentage can be determined by finding the line with ap, getting the PPID from column 3, and searching up the list for a process with that PID. The PPID is 718. Line 19 is another susie line and has PID 718. This indicates a login shell, the sh has a dash prepended. The PPID is 658 which is the PID of line 18. The PPID of 658 is 1, which is the init process, line 2. The init process is the ancestor of all user processes.

On Linux, the options and the format of the ps command are different.

```
ps -aux
USER      PID %CPU %MEM  SIZE   RSS TTY STAT START    TIME COMMAND
bin       100  0.0  0.9   816   300  ?  S    07:51    0:00 rpc.portmap
col       260  0.0  2.2  1076   704  4  S    07:51    0:00 login col
col       505  0.0  1.9  1132   616  4  S    12:43    0:00 -bash
col       566  0.0  1.1   844   360 p0  R    13:24    0:00 ps -aux
daemon    151  0.0  1.5  1020   472  ?  S    07:51    0:00 lpd
daemon    166  0.0  1.1   808   364  ?  S    07:51    0:00 atd
root        1  0.0  1.0   808   316  ?  S    07:51    0:03 init [3]
root        2  0.0  0.0     0     0  ?  SW   07:51    0:00 (kflushd)
root        3  0.0  0.0     0     0  ?  SW<  07:51    0:00 (kswapd)
root       98  0.0  1.0   808   320  ?  S    07:51    0:00 inetd
root      111  0.0  1.1   820   352  ?  S    07:51    0:00 syslogd
root      113  0.0  1.0   808   324  ?  S    07:51    0:00 klogd
root      141  0.0  1.6  1072   508  ?  S <  07:51    0:00 xntpd
root      161  0.0  1.2   824   376  ?  S    07:51    0:00 cron
root      177  0.0  1.2   876   400  ?  S    07:51    0:00 /sbin/cardmgr
root      535  0.0  0.0     0     0  3  Z    13:02    0:00 (sh <zombie>)
```

The SIZE column does not take into consideration overhead associated with tasks and should be increased by about 12K. The SIZE may also include areas of memory shared with other processes. The important information here in looking for hogs is %CPU, %MEM, and TIME. Note line 18: A *zombie process* is one that has died but not been cleared from the process table. This occurs when a parent process does not wait for a child process to terminate. The child process can not report its termination back to the parent so hangs. It uses no system resources. Eventually the system will clear the process slot.

The kill Command

Once you have learned to read a ps listing, you are ready to manage processes. The primary management method is to kill them. kill is used to send signals to processes. The signal may or may not terminate the process. Several options exist for the kill command. The most common are

```
kill -1 <pid>
```

The -1 signal is used to notify some commands to reread their configuration files. An example of this behavior is found in inetd the internet daemon. If changes are made to /etc/inetd.conf, executing kill -1 <pid_of_inetd> will force it to re-read the inetd.conf.

```
kill <pid>
```

With no options, kill is asking programs to close up and quit (equivalent to kill –15 PID). This is the method used by the shutdown command to close down all processes.

```
kill -9 <pid>
```

The -9 option is the unconditional kill. This should only be used as the last resort. Processes hit with a -9 do not get a chance to flush I/O buffers, close files or clean up work files.

Some processes cannot be killed. These include the system processes. Attempting to kill the init process, PID 1, will not work. The only way to end these processes is to shut down. Processes that are hung awaiting response from hardware will not die until the hardware responds or the system is rebooted.

UNIX and Disk Partitions

Unlike Windows NT, UNIX does not assign drive letters to disk partitions. UNIX creates a file system on each partition and the partition is then mounted onto an existing directory within the UNIX file system. The result of the UNIX approach is an extensible inverted tree file system that can cover multiple partitions on multiple disks (and multiple networked systems via NFS) without the user being aware of the actual partition or disk they are using. The application residing in /usr/medical could be moved to a new partition. The new partition is then mounted onto the /usr/medical directory. When users access the contents of /usr/medical, they are redirected to the mounted partition. All path names stay the same.

New partitions can be created and added to the system at any time. No reconfiguration or reinstallation is necessary when the new partition is mounted onto the old directory.

Author's Note

This makes the task of balancing the load of disk drives easier than the Windows method. Generally, Windows applications need to be uninstalled and reinstalled to be moved to another drive letter.

UNIX File System Structure

The UNIX file system structure starts at the root directory designated by a slash (/). Directories are created using the mkdir command. UNIX uses the (.) and (..) notations to indicate the current and parent directory, respectively.

Unlike other operating systems, UNIX separates the directory from the data concerning the file's location, ownership, size, and other control information. The directory contains the name, required for us to remember the file, and an information node or *inode* number that contains information about the file such as ownership, date of creation, last access, location of data, permissions, and so on. The inode number is the important information to the operating system, and the name is a reference to translate into the inode number. The `ls` command includes the `-i` option to list the inode number associated with each file.

By way of an analogy, the index card in a manual library card file is a pointer to a book on a shelf. Generally three cards were set up:

- By title

- By author

- By subject

There may be only one book, but there were three pointers to it. In the same way, directory names are pointers to inodes. The UNIX link command, `ln`, allows linking additional pointers to the inode.

Links

Links serve several purposes. A program called list could be written to maintain a list of names. Instead of having the program ask the user if she desires to add or delete, or instead of executing `list -a` for add or `list -d` for delete, links could be used. Link the program list to add and delete.

```
ln list add
ln list delete
```

The first step is to develop a program that provides the desired functionality. Add code at the beginning of the program to check the name by which the program was executed. In C and shell programming, the software examines argument zero of the command execution. For example, `list a` would have `list` as argument zero and `a` as argument one. Argument zero determines the action to be performed. With the links shown above, the program named list is linked to `add` and `delete`. When a user executed `add`, the program would examine argument zero and proceed to the `add` function.

These links are called *hard links* and work within a single file system. *Symbolic links* may be used to span file systems and to link directories.

> **Tip**
>
> *A good use for symbolic links is to move a directory and maintain the original name. For example, software is in place that requires programs to be installed in /usr/app. The /usr file system is running out of space. Plenty of space exists in /u. Move the contents of /usr/app to /u/app. Delete /usr/app. Create a symbolic link from /usr/app to /u/app: ln -s /u/app /usr/app. The application will be redirected to /u/app whenever it accesses /usr/app.*

At installation, many directories are created and populated with files. Each version of UNIX has its preference for where to place files. There is always a /bin and /usr/bin (binaries), /etc (system startup, shutdown, configuration), /dev (devices), /mnt (default mount point), and /usr (usually used for systems directories, sometimes for applications and home directories). In addition, there can be /home (home directories) and /sbin (shared binaries).

Both Solaris and SCO have an /etc/default directory with many default configuration files.

mount and umount Commands

Before a partition can be accessed, it must be mounted onto a directory. For partitions created at installation, this is installed at setup. Adding additional disk drives varies by UNIX flavor.

To add a second hard drive to Solaris, attach the new drive, and reboot with the boot -r option to reconfigure. The system will probe for new hardware and then will step you through the procedure to partition the drive, make new file systems, and mount the new file systems.

On SCO, to add a second hard drive, use the mkdev hd utility. This will ask questions about the type and location of the drive, EIDE (second drive on first controller) or SCSI, (SCSI ID, bus, adapter, LUN). For SCSI, you must relink the kernel and reboot. Re-execute mkdev hd, answering with the same parameters. Then you will be lead through fdisk, formatting, partitioning, making file systems and mounting.

Linux uses the Linux Installation & System Administration facility (LISA). Execute LISA, choose System Configuration, choose Hardware Configuration and then choose Hard Disks. LISA can be run from the GUI. Figure 2.12 illustrates the LISA Hard Disk configuration utility. If a second disk were available, it could be selected and fdisk would be run.

To mount a file system, the mount syntax is:

```
mount <device> <directory>
mount /dev/u /u
```

Line 2 would mount the device /dev/u on a directory /u. This syntax is from SCO. For Solaris, a mount command might be:

```
mount /dev/dsk/c0t0d0s7 /export/home
```

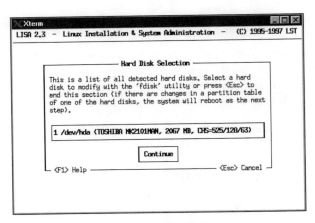

Figure 2.12. *Linux's LISA utility for adding a hard drive.*

Solaris names disk partitions based on their SCSI parameters. c0t0d0s7 represents controller number 0, target ID number 0, disk number 0, slice number 7. Note that the disk number is always 0 if the disk has an embedded controller, this is also called the *LUN* or *Logical Unit Number*. Embedded controllers are the norm. The s7 is the "slice" or partition within the UNIX file area on the disk. This use of the term *partition* should not be confused with the fdisk partitions.

File systems can be unmounted with the umount command. Solaris only allows root to mount and unmount file systems. SCO has an mnt and umnt command for use by users. Users are limited to working with file systems defined in /etc/default/filesys that have an indicator to allow user mounts. Both Solaris and Linux store their file system mount information in /etc/fstab. When a file system is in use, it cannot be unmounted. The words *in use* can mean that files are open or that a user's current directory is in the file system to be unmounted.

Troubleshooting Tip

A few months back, a client panicked because he could not mount a file system with his data. The panic was caused by lack of a backup less than 30 days old. The mount failed with an error message saying that the file system was not clean. Attempts to clean with fsck failed with a message that more space was allocated than existed on the disk.

The mount *command checks the status of the file system and will not mount a dirty system. He could not back up because it would not mount. After some thought, we used the* readonly *option to successfully mount the file system. We then made a couple of backups, reformatted the drive, rebuilt the file system, and restored the data. No data was lost and although his manager was not happy with the lost time, he never knew how close he was to disaster and the operator did not have to spruce up his resume.*

Booting UNIX

The first stages of booting a computer are the same on Intel or RISC regardless of the operating system. In both systems, there are *power on systems tests (POSTs)*. On RISC, the PROM identifies the active operating system and starts the boot process. In Intel, the BIOS searches for the bootable hard drive, either IDE or SCSI. Once the bootable drive is located, the master boot block code locates the active partition.

Up to this point, it doesn't matter if it is UNIX or NT. The partition boot code on Intel is operating system-specific. The boot code locates the boot area on the disk that holds the operating system and begins to load files. As UNIX boots, the kernel file is read and processes are spawned from the boot process.

One of the first processes to start is init. The init process is responsible for bringing the system to the correct state of operation. While Windows NT boots up to one ready state, UNIX has several stages known as *run levels*.

Run Levels

Run levels are used for different levels of operation:

- 0. Shutdown.
- 1. Single-user or maintenance mode. The system is only accessible from the console.
- 2. Multi-user mode. On SCO, this also includes networking.
- 3. Multi-user with networking for Linux and Solaris.
- 6. Reboot.
- s or s. Run level 1 with all file systems mounted.

The Startup Files

When left alone after turning on the power, bootup will proceed to level 2 on SCO and level 3 on Solaris and Linux. The files used to boot are dependent on the operating system.

> **Warning**
>
> *Do not edit the /etc/inittab file without a thorough understanding of what you are doing. This file is essential to booting.*

SCO Startup Files

SCO starts when the master boot loads the partition boot code. The SCO partition boot code then locates the /dev/boot partition and loads the boot program. This program displays a boot: prompt and will accept several options. The default is to leave it alone until it times out and starts to load UNIX. Entering **dir** at the boot prompt will provide a DOS style directory listing of the boot directory, which is very useful if the system will not proceed beyond the boot prompt. As UNIX loads, the init process takes over and reads through the /etc/inittab, starting processes according to the predefined list.

If manually booted by pressing Enter at the boot prompt, the process will stop at the single user mode to give the user the opportunity to enter the root password to do system maintenance. Otherwise, the user presses Control-D and the system continues up to run level 2.

The files that are used include /etc/rc0, /etc/rc1, and /etc/rc2. These Bourne shell scripts are run to bring the system to the run level indicated by the name. UNIX scripts or commands containing the letters rc are usually runtime commands for starting some program. In addition, two directories of scripts are run: /etc/rc0.d for shutdown and /etc/rc2.d for multi-user. For backward compatibility with the earlier SCO XENIX product, the /etc/rc.d directory maintains a series of numbered directories containing scripts that are also run when booting to multi-user.

It is permissible to add scripts to these directories for additional services. Do not remove scripts of unwanted services, but instead rename them to use lower case first letters. Only files starting with upper-cased first letters are executed.

Solaris

Solaris boot can be driven by either ufsboot (UNIX file system boot) for a computer with disk drives or inetboot for a diskless workstation. The ufsboot will look for a platform-specific boot program. On the Intel platform that is /platform/I86pc/boot/solaris/boot.bin, for SPARC it will vary by platform.

The /etc/bootrc script is started and prompts the user to enter boot parameters. Left alone, the system autoboots. Next the kernel is loaded. The kernel loads additional modules, mounts file systems and starts init to bring the system to the default run level.

The scripts run by init are located in the /etc/rc0.d, /etc/rc1.d, /etc/rc2.d, /etc/rc3.d and /etc/rcS.d directories based on the run level requested.

Linux

The Linux kernel is booted by default if the system is turned on and left alone. Linux uses the /etc/inittab to guide init through the startup. All the startup scripts for init are stored in subdirectories of /etc/rc.d. These include the rc0.d through rc6.d directories. An additional directory, init.d, keeps the actual copies of the scripts and links exist in the appropriate rc directories. The script file /etc/rc.d/rc is run by init with the run level as an argument. The rc script then locates the appropriate directory and executes the scripts.

Shutdown

Shutting down a UNIX system usually involves the shutdown command. Other options for shutting down include halt and reboot. There are differences by version.

Solaris

In Solaris, the shutdown command is as follows:

```
/usr/sbin/shutdown [-y] [-g grace_period] [-i init_state] [message]
```

- -y. Answers the any questions with a yes

- -g. Time to shutdown in seconds

- -i. Init level to proceed to

- message. The message to be sent to users

Linux

In Linux, the shutdown command is as follows:

```
/sbin/shutdown [-t sec] [-rkhncf] time [warning-message]
```

- -t. Time in seconds to wait before proceeding.

- -k. Don't really shut down; send the warning messages to everybody.

- -r. Reboot after shutdown.

- -h. Halt after shutdown.

- -n. Don't call init to do the shutdown but do it yourself. The use of this option is discouraged, and its results are not always what you'd expect. (Note: This warning is from the Linux documentation.)

- -f. Do a "fast" reboot.

- time. The time to shutdown. It can be in hh:mm format or in +minutes format. The time option is required.

SCO

The SCO shutdown instructions are the following:

```
/etc/shutdown [ -f file ¦ mesg ] [ -g[hh:]mm ]
[ -i[0156sS] ] [ -y ] [ su ]
```

- -f. Can be a file with a shutdown message. If mesg is enclosed in quotes, then the enclosed statement is used for a message.

- -g. Go to new init level in hours and minutes, hh:mm. The default is one minute.

- -i. New init level. Default is zero.

- -y. Answer the Do you want to continue? message with y.

- su. Shutdown to single user.

init

The shutdown command is a shell script that eventually runs the init command to change the run level. If you do not need to warn users, time can be saved by running init. Any of the run levels can be specified. For instance, to shut down completely:

```
init 0
```

Linux intercepts the init execution and runs shutdown regardless of your intentions.

Two other commands exist for halting the system are:

- The halt command, haltsys on SCO, will flush disk buffers and halt the processor. The halt command does not allow for the normal /etc/rc0.d scripts to gracefully shut down running processes. As a result of the abrupt shutdown, halt is not recommended on systems, particularly when networking is operational.

- The reboot command is the same as the halt command with the exception that it will restart the computer.

Both reboot and halt can be run on Solaris with an option to prevent synchronizing the in-memory disk information by flushing it to disk. This is not recommended, since it may result in corrupted disks. Shutdown without synchronizing may be necessary if the administrator has run the file system check, fixed errors, and wanted to reboot without in-memory file system information being written over top of the repaired information.

Author's Note

The init 6 *or* shutdown *with the* 6 *option is handy when you are dialed into a computer and need to reboot.*

A Short List of UNIX Commands

With all the GUI support on Windows NT and UNIX, there are still times when the command line is necessary. For UNIX, one use for command line is when dialed in over a serial modem connection, the GUI interfaces need more bandwidth. Another use is in single user mode when the GUI may not be available or is broken.

The following list of commands is not a complete listing of all UNIX commands, just those I find helpful.

File Manipulation Commands

more. Page files to screen one page at a time. Unlike the Microsoft use of more, in UNIX it is a verb:

```
more filename
```

pg. Page files, similar to more but with more options.

cat. Send complete file to screen, disk, or printer, and so on.

```
cat filename > /dev/lp0, sends file to parallel port
```

vi. Text editor, very powerful, but with a cryptic command syntax.

ls. List files, many options available.

cp. Copy files.

copy. Copy files and directories (SCO only).

grep. Search for strings in files. grep is an acronym for Global search for Regular Expression and Print. grep "customer" *.c searches all files ending in .c for the string customer.

rm. Delete files. There is no "are you sure" question. The -r option acts recursively. rm -r * will remove all files from the current directory downward. If the current directory is root, then the entire operating system is removed.

mv. Rename or move files.

ln. Link files to new file names.

Backup Commands

tar. Tape archive. Creates files in a tar archive format on hard disk, floppy disk, or tape. tar can be used to move entire directory substructures.

cpio. Copy in out. Creates backup archives that are more portable between UNIX flavors.

System Commands

uname -x. Prints out version, node name and other information about a UNIX system (Solaris and SCO).

uname -a. Prints out operating system name, node name, version date, and time on a Linux system.

A listing of the bin directories will reveal a wealth of utilities and system commands. A good book on shell programming will provide information on the use of many shell executables to build new scripts. Utilities such as cut, paste, sed, and other powerful UNIX tools have been used by administrators for years to enhance their systems.

Chapter 3

Microsoft TCP/IP on Windows NT 4.0

- **Microsoft Networking**
  Learn about Microsoft networking and NetBIOS, along with a little history.

- **Browser Service**
  Microsoft networking depends heavily on browsing. Learn what browsing is, how it works, and how to reduce its impact on network performance.

- **Dynamic Host Configuration Protocol (DHCP)**
  DHCP can reduce the work of the systems administrator in controlling TCP/IP IP addresses. You explore DHCP and its options in this chapter.

- **Windows Internet Configuration Protocol (WINS)**
  WINS is used to reduce broadcast traffic and convert NetBIOS computer names into IP addresses.

- **Server Message Block**
  Server Message Block (SMB) is the software format for data flow on Microsoft networks. SMB is being replaced by Common Internet File System (CIFS).

- **TCP/IP Utilities**
  Discover the utilities included in Microsoft TCP/IP. Learn how to troubleshoot your network connection with IPCONFIG and NBTSTAT.

- **The NET Command**
  The NET command is a command line utility with 22 option groups. See how this command can be used to augment the mouse and GUI components.

- **Setting Up TCP/IP on Windows NT with the Network Applet**
  Microsoft wraps up all networking controls in a single applet in the
  Control Panel. Learn how to control your network environment and take
  advantage of Microsoft capabilities.

Microsoft Networking

For many years, Microsoft networking revolved around the NetBIOS application programming interface (API) and the NetBIOS Extended User Interface
(NetBEUI) transport protocol. The NetBIOS interface uses machine names
rather than numeric addresses to maintain the identification of computers.
Each NetBIOS name has to be unique within the network. The NetBEUI protocol was well suited for the DOS-based PC, requiring very little memory and
performing quickly. NetBEUI has its flaws; compared to today's Internet,
NetBEUI is not routable and is limited to small local area networks (LANs).

With the onslaught of the Internet and the TCP/IP protocol suite, Microsoft
changed the primary protocol of Windows NT Server as of Version 3.51 from
the NetWare-compatible IPX/SPX to TCP/IP. NetBEUI remains an option for
the small LAN.

As Microsoft developed TCP/IP for Windows NT, the NetBIOS heritage was
accommodated in the protocol. NetBIOS is deeply embedded in Microsoft networking and compatibility needed to be maintained. To provide compatibility
with the NetBIOS-oriented networking applications, Windows NT runs
NetBIOS over TCP (NBT). NBT provides a NetBIOS API for the TCP/IP protocol, allowing protocol independence for the thousands of network-enabled
Microsoft applications.

> **Author's Note**
>
> *NetBIOS names are 16 bytes in length—15 characters plus the 16th char-
> acter usually displayed in hexadecimal indicating the role of the name. A
> NetBIOS name of BIGCOMPUTERNAME, which is 15 characters in
> length, would have a hex value appended of <00> for the computer name
> itself and <03> for the Messenger Service running on that computer. Other
> services have different suffixes. These suffixes are the method NetBIOS
> uses to advertise services available from a computer.*

The difference between NetBIOS names and host names is that NetBIOS names
are in a flat namespace whereas host names can be used to define a hierarchi-
cal namespace using Domain Name Service (DNS). An NT machine could be
named Server1 as a NetBIOS name and Server1.unit.company.com as a fully
qualified host name. Windows NT 4.0 uses different methods to resolve
NetBIOS names and hosts names.

Browser Service

The *Browser Service* makes the Network Neighborhood and browsing for resources on remote computers possible. Browsing is based on NetBIOS names and consists of two major pieces:

- Providing a list of computers to a client
- Maintaining lists of computers on selected servers

Browsing is turned on by default in Microsoft networking.

Setting Up the Browsing Process

Servers that maintain a browse list are called *browsers*. Windows NT servers and workstations that do not maintain a browse list are potential browsers. The basics of the browser process on servers are as follows:

- When a domain's PDC boots, it assumes the role of domain master browser.
- When a BDC boots, it becomes a backup browser if a browser already exists on the subnet; otherwise it becomes a subnet master browser.

Every 12 minutes, the following occurs:

- Each domain master browser contacts a WINS server for a listing of all domains. Domain master browsers exchange browse lists.
- Each subnet master browser contacts the domain master browser to update the browse lists.
- Each backup browser contacts its subnet master browser to retrieve an updated browse list.
- Each system with a server component announces itself to the subnet master browser.

Every 15 minutes, each subnet master browser announces itself to the other subnet master browsers.

With all the traffic described, you have only begun the browsing process by setting up the data to be used. As more computers are added to a network, master browsers make a determination on the need for more backup browsers. All NT versions are potential browsers and, whenever the need arises, a potential browser is promoted to backup browser.

If a master browser shuts down or a computer cannot locate the master browser, it initiates a *browser election*. Computers win browser elections based on their operating system version and several other factors.

Initiating Access to the Browse Lists

Now that you have all the browsers up and running, fully capable of collecting data, how do clients get the browse lists?

1. When a client needs to locate another computer, it retrieves a list of backup browsers from the subnet master browser.

2. The client contacts a backup browser and retrieves a list of servers.

3. The client contacts the server and retrieves a list of shared resources.

The relative impact on the network of browsing is heavy compared to other services. While the Browser service is useful when looking for resources on the network, it creates a large portion of the server-to-server traffic on a Microsoft network. Every computer that has a Server service running will announce itself every 12 minutes, whether or not it has resources to share.

Reducing Network Announcements

To reduce the network announcements, turn off the Server service when not required. Turning off the Server Service means that the computer is no longer able to provide services, such as File and Print Services, to clients. The means of disabling the service varies with the Microsoft operating system.

For Windows NT:

1. Select Control Panel, Services, Server, Disable; after doing this, you may no longer remotely administer the computer, and users may not access resources on the computer.

2. To hide the Server service while still being able to access the computer for remote administration, at a command prompt, enter:

   ```
   net config server /hidden:yes
   ```

For Windows 95, turn off File and Print Sharing if not used. This is accomplished through the Network applet in Windows 95. Select File and Print Sharing and clear the selections for I Want to Share.

For Windows for Workgroups, add the following entries in the System.INI file located in the Windows folder:

```
[Network]
NoSharingControl=1
MaintainServerList=No
```

Dynamic Host Configuration Protocol Service

The Dynamic Host Configuration Protocol (DHCP) service can be loaded onto an NT server. This service provides automatic assignment of IP addresses to DHCP client computers. The DHCP server might optionally hand out information on the DNS server and WINS server.

When a DHCP client boots, it loads a limited version of TCP/IP and broadcasts a request for a DHCP server. All available DHCP servers respond with an IP lease offer. The client selects the first response and broadcasts a message requesting the offered IP address. The DHCP server responds with an acknowledgment. The client loads a full copy of TCP/IP and completes the boot process.

Based on the length of the lease, the clients request a lease renewal at the halfway point in the lease. If not renewed by the 87.5% point, the client broadcasts a request for a new lease assignment. If the client does not receive a new lease by the expiration time of the old lease, the IP address reverts to 0.0.0.0 and use of TCP/IP is discontinued. The client will continue to broadcast for a new lease.

DHCP services can greatly reduce administrative overhead in an IP environment. While DHCP servers may occasionally have problems, those problems are infrequent enough to make the service worth using.

DHCP servers can provide a client with more than an IP address. From the DHCP_Options menu, select the range for options: Global, Scope, or Default. Within these options, DHCP can assign many network parameters. For Microsoft clients, only five of the options will be used:

- Router
- DNS Servers
- WINS/NBT Node Type
- WINS/NBNS servers
- NetBIOS scope ID

Other non-Microsoft clients may be able to use other options.

Unlike many services, such as domain control, WINS, DNS, and browsing, DHCP has no backup server that maintains a copy of the DHCP database. Multiple DHCP servers may be configured within a network, but no server will back up another server.

Installing a DHCP Server

DHCP service must be installed on a Windows NT server; NT Workstation cannot provide this service. A DHCP server must have a static IP address assigned. It cannot be a client of another DHCP server.

To create a DHCP server:

1. Install the DHCP service from the Network applet in the Control Panel.

2. Select the Services tab.

3. If Microsoft DHCP Server is not listed (make sure to look alphabetically under M for Microsoft, not D for DHCP), click Add.

Figure 3.1 illustrates the install process. If you have not copied the entire I386 folder from the CD to disk, then you need the installation CD.

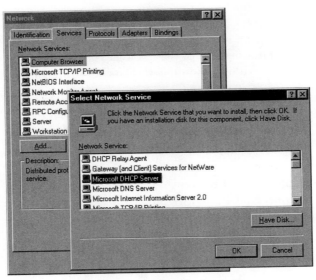

Figure 3.1. *Select the Microsoft DHCP server to be loaded.*

Configuring DHCP

After the software has been installed, you must restart the computer to configure DHCP. DHCP is managed through the DHCP Manager option in the Administrative Tools menu.

The steps for configuration are as follows:

1. Create a scope defining a range of IP addresses to be controlled by the server. With the DHCP Manager open, double-click Local Machine under the DHCP Server column to designate the server to be administered. Click Scope, and select Create from the drop-down menu. Figure 3.2 illustrates the Create Scope window that appears.

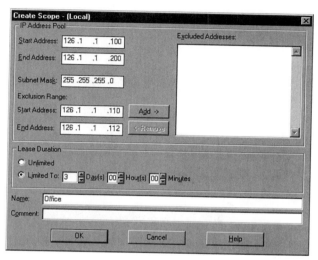

Figure 3.2. *Creating a DHCP scope.*

2. Enter the beginning and ending IP addresses for the scope. Within the range of addresses may exist addresses that have been assigned and need to be excluded. Enter the addresses into the Exclusion Range Start and End addresses and click Add. Multiple exclusion ranges might exist. Exclusion ranges should be used for non-DHCP enabled computers and other network devices such as printers.

3. Enter the amount of time for the lease in the Lease Duration area. Lease duration defaults to three days. For offices with a volatile work environment of portable computers with users on the network for short periods, a shorter lease may be desirable. For stable environments, longer leases may be desirable to reduce the lease renewal traffic. Lease renewal traffic is not excessive with only two packets being required to renew a lease.

4. The name of the scope should be descriptive. Enter comments as desired.

5. Once the scope has been created, check the Scope drop-down menu to see if the scope is active. If the scope is highlighted and the Deactivate option appears on the drop-down menu, then the scope is active.

6. Double-clicking on the scope now produces a list of the clients in the scope. Figure 3.3 illustrates the scope's active leases. The properties for the Mina entry are displayed in the lower right hand corner. The lease expires three days from the date of the original lease acquisition. The hardware or MAC address is also displayed, described as the Unique Identifier.

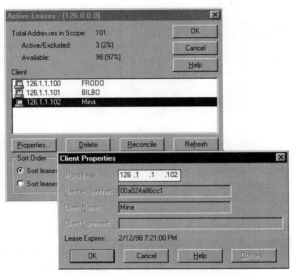

Figure 3.3. *The Active Lease window of a DHCP scope.*

Lease Reservations

As a final note on DHCP servers, *lease reservations* can be made for DHCP clients. Reservations are useful to make a server that requires a fixed IP address able to receive the IP address through DHCP so that other options may be automatically assigned.

For example, an NT print server is to be given a fixed IP address for access by a UNIX computer. To maintain as much compatibility as possible with the Microsoft network, the administrator wants the WINS and DNS server addresses given to the print server at boot time. The administrator configures a lease reservation for the print server. When the print server boots, it requests an IP address from its DHCP server. The DHCP server provides the print server with the same address each time, also supplying the addresses of the WINS and DNS servers.

Windows Internet Name Service

WINS registers NetBIOS names and IP addresses as computers boot. The client sends a name registration request to its WINS server. The WINS server verifies that the name is not already claimed by another client. If the name is currently registered, the WINS server makes three attempts to contact and verify the previous claimant. If the previously registered computer responds to the challenge, the new computer is denied registration; otherwise, the previous claimant is dropped from the database and the new computer is registered.

When NetBIOS name resolution is required, WINS servers can be queried for the IP address. Only if the WINS server cannot resolve the name does a broadcast occur, therefore WINS servers reduce broadcast traffic.

WINS servers can be configured to exchange information with each other. Servers working together are configured as push and pull partners. Since broadcasts are usually not forwarded through routers, WINS servers can provide internetwork and interdomain name resolution capabilities by maintaining information from their partners.

WINS *partners* replicate their databases periodically. Multiple WINS servers enable WINS resolution over wide area networks (WANs). Replication times can be configured to reduce replication traffic during busy periods of the day.

Starting with NT 4.0, if the primary WINS server for a client cannot resolve a request, the client sends the request to the secondary server if one is configured. If the secondary server can resolve the name, it becomes the primary until the computer is rebooted or another name resolution attempt results in another role reversal.

Once an NT server is configured as a WINS server, it begins to register names and IP addresses. In Figure 3.4 the PDC, GANDALF, was configured as the WINS server, and FRODO was configured as a WINS client. The NetBIOS-over-TCP protocol registers all services with the server.

The first item in the list is the domain master browser service on 126.1.1.4 (GANDALF). The HENRIKSEN domain is registered with a <1B> hex suffix indicating to other domain controllers on subnets that this is the domain master browser location. Recall that the PDC is always the domain master browser. The <1B> hex entry allows browse lists to be constructed by all subnet browsers working with the domain master browser.

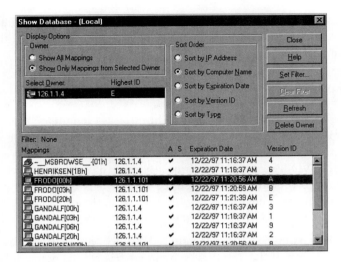

Figure 3.4. *WINS server database.*

Entries with a <00> hex suffix register the computer name. The <03> hex suffix is the messenger service. The <20> hex entry is the Server service. GANDALF has registered the <06> hex service indicating a Remote Access Server (RAS) service.

Disappearing at the bottom of the scroll region are more entries for the HEN-RIKSEN domain. A <1C> hex suffix registered by GANDALF, the PDC, is a group entry. Note the icon for the master browser is a group entry icon, with a list of up to 25 domain controllers. The <1E> hex suffix is registered by all browsers and potential browsers, and is used for browser elections and announcement requests sent by master browsers.

Static mappings may be inserted in the WINS database to allow WINS clients to locate non-WINS enabled computers. These entries might be for a UNIX computer.

When non-WINS Microsoft operating systems need to resolve a NetBIOS name, a WINS proxy server can be configured to listen for name resolution broadcasts and forward them to a WINS server. The WINS proxy may resolve the name from its own name cache. One use for a WINS proxy is to set up client Windows computers as non-WINS clients to reduce the WINS database size while a WINS proxy enables WINS resolution. This solution is similar to disabling the Server service on clients to reduce unnecessary broadcasts.

Server Message Block

Resource sharing under Microsoft native networking is performed using *Server Message Blocks (SMB)*. SMB is best described as a protocol data unit which is transmitted across the physical network connection from one computer to another.

Microsoft resource sharing is based on the SMB protocol. To share resources with non-Microsoft computers, the Microsoft computer must be enabled to understand another networking data protocol, or the non-Microsoft computer must be enabled to work with SMB.

SMB data is placed in network packets to be delivered by NetBEUI, TPC/IP or IPX. An SMB packet could be analogous to a letter addressed to another computer (NetBIOS name) and delivered by courier (TCP/IP).

SMB is the basis for a new protocol under development—*Common Internet File System (CIFS)*. CIFS is a multi-vendor project designed to provide a rich file access service without ties to a specific name service, such as NetBIOS. CIFS allows common resource access from heterogeneous operating systems on a network in a more advanced manner than SMB.

With CIFS, a user wanting to download only the first page of a 2 megabyte document would be able to specify only the first page as opposed to current protocols that required download of the entire document.

TCP/IP Utilities

Microsoft includes many of the usual TCP/IP utilities: FTP, Telnet, PING, RSH, REXEC and RCP. Usually the "r" commands (RSH, REXEC and RCP) are thought of as UNIX-to-UNIX commands, but they exist and work in Windows NT.

PING, FTP, and Telnet all use the standard UNIX syntax. By default, PING will send four messages and then quit. With most command line interface NT programs, help is available by entering the command name followed by a slash question mark:

```
ping /?
```

The Windows NT versions of REXEC and RSH both run commands on remote hosts, such as UNIX hosts. One difference is that REXEC prompts for a password and RSH does not. For RSH to work, the account name must be in the .rhosts or the /etc/hosts.equiv file on the remote UNIX computer. The NT version of RCP includes a -h option for copying hidden (DOS) files. RCP has the same authentication requirements as RSH. Neither RCP nor RSH prompt for a password.

The IPCONFIG Command

Most of the Microsoft troubleshooting utilities are command line functions. IPCONFIG offers the following options:

```
IPCONFIG [/? | /all | /release [nic] | /renew [nic]]
```

- /?. Produces a help screen.

- /all. Provides a total listing of IP configurations.

- /release. Releases a DHCP assigned IP address. If multiple network interface cards exist, the adapter may be specified.

- /renew. Renews a DHCP assigned IP address, optionally for a specific adapter.

By default, IPCONFIG lists only the IP address, subnet mask, and default gateway as shown in Figure 3.5.

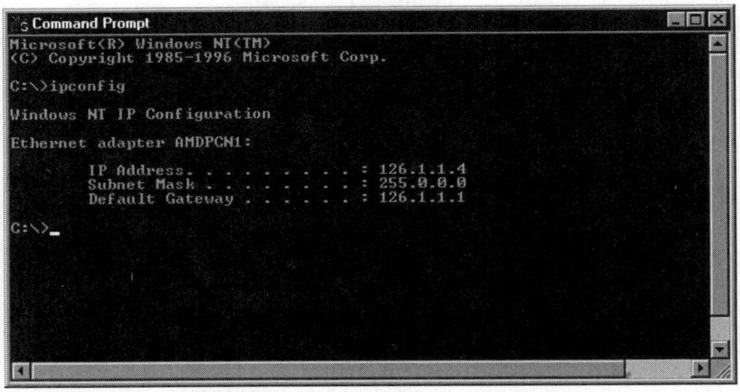

Figure 3.5. *The* IPCONFIG *default display.*

The IPCONFIG /all provides a full listing of the IP configuration. Figure 3.6 illustrates /all. The /all option is important enough that several questions in Microsoft's TCP/IP Certification test are based on problem solving using this display.

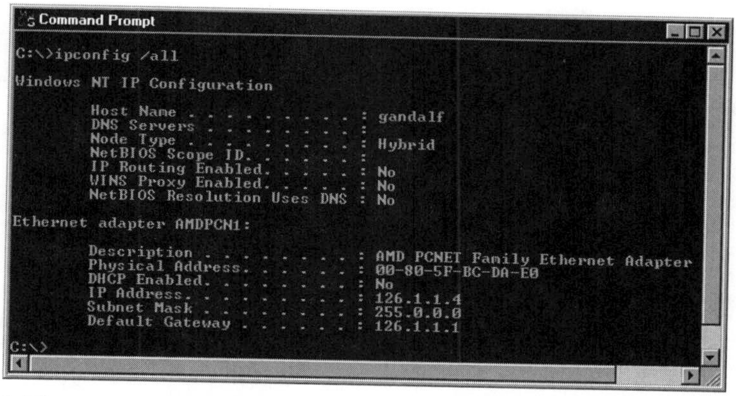

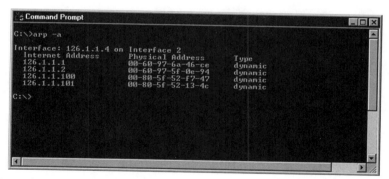

Figure 3.6. *The* IPCONFIG /all *display.*

Address Resolution Protocol

To view the current contents of the address resolution protocol (ARP) cache, the ARP -a command provides a listing as shown in Figure 3.7. ARP may be used to add a static IP address to an Ethernet address entry with the ARP -s *IP_address Ethernet_address* syntax. This is used in setting up network devices with a known hardware or Ethernet address that must be configured by Telnet.

ARP may also be used to delete cache entries. The arp -d *IP_address* syntax removes an ARP cache entry.

Figure 3.7. *The ARP cache listing.*

The NBTSTAT Command

The NBTSTAT command is used to obtain information on the NetBIOS over TCP or NBT protocol. NBTSTAT /? displays the help screen as shown in Figure 3.8.

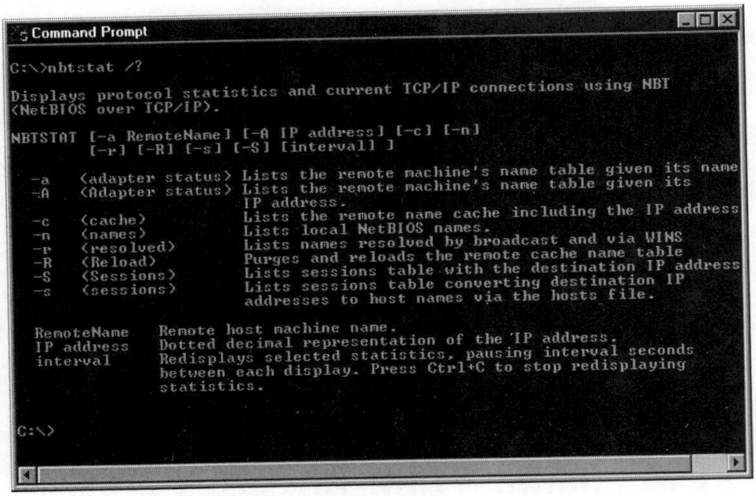

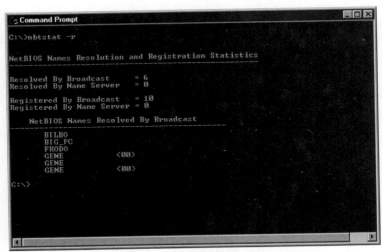

Figure 3.8. *The NBTSTAT help window.*

To determine how NetBIOS names are being resolved—by broadcast or WINS—use the NBTSTAT -r command. In Figure 3.9, nine names are resolved by broadcast. Twelve names were registered by broadcast. The entry for HEN-RIKSEN with the <1B> suffix is a domain name registration. More information can be obtained by using the -n option to list the local NetBIOS name table.

Figure 3.9. *The output of* NBSTAT -r. *All resolutions by broadcast.*

To track down NetBIOS connections, the NBTSTAT -s command lists all connections with the state, remote host and the amount of input and output. Figure 3.10 illustrates the NetBIOS Connection Table listing.

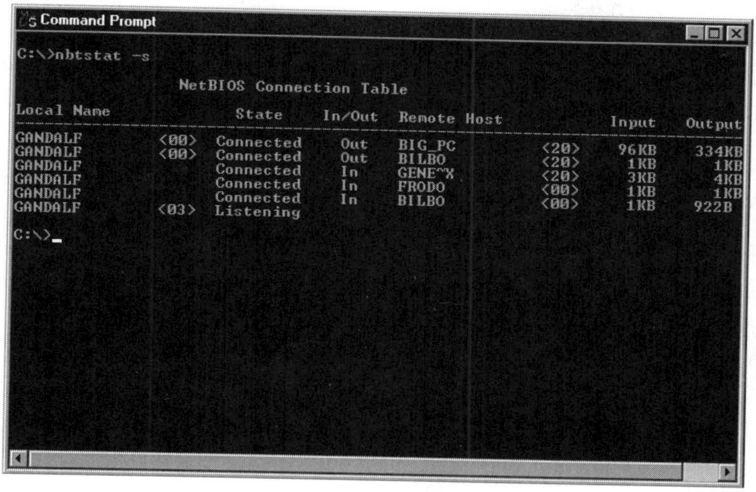

Figure 3.10. *NetBIOS Connection Table listing* (NBTSTAT -s).

The NET Command

From its DOS origins, Windows NT continues to maintain the NET command. The NET command is a command line interface providing control over many facets of NetBIOS-based networking.

The help message for the NET command lists 22 option groups. I refer to them as *option groups* because there is a help screen for the groups.

The syntax of this command is:

    NET HELP command

or

    NET command /HELP

Commands available are:

NET ACCOUNTS	NET HELP	NET SHARE
NET COMPUTER	NET HELPMSG	NET START
NET CONFIG	NET LOCALGROUP	NET STATISTICS
NET CONFIG SERVER	NET NAME	NET STOP
NET CONFIG WORKSTATION	NET PAUSE	NET TIME
NET CONTINUE	NET PRINT	NET USE
NET FILE	NET SEND	NET USER
NET GROUP	NET SESSION	NET VIEW

NET HELP SERVICES lists the network services you can start. NET HELP SYNTAX explains how to read NET HELP syntax lines. NET HELP *command* ¦ MORE displays Help one screen at a time.

The NET HELP VIEW command lists additional information on the view options. NET VIEW can be used to view shares from a computer (NET VIEW \\computername) or (NET VIEW /DOMAIN:*domainname*) will display all computers in the domain.

Setting Up TCP/IP on Windows NT with the Network Applet

Windows NT has most of the networking configuration contained in the Network applet in the Control Panel. Navigate there by choosing Start, Settings, Control Panel, Network. Configuration can be done from the Network applet in the graphical mode. Some commands for configuration and testing execute from a command line prompt.

Computer Identification

The first screen to appear in the Network applet is the Identification window, shown in Figure 3.11, with a computer name of GANDALF and a domain name of HENRIKSEN. These names are not case-sensitive, but are upshifted by NT when entered and displayed.

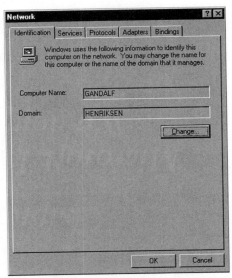

Figure 3.11. *The Identification window of the Network applet in the Control Panel.*

Network Services

Selecting the Services tab displays a window like Figure 3.12. The network services include three basic services: Server, Workstation, and Browser.

The Server service provides the Windows NT computer with the ability to provide services to other computers. Server announces itself every 12 minutes to the master browser. The announcements are the basis for the browse lists that appear in Network Neighborhood.

The Workstation service, which appears on servers as well as workstations, accesses resources on remote computers for file and print sharing. Problems with an inability to access any remote resources may be with the Workstation service.

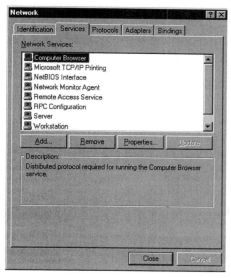

Figure 3.12. *The Services window of the Network applet.*

Network Protocols

Figure 3.13 illustrates the protocols selected for the network. In this case, TCP/IP is the only protocol. For efficiency, do not run more protocols than required. Each protocol carries overhead, not only on the local computer in terms of memory and CPU cycles, but in network traffic. Every Server service announcement and every browse request is transmitted over all enabled protocols.

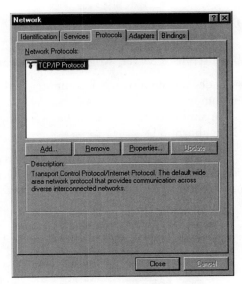

Figure 3.13. *The Protocols window of the Network applet.*

TCP/IP is the primary protocol for Windows NT. TCP/IP is the protocol used for NT to UNIX communications. For these reasons, we will ignore the IPX and NetBEUI protocols and concentrate on TCP/IP.

Clicking the Properties button on the Protocols window with TCP/IP Protocol highlighted displays the Microsoft TCP/IP Properties window.

The IP Address
The first tab is the IP Address tab shown in Figure 3.14.

Note that Adapter is shown with a drop down arrow to the right. Multiple adapters may be installed to create a multi-homed host capable of routing IP packets.

If a DHCP host is available, Windows NT can be configured as a DHCP client and receive an IP address from the DHCP server as described earlier.

For computers configured as servers of a service, such as the DHCP server or a DNS server, a static IP address is required. For these servers, select Specify an IP Address. Enter the IP address, subnet mask and, if necessary, enter a default gateway. A default gateway is required when computers on a subnet need a router that will forward packets for computers not on the local subnet.

The Advanced options include assigning multiple IP addresses to a single network card, and adding gateways and two security features.

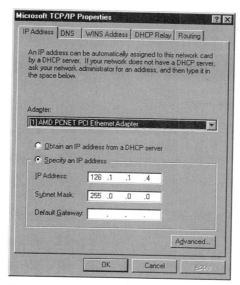

Figure 3.14. *The IP Address tab of TCP/IP Properties.*

The first security feature is used with virtual private networks (VPNs) over the Internet. It permits filtering of packets from the Internet for Point to Point Tunneling Protocol (PPTP).

The second security feature allows restriction of TCP and UDP ports and protocols. Specific TCP functionality may need to be restricted to disallow certain types of connections. Normally, TCP and UDP ports are restricted on Internet servers to protect them from intrusion. For example, if someone discovered that NT Internet servers were being compromised by a flaw in the bootserver port, the Security service could be used to filter out all requests for port 2016 on both UDP and TCP. Within an intranet, restricting ports can also result in loss of functionality.

Domain Name Service

Domain Name Service (DNS) is supported by Microsoft with a twist. Microsoft DNS allows a DNS server to check WINS for name resolution. In the DNS window, insert the DNS domain name in the block below the Domain: prompt.

Author's Note

Do not confuse DNS with the Windows NT domain name. A DNS domain is defined by the range of computer names and IP addresses it can resolve. An NT domain is a group of computers with a common

continues

Continued

> *accounts database. For example, a DNS domain could be* larc.nasa.gov, *the Langley Research Center belonging to NASA. The DNS domain encompasses many types of computers including UNIX, NT, Windows 95, and mainframes. On the Langley Research center, there could exist an NT domain in the engineering group with an NT domain name of* LARC-ENG. *We are concerned here with the DNS domain,* larc.nasa.gov.

The DNS Service Search Order area contains a listing of DNS servers. Up to three DNS servers may be listed. The Domain Suffix Search Order is used when attempting to resolve a host name into a *Fully Qualified Domain Name (FQDN)*. The first domain name appended to the host name is the local domain. If the search fails, the domain names listed in the Search Order area will be appended to the host name in the order listed.

Figure 3.15 shows the DNS configuration with a single DNS server address and two alternate domain suffix names.

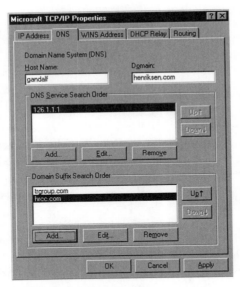

Figure 3.15. *The DNS tab of TCP/IP Properties.*

The Windows Internet Naming Service

Now you need to decide whether to provide a WINS server to the client computer. If DHCP is being used, the WINS server can be specified as a DNS setting to avoid setting all the clients.

Figure 3.16 illustrates the WINS setup.

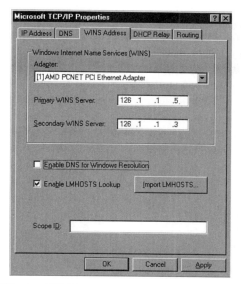

Figure 3.16. *The WINS tab of TCP/IP Properties.*

Two WINS servers may be assigned. The primary is queried first when a client is requesting name-to-IP address translation. Starting with Windows NT version 4.0, if the primary WINS server cannot satisfy a request, the secondary server is queried. In prior versions of NT, if the primary WINS server cannot supply the information, the secondary is ignored.

Clicking the Enable DNS for Windows Resolution box sets the name resolution order. Names of more than 16 characters are automatically sent to a DNS server, and names of 16 characters or less are sent to a WINS server.

Checking the Enable LMHOSTS Lookup box instructs the system to load a static file, LMHOSTS, and resolve names from the LMHOSTS file. The file is similar to the /etc/hosts file on a UNIX system. It does not list fully qualified host names or aliases. The LMHOSTS file may be required to find a domain controller on a different subnet to allow initial logon.

The Import LMHOSTS button allows importation of an LMHOSTS file from another folder or system and copies it to the <winnt root>\System32\Drivers\ Etc\LMHOSTS file.

Placing a name in the Scope ID text box enables you to create an isolated group of computers on an intranet that can only communicate with each other. This situation would be analogous to putting them into a different workgroup. It's not the same as a workgroup because they still log into the domain. They are isolated from other computers in the domain. This functionality is not often used.

DHCP Relay

When a computer requires access to a DHCP server, it must broadcast a request. If the DHCP server is not on the same subnet and the routers are not configured to forward bootp requests, a DHCP relay agent can fill in. The *DHCP relay agent* listens for DHCP clients and forwards the requests to a DHCP server on a different subnet. Figure 3.17 illustrates the DHCP Relay tab.

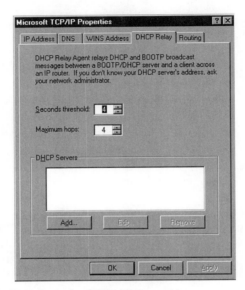

Figure 3.17. *The DHCP Relay tab of TCP/IP Properties.*

Routing

Figure 3.18 illustrates the lone option on the Routing tab. For a multi-homed host to automatically route packets, click on Enable IP Forwarding. Starting with Windows 4.0, the *Routing Information Protocol (RIP)* for IP is available. Prior versions of Windows NT have to be manually configured for static routing. RIP listens to the other routers and builds a list of known networks and forward packets accordingly.

Multiple Adapter Installation

Multiple adapters may be installed on a Windows NT computer. Figure 3.19 illustrates the Adapters tab with the Properties window opened also. Adapters may be added and removed using this tab.

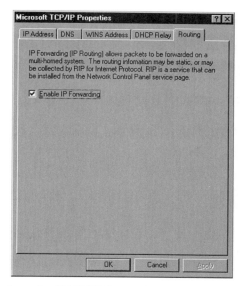

Figure 3.18. *The Routing tab of TCP/IP Properties.*

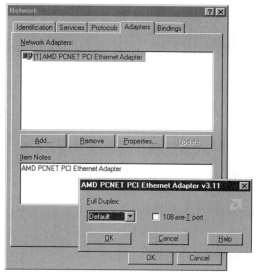

Figure 3.19. *The Adapters tab of the Network applet.*

Bindings

Each protocol and service must be bound to the appropriate adapters. *Binding* is a process of linking protocols and services to adapters. In Figure 3.20, the binding for all adapters is selected and the binding for the AMD Ethernet card is expanded to show that TCP/IP, WINS client, and Network Monitor Agent are all bound to the adapter. The WINS client is bound to the NetBIOS interface, the Remote Access Server, the Server service, and the Workstation service.

Troubleshooting Tip

Often, problems result from bindings not being complete. These problems reveal themselves as non-working network components, such as being unable to reach computers outside the local host. Bindings are automatically regenerated when exiting the Network applet. If a failure occurs, go back and click OK on the Bindings tab and check to see if it reconfigures the bindings. If all else fails, add and then delete a protocol that you are not using.

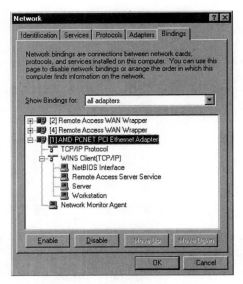

Figure 3.20. *The Bindings tab of the Network applet.*

Chapter 4

UNIX TCP/IP

- **Setting Up TCP/IP on UNIX**
  Find out more about the configuration files and script files that start up TCP/IP.

- **NIS**
  Network Information Services is a centralized account administration system for UNIX.

- **NFS**
  Network File System enables you to share files with native UNIX file sharing. You learn about the configuration files and how to use them.

- **DNS**
  Learn how Domain Name Service—the name service of the Internet—is configured.

- **DHCP**
  Solaris offers a DHCP server; explore the files and configuration.

- **Trusted Hosts and Users**
  Trusts—UNIX style—allow access to remote hosts without passwords. Discover how they work and the security problems that can exist.

- **TCP Utilities**
  Check up on TCP, the tools for diagnosis, plus some standard UNIX TCP tools.

TCP/IP on UNIX

TCP/IP and UNIX have an intertwined past. In 1983, the TCP/IP protocols were adopted as the standard for ARPAnet, the precursor to today's Internet. The Defense Advanced Research Projects Agency (DARPA) funded Bolt, Beranek and Newman to implement TCP/IP in Berkeley (BSD) UNIX. Thus began the long relationship between UNIX and TCP/IP. Other protocols have been ported to UNIX, but TCP/IP is the standard UNIX networking protocol.

> **Author's Note**
>
> *This book is written for systems and network administrators of either UNIX or Windows NT. Administrators should have a working knowledge of the TCP/IP protocol and the terminology of networking. A full discussion of the TCP/IP protocol stack, IP addressing, subnets, routing, address resolution, and ports is beyond the scope of this book. This chapter concentrates on configuring TCP/IP on UNIX and the TCP components and tools.*

Setting up TCP/IP on UNIX

TCP/IP configuration is contained in several text files. These files may be configured through a GUI or character-based interface. The files can be edited with a text editor in many cases.

> **Warning**
>
> *While the Windows NT administrator may be more comfortable with Microsoft Word, Notepad, or other Windows-based editing programs, be careful not to have TCP/IP configuration files saved in files with extensions added such as .doc or .txt. These files will not be read as configuration files by UNIX or Windows. Even worse is saving the file with the correct name, but as a Word document. UNIX will not read Word documents as text files.*
>
> *A student once asked if WordPerfect for UNIX was okay for editing system files if he remembered to save them in text format. The answer was, "I would not want to bet my system on your ability to remember saving in text format." If the file edited and saved in this manner is a critical boot file, refer to the recovery procedures in your UNIX vendor's manuals.*

The /etc/hosts File

The /etc/hosts file is a list of IP address-to-host name mappings. Host names and aliases are local to the computer. TCP/IP communicates using IP addresses, not host names, and therefore requires a method for mapping human readable host names to IP addresses. In contrast, NetBEUI does not have a networking layer that depends on network addresses for inter-network routing, using instead broadcast packets to resolve NetBIOS names to MAC level hardware addresses.

If the IP address 192.168.53.27 represents a computer with a node name of Porkchop, the /etc/hosts file on another computer could have an entry that referred to the computer as Porky. No harm would be done. When referring to the computer locally, Porky would be translated to 192.168.53.27. It is better, however, to use consistent naming.

The /etc/hosts file is the equivalent of the Windows NT <winnt_root>\System32\ Drivers\etc\HOSTS file. When copying a hosts file between UNIX and NT, do not forget the file conversion necessary to get the correct end-of-line characters. Most UNIX systems have a UNIX-to-DOS or DOS-to-UNIX file conversion facility.

The entries in the /etc/hosts file use the following syntax:

```
<ip_address> <hostname [alias list]>
192.168.53.27 Tuscany.mycompany.com Tuscan Toscano T
```

The /etc/hosts file is not case sensitive. The host name could be TUSCANY, tuscany or TuScAnY. TCP/IP will not care. The host names may have aliases. The computer in the above example can be referred to by its Fully Qualified Domain Name (FQDN), Tuscany.mycompany.com, or by any of the aliases: Tuscany, Toscano or T. For a small network not connected to the Internet and not using DNS, the FQDN is not required.

When the hosts files become too long to be manageable, or if the names in the network change often, a name service should be employed such as Domain Name Service (DNS).

The /etc/services File

The /etc/services file is a text file of Internet services with their port numbers and protocol types. All networking programs should look at the /etc/services file or an equivalent source to get the port number and protocol for a service. The administrator should not have to edit these files in a normal environment.

Port numbers are assigned by the *Internet Assigned Numbers Authority (IANA)*. Port numbers below 1024 can only be bound to by root, thereby allowing client computers to trust that those services running on these ports are authentic and not a user-created rogue service.

An example of a /etc/services file is

```
# Network services, Internet style
#
# IANA
# Internet Assigned Numbers Authority
# ftp://ftp.isi.edu/in-notes/iana/assignments/port-numbers
#
tcpmux        1/tcp
echo          7/tcp
echo          7/udp
discard       9/tcp           sink null
```

```
discard      9/udp          sink null
systat       11/tcp         users
daytime      13/tcp
daytime      13/udp
netstat      15/tcp
qotd         17/tcp         quote
chargen      19/tcp         ttytst source
chargen      19/udp         ttytst source
ftp-data     20/tcp
ftp          21/tcp
telnet       23/tcp
smtp         25/tcp         mail
```

The inetd.conf File

The primary method of starting Internet services is through the Internet super server daemon: *inetd*. The alternative to inetd would be to start each service at boot time and have them wait for an incoming TCP message to connect with them. That would involve a large number of programs running in the background using memory and processor resources. The inetd daemon intercepts calls for Internet services, looks up the request in the inetd.conf file, executes the service, and hands over the connection.

The inetd.conf file is found in the /etc directory in SCO and Linux and in the /etc/inet directory on Solaris. The format is

```
service sock_type protocol nwait user server_program server_program_args
ftp      stream  tcp      nowait root   /etc/ftpd     ftpd
telnet   stream  tcp      nowait NOLUID /etc/telnetd  telnetd
shell    stream  tcp      nowait NOLUID /etc/rshd     rshd
login    stream  tcp      nowait NOLUID /etc/rlogind  rlogind
exec     stream  tcp      nowait NOLUID /etc/rexecd   rexecd
finger   stream  tcp      nowait nouser /etc/fingerd  fingerd
#uucp    stream  tcp      nowait NOLUID /usr/lib/uucp/uucpd   uucpd
# Enabling this allows public read files to be accessed via TFTP.
#tftp    dgram   udp      wait   nouser /etc/tftpd    tftpd
# This is the more secure method, since only files from /tftpboot can
# be accessed via TFTP.  This must be root in order to do the chroot
# to /tftpboot.  /tftpboot must be created by hand.
#tftp    dgram   udp      wait   root   /etc/tftpd    tftpd -s /tftpboot
```

> **Tip**
>
> On Solaris, programs usually begin with in.—for example, in.ftpd and in.telnetd.

In the sample inetd.conf, the trivial file transfer protocol daemons (tftpd) are commented out because they can be considered a security risk. The tftp protocol does not require passwords. For security, tftpd can be run with the -s option limiting access to the tftpd directory. The tftp protocol is used with booting diskless workstations and other systems that require a download of information but do not have enough stored data to have a password. The inetd.conf file does not normally require editing.

Startup and Configuration of TCP/IP

TCP/IP is configured by the boot process. The configuration of TCP/IP varies with each flavor of UNIX system. The TCP/IP interface configuration command is `ifconfig`. Executing `ifconfig` with no options displays the current configuration. An *interface* is a mapping of TCP/IP parameters (IP address, netmask, and so on) to a network card.

Solaris Startup

Solaris uses a three-part startup procedure for TCP/IP. The first part is the execution of the script /etc/rcS.d/S30rootusr.sh. You might recall from Chapter 2, "An Introduction to UNIX," that the rcS.d scripts are single-user mode startup scripts. This script performs all configuration necessary to mount the "/usr" file system via NFS. This includes configuring the interfaces and setting the machine's hostname. During this phase, the script looks for the /etc/hostname.* files. These files define the hostname to be used on each interface. On Compaq DeskPro XL 5100's with a built-in network connection, the file is /etc/hostname.pcn0, the first pcn adapter.

From the hostname lookup, the hosts file is searched to determine the IP address of the interface. The /etc/netmasks file is referenced to set interface netmasks.

The second phase is the /etc/rc3.d/S69inet script. This script configures everything that can be configured before Network Information Services (NIS) is started. This step includes IP routing, setting the NIS domain name and setting tunable parameters.

The third script to run, /etc/rc3.d/S72inetsvc, performs all configuration dependent on NIS. In case any configuration parameters are NIS dependent, it re-runs the `ifconfig` command.

Solaris Configuration

TCP/IP is configured during setup. Reconfiguring Solaris' network parameters is performed using the sys-unconfig utility. The sys-unconfig sets the network configuration back to the unconfigured status. The actions of sys-unconfig are to:

- Restore the default /etc/inet/hosts file

- Remove the *nodename* in /etc/*nodename*

- Remove the default interface in /etc/hostname.*interface*[0-9]

- Remove the default domain name in /etc/*defaultdomain*

- Restore the timezone to PST8PDT (west coast)

- If enabled, disable NIS and NIS+

- Remove entries in /etc/net/*/hosts (loopback networks)

- Remove the /etc/inet/netmasks

- Remove the root password in /etc/shadow

- Reboot

After the reboot, Solaris runs sysidtool, comprised of sysidnet, sysidnis, sysidsys and sysidroot. Sun does not recommend running these manually.

If all you wanted to do was change the IP address, edit the /etc/hosts file. This can be done from the command line with an editor such as vi or from the Admintool in the GUI. To run the Admintool, type **admintool** and press Return in either a command tool or shell tool in the GUI. Click on Browse and select the Hosts option. Figure 4.1 illustrates adding a new system to the hosts file.

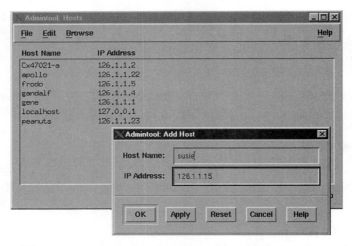

Figure 4.1. *Adding a new system to the hosts file with the Solaris Admintool.*

SCO OpenServer Startup

TCP/IP starts up in the boot process from the /etc/inittab table running /etc/tcp as the system goes to single-user mode. The defaults for domain name, netmask and broadcast settings, are in the /etc/default/tcp file. The /etc/tcp script executes the /etc/default/tcp script to obtain the settings and executes `ifconfig` to configure the loopback and the network interfaces:

```
ifconfig lo0 127.0.0.1 perf 57344 57344 1
ifconfig -p net0 126.1.1.1  netmask 255.0.0.0 broadcast 126.255.255.255 perf
4096 8192 1
```

With the embedding of the `ifconfig` information directly in the /etc/tcp script, the script does not have to reference files such as /etc/hosts or /etc/hostname.interface[0-9].

When the operating system proceeds to multi-user, run level 2, the tcp script is run a second time from the /etc/rc2.d directory to complete the startup procedure.

Also in the /etc/rc2.d directory are other scripts used in networking depending on the software installed:

- S45netbeui
- S85nis
- S86netbios
- S89nfs

Scripts are executed in ASCII sorted order, so S45netbeui executes prior to S85nis and, since it is independent of TCP/IP, NetBEUI can be invoked before the TCP/IP start up completes. The startup order ensures that the S85tcp script runs before the S86netbios and S89nfs scripts that are dependent on the TCP/IP being configured and running.

SCO Configuration

The GUI for SCO provides the configuration tools for WAN and LAN adapters and protocols, as shown in Figure 4.2.

Tip

To change the /etc/hosts file use a text editor such as vi.

Linux Startup

Linux starts TCP/IP as it moves to run level 3. In the /etc/rc.d/rc3.d directory, the script file S15inet is executed to bring up the network. The /etc/sysconfig/network script is run within the S15inet script to determine the network configuration. The network file contains following two pieces of information:

```
NETWORKING=yes
```

```
HOSTNAME=peanuts.henriksen.com
```

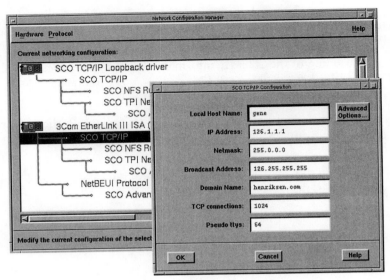

Figure 4.2. *The SCO network/ administration GUI. The Advanced Options button* *allows setting the system to be a router.*

The TCP configuration is in the /etc/system.cnf file. The following appropriate lines for TCP are extracted:

```
# First Ethernet Connection:
#
CONF_eth0_STAT="up"
CONF_eth0_DEV="eth0"
CONF_eth0_NAME="peanuts.henriksen.com"
CONF_eth0_IP="126.1.1.23"
CONF_eth0_MASK="255.0.0.0"
CONF_eth0_NET="126.0.0.0"
CONF_eth0_BCAST="126.255.255.255"
#
```

Linux Configuration

Configuring TCP/IP on Linux is accomplished from the GUI. When the netcfg icon is double-clicked, the window shown in Figure 4.3 appears. The hosts file, network configuration, and name server can be configured from this window.

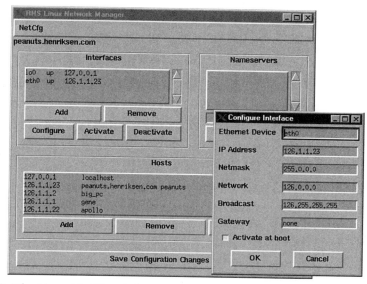

Figure 4.3. *The Linux NetCfg window.*

NIS

Network Information Service (NIS) enables centralized management of the accounts database and other files on UNIX. The files to be managed by NIS are at the discretion of the administrator. The /etc/passwd, /etc/group, and /etc/hosts are good candidates for centralized administration. The files that are host-specific such as the list of file systems to be mounted is not appropriate. In addition to systems files, NIS can be configured to handle site-specific files and their indexes: for instance, an internal phone book.

NIS is built on the client/server model. NIS servers contain data files called *maps*. Clients request map information from servers. Servers are divided into two categories: *master* and *slave*. The relationship and activities are similar to the PDC/BDC relationship and activities.

All map maintenance is performed on the master. Changes made on the master are then replicated to the slave servers. When clients need NIS information, they contact an NIS server.

NIS organizes maps by domain. A single NIS master can control several NIS domains. Clients will usually belong to a single domain, but can belong to multiple domains.

NIS Master Setup

It is very important in setting up NIS that the master be set up before attempting client or slave setup. The process deteriorates rapidly if some clients try to start before the master is ready.

The master needs a domain name. On Solaris, this is maintained in the /etc/defaultdomain file. To make the domain name permanent, create the defaultdomain file and insert the domain name. The /etc/init.d/inetinit script sets the domain name at boot. On SCO, the /etc/nis script sets the domain name. To set the *domainname* variable for the current boot session:

```
domainname <name>
```

After the domain name has been set, the initialization of the master can begin. The files to be included in the NIS distribution should be carefully examined. Unwanted entries should be removed to avoid propagating possible problems.

Be certain that the NIS master password file, /etc/passwd, does not contain an entry like +::0:0::. This entry is used on clients to indicate that they want to include NIS password data in their /etc/passwd file. Having this entry in the master's password file creates a user named + with no password.

Once the files have been cleaned of extraneous information, the ypinit program can be run to set up the database. For Solaris, run /usr/sbin/ypinit. For SCO, run /etc/yp/ypinit. For Linux, run /usr/libexec/nis/ypinit. For the master, ypinit should be run with the -m option:

```
# /usr/sbin/ypinit -m
```

The script for building the master asks a few questions and builds the database.

In order for NIS to operate successfully, you have to construct a list of the NIS servers. Continue to add the names for YP servers in order of preference, one per line. When you are done with the list, press Control-D or Return on a line by itself.

```
next host to add:  apollo
next host to add:  venus
```

The current list of yp servers looks like this:

```
apollo
venus
```

```
Is this correct?  [y/n: y]
Installing the YP database will require that you answer a few questions.
Questions will all be asked at the beginning of the procedure.
Do you want this procedure to quit on non-fatal errors? [y/n: n]
There will be no further questions. The remainder of the procedure should take
5 to 10 minutes.
Building /var/yp/red/ypservers...
Running /var/yp /Makefile...
updated passwd
updated group
updated hosts
make: Warning: Don't know how to make target '/etc/ethers'
Current working directory /var/yp
updated networks
updated rpc
updated services
updated protocols
make: Warning: Don't know how to make target '/etc/netgroup'
Current working directory /var/yp
make: Warning: Don't know how to make target '/etc/bootparams'
Current working directory /var/yp
/var/yp/red/mail.aliases: 3 aliases, longest 10 bytes, 52 bytes total
/usr/lib/netsvc/yp/mkalias /var/yp/`domainname'/mail.aliases
/var/yp/'domainname
'/mail.byaddr;
updated aliases
updated publickey
updated netid
/usr/sbin/makedbm /etc/netmasks /var/yp/'domainname'/netmasks.byaddr;
updated netmasks
couldn't find /etc/timezone
updated auto.master
updated auto.home
make: Warning: Target 'all' not remade because of errors
Current working directory /var/yp
apollo has been set up as a yp master server without any errors.
If there are running slave yp servers, run yppush now for any data bases which
have been changed.  If there are no running slaves, run ypinit on those hosts
which are to be slave servers.
```

NIS Slave Server Setup

To initialize a slave server, set the domain name on the slave server. Execute
ypinit on the slave server with the -s option and the name of the master:

```
ypinit -s apollo
```

The slave must be able to contact the master by broadcast; they must be on the
same IP network. If not, the slave must first be set up as a NIS client to access
the NIS master.

NIS Client Setup

Setting up an NIS client requires three steps:

1. Set the domain name in the client.

2. Place NIS markers in files that will be augmented by NIS information.

3. Start the *ypbind* daemon.

Some local client files are replaced by NIS and others are augmented. The replaced files should not be removed because you might need them later. For example, the /etc/hosts file can by replicated by NIS. The client uses the local /etc/hosts file during boot and switches over to the NIS /etc/hosts once NIS starts. A system may only require the local host and its own name and address in the /etc/hosts file.

Netgroups

Netgroups are a shorthand method of establishing groups of users and hosts in NIS. These groups can be used in NFS and the trusted hosts files. The format of the netgroup is

```
Name (hostname, username, domain name)
```

Example:

```
Trusted-hosts (apollo,-,),(venus,-,),(mars,-,)
```

The hosts apollo, venus and mars are trusted. The - in the username does not match any username, so no usernames are included. The example above could be in an NFS permissions setting in the /etc/exports file:

```
/u  -access=trusted-hosts
Trusted-users (,gene,),(,susie,),(,melissa,),(,mina,)
```

The listed users from any domain are trusted users. The example above could be placed in a .rhosts file, for instance.

NFS

Network File System (NFS) is the UNIX protocol for sharing data. NFS is an application that uses TCP/IP for a transport. NFS has a client and server aspect. A UNIX computer can be both a client and a server simultaneously. NFS shares files with other systems. NFS assumes the remote host computer will provide security for the NFS data. NFS servers can limit the access of remote servers.

SMB, by contrast, shares files with users. SMB authenticates user access rights, not system access rights. The difference is from the origin, NFS was developed on multi-user systems with strong local system security. SMB was developed for PCs with almost no local security for getting onto the system so the server had to enforce the security.

NFS is a stateless protocol. A stateless protocol does not keep any information on the state of the client. The reasoning behind a stateless protocol is for crash recovery. Neither client nor server maintains a crash recovery log. If the server crashes, it begins to answer the NFS client requests when it reboots as though nothing had happened. To an NFS client, a crashed server appears to be a very slow server.

Generally, UDP is the transport. UDP provides an *unreliable service*, which means that delivery is not guaranteed. The programs are responsible for checking for delivery and ensuring packets are assembled into the correct order.

Each NFS request contains all the information necessary to process the request so that the server does not have to maintain information on the client's work in progress. Each request will contain complete information about the request. For instance, a write operation will contain the file handle, the offset into the file and the length of the write. In normal UNIX writes, a buffer is written to wherever the current file descriptor points. The state in the file descriptor is not maintained by the NFS server.

Many NFS requests can be carried out multiple times without harm, such as reading a disk block. Some NFS implementations maintain a cache of recent requests and drop duplicate requests that arrive within a limited time span for performance reasons. When duplicate requests are not dropped, the server performs additional disk I/O and increases the network traffic by transmitting the requested data to the client. NFS servers notify clients when a call is completed by UDP.

A client will not issue a new request to the server until the current request is acknowledged. If the request times out, the client retransmits the request.

If a client crashes and reboots, the server will begin to answer requests when the client is up without any knowledge of the crash.

The NFS Server Component

NFS server is started from an NFS script in either /etc/rc2.d (SCO), /etc/rc.d/rc3.d (Linux) or /etc/rc3.d (Solaris). To start an NFS server, the file with the exported file system list is checked to see that a reason exists as to why it should become a server. SCO OpenServer and Linux use the /etc/exports file to list shares. Solaris uses the /etc/dfs/sharetab.

If the NFS start script determines that shareable file systems exist, two process-es are started: mountd and nfsd. mountd is a daemon that processes incoming requests from clients to mount an NFS share. nfsd processes incoming data requests.

In Solaris, nfsd is a multithreaded process that starts with 16 threads by default. The number of threads can be adjusted by editing the script and changing the number 16 up or down. In SCO, the nfsd syntax permits setting the number of UDP and TCP server daemons. Changing the number of threads or daemons depends on performance. For instance, with SCO OpenServer, checking a ps listing to determine the amount of CPU time used by each nfsd can provide guidance on adjusting the number of nfsd's running. If all nfsd's have an equal amount of time, add additional nfsd's until one accumulates no time, indicating that enough are running to satisfy all requests.

Linux nfsd allows multiple copies of nfsd to be run. Linux runs these as user level processes as opposed to SCO and Solaris that run them as system level processes. When multiple copies are run, they cannot share a common file han-dle cache and writes are disabled. This may be useful for publicly accessible FTP areas where no writes are desired. Use a single nfsd, if writes are required.

> **Warning**
>
> *All user IDs should be the same throughout the UNIX network when using NFS. When a client mounts an NFS share onto its file system, the UID ownership of files is looked at through the local /etc/passwd file, not the remote one. A user named karen, UID 223, owns a file on an NFS share that is mounted on another computer. User lisa, UID 223 on the NFS client, "owns" the file by virtue of having the same UID. NIS is one method of keeping UIDs and GIDs identical on all UNIX computers on the network.*

The Export Syntax

The syntax for the /etc/exports file is

```
Directory [options]
```

`Directory` is the pathname of a directory (or file).

The options include the following:

- ro. Export the directory read-only.

- `rw=hostname[:hostname]`.... Export read/write to the hosts listed, read-only to all others.

- `anon=uid`. Use uid for anonymous or unknown users, for security, a remote root user is always considered unknown unless specified in the root option.

- `root=hostname[:hostname]`.... Allow root access for listed hosts.

- `access=client[:client]`.... Allow clients in list to mount share.

Tip

NIS *netgroups can be used as a client with the form* `@netgroup`. *Only the host portion of the* `netgroup` *string is used.*

Examples of the export lines are

```
/u #export to the world
/u2 -access=tuscany:umbria #export to these machines
/u3 -root=firenze #give root access to firenze
/u4 -anon=0 #give all machines root access
/usr/bin -ro #export read-only to everyone
/usr/man -access=zip,anon=-3,ro #several options on one line
```

When the file containing the exports list is modified, the `exportfs -a` (SCO OpenServer and Solaris) command should be used to update the exports.

Both SCO and Solaris disallow sharing a directory and a child of that directory. For instance, you cannot share /home and /home/users.

Linux varies from the UNIX NFS by allowing both a directory and a child of that directory to be shared. Linux adds additional options to the export line. One option, `all_squash`, prevents remote user IDs to be used on the server; they are mapped to the anonymous user.

The NFS Client Component

On the client computer, *block I/O daemons (biod)* handle the read and write requests from the client application. NFS is implemented in the kernel for performance. The kernel issues more read requests to the biod daemons than the application requests from the kernel. This allows a read-ahead buffer cache to be maintained, improving NFS performance. The biod also implements write-behind caching.

To access a remote NFS file system requires use of the `mount` command. The `mount` command should be placed in system files that are used to mount file systems at boot for remote shares that always need to be accessed. For Linux, the /etc/fstab is the mount file. Manage the fstab with the file system tool in the GUI as shown in Figure 4.4. NFS shares can be mounted at any time with the mount command.

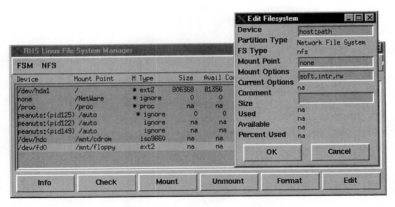

Figure 4.4. *Creating an NFS file mount in Linux.*

Mounting a remote NFS file system permanently on SCO requires an entry in the /etc/default/filesys file:

```
bdev=apollo:/export/home \
        mountdir=/u/home mount=no fstyp=NFS \
        desc="Home directories on Apollo" \
        rcmount=yes \
        mntopts="nosuid,rw"
```

The preceding entry was created through the SCOadmin GUI, as shown in Figure 4.5. mount=no states users may not mount or umount this connection. rcmount=yes indicates the mount should be performed at multi-user time during boot. The mntopts="nosuid,rw" says to make this a read/write mount and ignores set UID and set GID bits on execution. nosuid is a security feature.

On Solaris, the entry would be placed in the /etc/vfstab. A sample entry would be:

```
mount -r server1:/usr/man /usr/man
```

The -r option mounts the filesystem as read-only.

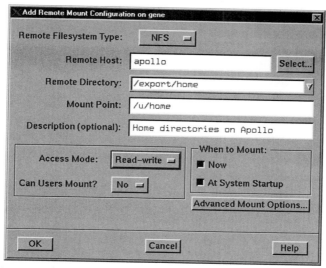

Figure 4.5. *Mounting an NFS share on a SCO UNIX system.*

DNS

Domain Name System (DNS) is a distributed database of host information. Local domains maintain their own information plus pointers to other systems outside of their domain. Files hold data translating host names to IP addresses and reverse lookup from IP address to host name.

The files required are the same for different versions of UNIX. Data is managed by editing the configuration files. None of the three operating systems—Solaris, SCO, or Linux—include a DNS configuration GUI like the one that comes with NT.

If you need to set up DNS on a UNIX machine, see Appendix B, "References," for books on DNS. A discussion of setting up and testing DNS is beyond the scope of this chapter.

DHCP

Solaris is the only flavor of the three that offer a DHCP Server service. SCO OpenServer will include a GUI-configured DHCP in release 5.0.5. Configuration is performed through `dhcpconfig` which also offers configuration of a dhcp/bootp relay.

The configuration program is a character-based application that asks a series of
questions and builds a database for the network. Checking on use of the
DHCP service is done by looking at the file /var/dhcp/<*network_number*>.
Prior to assigning a lease, the configuration builds a table of all the available
addresses and pings for those addresses to make certain they are available. The
database lines look like

```
00        00       126.1.1.101     126.1.1.22      0       apollo
```

Once an address is assigned, the line looks like

```
0100805F52F747 00      126.1.1.101     126.1.1.22      888528021      apollo
```

The fields are MAC address, flag (0 is a dynamic assignment), assigned IP
address, IP address of DHCP server, number of seconds from January 1, 1970
until lease expiration and the name to look up in the dhcptab file for configuration parameters.

Multiple ranges of addresses can be handled by a single server.

Trusted Hosts/Users

When using the UNIX rlogin, rexec, rsh and rcp utilities, users and systems can
be configured for trusted access. The rcp and rsh utilities do not allow for
password entry. If the user executing the command does not have trusted
access to the remote system, the command fails.

> **Warning**
>
> *The use of trusted hosts and trusted users can result in unexpected access
> if the usernames are not centrally controlled. A user Susie Henriksen has
> an account,* susieh, *on a system named oak. Susie Holden has an
> account,* susieh, *on pine. Pine is a trusting host for oak. Susie on oak
> could access the resources of* susieh *on pine with no password.*

/etc/hosts.equiv

When a hosts.equiv file is used, a user may log in to the trusting host, assum-
ing an account of the same name, without a password. The same level of trust
holds for copying files (rcp) or executing commands (rsh). The hosts.equiv does
not work for root.

Trusted host access is configured with the /etc/hosts.equiv file. The format is
one system name per line:

```
hostname [username]
```

This is one case where the host name must be the official name, not one of the aliases. If just the hostname is used, all users from the system hostname can access the system as a trusted user if they have the same account name.

> **Warning**
>
> *If the hostname and a username are listed, the user can access the host as any user! This could be a serious security problem.*

Access can be denied with a minus sign:

```
-hostname
```

The + and - signs should be used with caution. For instance,

```
+username
```

allows the named user to access the system from any host. The parsing looks for the first match, so

```
+
- hostname
```

will not disallow *hostname*.

NIS netgroups may be used with the + or - options.

.rhosts

If the hosts.equiv file is too broad, or you need root-trusted access, use the .rhosts file. The .rhosts file is placed in the home directory of the trusting user. The .rhosts file syntax is the same as the hosts.equiv. The .rhosts file is the only way for root to have trusted access.

The .rhosts file for root should be owned by root and have permissions of 600. If the permissions are other than read/write only for the owner, trusted access will fail. This is a good rule for all .rhosts in order to prevent manipulation by another user.

TCP Utilities

Several utilities are available for checking TCP/IP. There is no network application available as a basic component of these operating systems.

- *ifconfig.* the interface configuration utility (see Figure 4.6). With no options, ifconfig prints the current information on the interfaces.

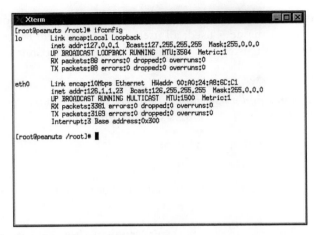

Figure 4.6. *The ifconfig utility on Linux.*

- *netstat.* Network statistics (Solaris, SCO, Linux).

```
# netstat -r
Routing tables
Destination      Gateway       Flags    Refs    Use    Interface
24.2.55.0        gandalf       UGHS      0       0     net0
126              gene          UC        1       0     net0
gene             localhost     UGHS      6      52     lo0
localhost        localhost     UH        2     204     lo0
224              gene          UCS       0       0     net0

# netstat -i
Name  Mtu   Net/Dest  Address   Ipkts Ierrs Opkts Oerrs  Collis Queue
lo0   8232  loopback  localhost 1108  0     1108  0      0      0
pcn0  1500  126.0.0.0 apollo    1691  0     1102  0      0      0
```

- *llistat (SCO only)*. Display network adapter statistics.

```
Device          SNPA/MAC address        Factory Address
/dev/net0       00:60:97:6a:46:ce       00:60:97:6a:46:ce


                Multicast address table
                - - - - - - - - - - - - - - - - - - - - - -
                03:00:00:00:00:01
                01:00:5e:00:00:01


                                    FRAMES
      Unicast  Multicast  Broadcast  Error     Octets    Queue Length
      - - - - - - - - - -  - - - - - - - - -  - - - - - - - - -  - - - - - -  - - - - - - - - - - - -  - - - - - - - - - - - -
In:    866       373        1379       2       308756              0
Out:   979       375         100       0       174583              0
```

- *ping*. On SCO OpenServer and Linux, will run indefinitely, Solaris
  returns a *<host>* is alive message. ping has several options, a useful one
  on SCO and Linux is -c, the count of pings to be sent.

When writing scripts, ping can be used prior to an attempted file transfer to
check that the target computer is up. By checking the return value of the ping
command, the script can determine whether the remote system is available.
Using the -c option on Linux and SCO prevents ping from pinging indefinitely.

Part **II**

File Sharing Between UNIX and Windows NT

Chapter 5

Windows NT-Based Solutions

- **Network File System**
  Learn how NFS works.

- **Solstice NFS Client and Network Client**
  Examine two products from the company that created NFS.

- **The Hummingbird NFS Maestro Family**
  Hummingbird sells an NFS client, NFS server and NFS gateway for NT.

- **Case Study: NASA**
  Learn how one NASA site implemented NFS on NT.

- **The Intergraph NFS Suite**
  Intergraph offers an NFS client, NFS server and NFS gateway.

Network File System

For the Windows NT-literate administrator dealing with a UNIX computer on the network, the simplest solution to solve your NT/UNIX connectivity problems may be to add software to the Windows NT environment. Dealing with UNIX can be a daunting task for the Windows-oriented administrator. If the connectivity problem can be solved on the Windows side of the equation, the configuration will be more natural to an NT administrator.

Another consideration in selecting a software solution to the connectivity problem is how many UNIX systems and how many Windows NT systems are involved. If the software is to be purchased, the answer can be to add software to the operating system that has the fewest systems on the network, thereby reducing purchase cost. Another answer lies in the software that permits one NT computer to re-share UNIX data in Windows-native SMB format with the other Windows computers.

Why select an NT NFS product over a UNIX SMB product? With large NFS installations with UNIX, NIS provides a very stable name service, creating a highly scalable solution. The statelessness of NFS connections provide better handling of loss of connections than SMB connections.

The Network File System Protocol

Windows NT can communicate with UNIX by learning to speak the Network File System (NFS) file sharing language. NFS was created by Sun's Bill Joy, who also created the C shell for UNIX. Depending on which UNIX version is used, the terminology for sharing can be referred to as *sharing* or *exporting file systems*.

NFS on UNIX exports or shares a file system. The NFS client then maps the network share. On UNIX, the client software uses the mount command to map the drive to a mount point on the local file system. A *mount point* is a directory. For persistent connections, UNIX uses a text file to store the information on shares and remote drive mappings. The file for shares is the /etc/exports file on most UNIX systems, /etc/dfs/dfstab on Solaris. The exports file must be in place for the NFS server daemons to start. A script file, such as /etc/nfs, generally starts the NFS processes.

> ### Tip
>
> *If you forget to create the exports file, you can create it and then restart NFS on OpenServer with*
>
> ```
> /etc/nfs stop
> /etc/nfs start
> ```
>
> *Check your system to verify that this method will work for you.*

On the UNIX computer, the file must exist at boot time for the NFS server daemons to be initialized. This is true with some of the Windows-based NFS products. At least one of the Windows products maintains a dummy entry in its equivalent of the /etc/exports file to bring the NFS services up without initialization errors.

The exports file may be edited with any UNIX text editor. The format is shown below:

```
<directory>  <options>   <access rights>
/u    -access=:venus:mars,root=mars
```

In the preceding example, access is limited to two computers, venus and mars, and root privileges are granted to mars.

Some versions of NFS do not allow exporting components of an exported tree. For instance, you can not export /u and /u/common. You can not export /u/common and then try to add an export for /u. Another restriction is on daisy-chained exports. Venus cannot mount a file system from mars and then export it for other clients.

When using the mount command to mount an exported file system, several options can be used, including but not limited to:

- -f NFS. Designates the file system as NFS

- -r. Read-only

- -soft. Returns an error if the server does not respond

- -bg. Runs the mount command in the background; useful during automatic mounts on bootup

- -noac. Disables caching; impairs performance but guarantees synchronization with the server

- -intr. Allows use of keyboard interrupts to kill a process that is hung while waiting for a response on a hard-mounted file system

The options to the mount command vary by operating system. Be careful to check your system documentation.

Troubleshooting Tip

Be careful to make the computer names the same as the names in the name service being used, whether DNS or the /etc/hosts file. Associating an IP address with the name venus means that the machine responding to the IP address is considered to be venus by the local computer, whether or not it is named venus. Names are not case-sensitive.

To check the existence of exported file systems, run the exportfs program, which lists all exported file systems. If you modify the /etc/exports file, you can export the newly-added directories with:

```
exportfs -a
```

While NFS will be around for a while, the popularity of NFS for Windows/UNIX connectivity is declining as UNIX includes Server Message Block (SMB) functionality in new releases. NFS is a mature product with good file-locking capabilities and stability. NFS can be implemented on operating systems other than Windows NT and UNIX. Many Windows 3.x and Windows 95 NFS implementations are available.

NFS Gateways

In addition to NFS, NFS gateways can be installed on Windows NT to provide access to NFS data for occasional users on non-NFS enabled Windows/DOS clients. Two NFS gateways from Hummingbird and Intergraph are examined in this chapter. NFS client and server capabilities for Windows NT are presented, as well.

The method of installing a new file system recognition driver on NT is to provide new dynamic link libraries (DLLs). These will be installed as optional file system providers for the Multiple Provider Router (MPR), alongside the native SMB service, much as NetWare drivers are added.

In addition to new file system providers, it is necessary to include new DLLs for the Multiple UNC Router that has the responsibility of resolving network names whether in UNC (\\server\share) convention or NFS (server:/share) convention. This task should occur when the software is loaded.

When NFS is loaded on to a Windows NT computer, there are two networks listed in Network Neighborhood under the Entire Network:

- The Microsoft Windows Network

- The NFS network, which may have different names depending on the NFS product installed

Each of these can be browsed separately.

The software listed here is referenced in Appendix A, "Products for File and Print Sharing," by product name. Many of these packages can be downloaded for free trials.

Solstice NFS Client and Network Client

Sun Microsystems offers Solstice NFS Client as a Windows NT/Windows 95 NFS client. Solstice NFS works with Network Information Services (NIS) or the successor to NIS, NIS+. Solstice can use DNS or the hosts file for hostname resolution. Upon installation, name resolution defaults to Windows Networking.

Figure 5.1 illustrates how Solstice NFS Client fits into the Network Neighborhood. Clicking on Network Neighborhood reveals the Entire Network option and the NetBIOS registered computers. Double-clicking Entire Network opens a window showing the Microsoft Windows Network and the

Solstice_NFS_Network. Double-clicking the Solstice_NFS_Client icon reveals the NFS Servers and NFS Automount Maps entries. Double-clicking the NFS Servers brings up a window showing two computers.

Now the territory becomes more familiar to the Windows user. Double-clicking Gene lists the shared folders available, and double-clicking Frodo lists the shared folders available there. The point here is that one of those computers is a UNIX computer running NFS and the other is a Windows NT computer running the Solaris Network Client NFS Server. Unless the names of the shares give away the operating system, it is almost impossible to figure out which is UNIX.

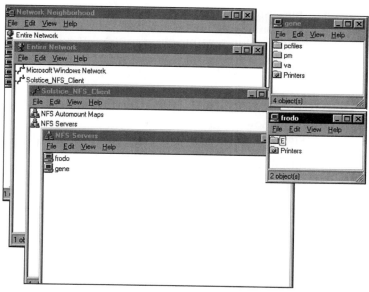

Figure 5.1. *Exploring the NFS network from Entire Network to the shared folders and files.*

Network Drive Mapping

Mapping a network drive is done in the same manner as for a Microsoft Windows network shared folder:

1. Click on the folder.

2. Choose File, Map Network Drive.

Installation

Installation of Solstice NFS Client is easy. A Windows Install Wizard runs the setup. After the setup is complete, restart the computer. With no further tuning, I was able to click my way through the network to find my UNIX computer's NFS shares, as shown in Figure 5.1.

Sun has created a method of automating installs for Solstice NFS Client by allowing the setup in administration mode to create setup data files. The installation may then be run from batch files specifying the setup file.

Share Naming Conventions

Solstice NFS works closely with the Windows NT Multiple Provider Router (MPR) to convert NFS names to Universal Naming Convention (UNC) names used by NT. For instance, a UNIX NFS share would be defined as `server:/sharename` while a UNC name for the share would be `\\server\share`. When the MPR sees an NFS name, it passes it to the provider DLLs registered with it. The NFS provider DLL recognizes the name and converts it to UNC convention.

Adding Remote NFS Servers

By default, Solstice NFS Client only searches the local subnet for NFS servers. UNIX has no equivalent of the browser service that builds lists of servers throughout the domain. Figure 5.2 illustrates adding computer names to the NFS browse list. These computers must be able to be found via a name service such as DNS or the local hosts file (winnt\system32\drivers\etc\hosts). The format for the hosts file can be found in the sample HOSTS file, HOSTS.SAM, located in the same folder.

In spite of indications in the Windows NT Resource Kit that host names are case-sensitive, they are not. They were, though, case-sensitive in Windows NT 3.1.

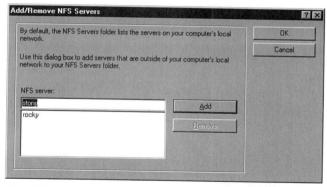

Figure 5.2. Adding NFS servers outside of the local subnet to the browse list.

NFS Automount Maps

NFS provides a means of allowing UNIX computers to automatically mount remote shares as needed. The process of automatically mounting is called *automounting*. Automount works with maps that define the mappings. This is similar to a user login script. The automount system is designed to work with the NIS or NIS+ system.

Changing the Default Settings

To change the default settings for Solstice NFS, navigate to the Network applet in the Control Panel. Under the Services tab, select Solstice NFS Client. The Security tab offers the opportunity to set an Authentication server.

At logon, the NT user is required to log onto the NT domain. Immediately following the NT logon window, the NFS logon appears. An account (not necessarily the same name as the NT account), a password, and an authentication server are required. The information requested is a UNIX account and password that must exist on the computer serving as the authentication server. The default authentication server can be set to a specific server rather than broadcasting for one.

Figure 5.3 illustrates the server setting. The top half of the tab lists the default file creation permissions on the NFS shares. These are UNIX permissions. These can be set by the administrator. The permissions shown are the standard for traditional UNIX security:

- read/write/execute for the owner
- read/execute for the group
- read/execute for all others

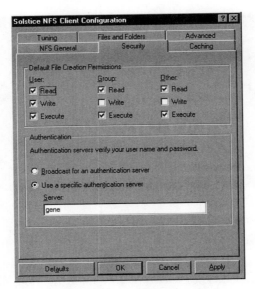

Figure 5.3. *Setting file permissions and a specific authentication server.*

Solstice NFS supports caching of data and file names in memory. Caching is controlled by the Caching tab. Figure 5.4 shows the default caching attributes. The Attribute Cache area maintains relatively stable information on file size and modification time. Smaller intervals assure early detection of file changes but increase network traffic.

The Data Cache area stores information on previously read files. If the computer has available memory, data caching improves NFS performance. The Automatic setting allows NFS to base the amount of cache on free memory, much as NT's own File Cache Manager does.

Warning

Setting a high value to force better NFS performance could adversely affect a computer with a low free memory by increasing the use of swap space.

The File Name Cache area stores mappings of long file names to the DOS 8.3 file name convention. This cache is necessary for applications that do not support long file names.

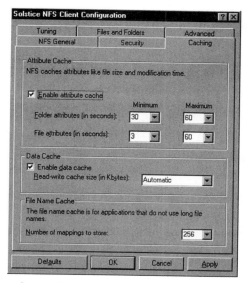

Figure 5.4. *Attribute caching values in the Caching tab.*

NFS Server Service

Solstice Network Client provides an NFS Server service for Windows NT. In Figure 15.1, Frodo is a Windows NT computer running the Solstice Network Client NFS Server. It looks indistinguishable from a UNIX NFS server to an NFS client. To enable the NFS Server service:

1. After installing Network Client, from the Network applet in the Control Panel, select Services, Solstice File Sharing.

2. Click on properties.

Figure 5.5 illustrates the configuration for file sharing. The Enable Solstice NFS Server check box is not checked by default. Once enabled, folders can be shared through a new NFS tab.

Sharing Folders for UNIX Access

When sharing folders for UNIX access, the process is similar to sharing for Windows networking:

1. Right-click on the folder and select Properties. A new NFS tab appears in addition to the normal tabs.

2. Click NFS Sharing and the tab looks like Figure 5.6.

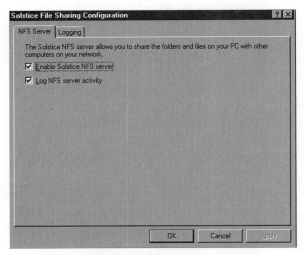

Figure 5.5. *Enable NFS Server through the Solstice File Sharing Configuration properties.*

The share options include Share Name, Access Type, and Access Restriction. The limit here is on machines accessing the share, not on NT users or groups. Remember that the purpose of NFS sharing on NT is to share data with UNIX computers whose users may not have NT accounts. When Access Restrictions is set to Restricted, an access list can be configured to restrict the hosts.

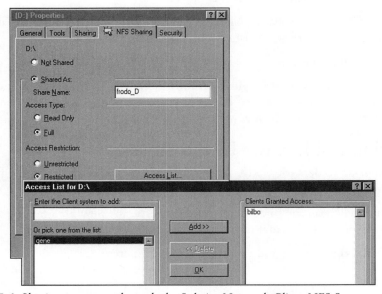

Figure 5.6. *Sharing resources through the Solstice Network Client NFS Server.*

> **Warning**
>
> *On Windows NT with an NTFS file system, Solstice Network Client NFS Server exports the security attributes of the user on the local (sharing) system to any remote user with full access to the system. For instance, if NFS Server is started by the administrator, those privileges are granted to the remote user. Be careful to restrict access to trusted hosts and to treat any data shared as public. Limit the shares to read-only if practical.*

The Hummingbird NFS Maestro Family

Hummingbird is one of the major suppliers of NFS software for Windows. The NFS Maestro family consists of three NFS products:

- NFS Gateway

- NFS Server

- NFS Client

NFS Client is designed for Windows clients requiring access to NFS data (Windows clients accessing UNIX data). NFS Server allows an NT computer to share data with other NFS-enabled computers (UNIX clients accessing NT hosts). NFS Gateway provides a gateway to NFS data through an NT computer for Windows clients requiring occasional access.

Hummingbird NFS Maestro Gateway

For networks with clients requiring occasional access to shared NFS files, a gateway is often more cost effective than client-based NFS. Hummingbird offers a gateway as an extension of its popular NFS Maestro. The gateway computer connects to an NFS share on a remote computer, probably UNIX, and re-shares the information as a Microsoft network share. This provides Microsoft users access to the UNIX-based data without the necessity of loading NFS client software.

Loading the gateway software is as easy as you would anticipate for a CD-based installation. After the software is installed, a Maestro application attempts to determine the best configuration to optimize transfer rates. This process can take 45 minutes, but improves performance. Figure 5.7 illustrates the process of determining the best transfer rates.

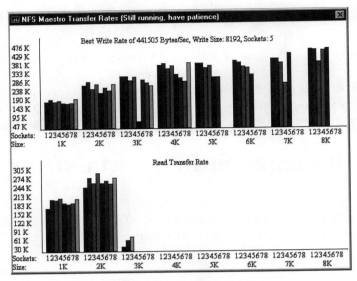

Figure 5.7. *Computing the most effective transfer method.*

Tip

When preparing to run the transfer computations, you are asked to supply a share name for which you can browse NFS servers, a user name, and a password. If you installed NFS as Administrator on NT and are using a share on UNIX as root, ensure that the NFS share allows root access from the machine on which you are running the test, otherwise you will get write errors. NFS translates a remote root access as an anonymous user for security reasons.

The NFS Maestro Gateway installs as an NT service and may be seen in the Control Panel, Services applet. By default, the service starts automatically.

Connecting to NFS Shares

After installation, the gateway needs to be connected to NFS shares that will be re-shared to Windows clients. Figure 5.8 illustrates the menu for NFS Maestro Gateway.

The NFS Gateway menu contains the same programs as are contained in the program group of the NFS Maestro icon. For repeated executions of Maestro programs, the icon provides faster access.

Connecting to shares is done with the NFS Network Access program. Figure 5.9 illustrates the NFS Network Access window with the Browse Network

Connections option open. Highlighting a shared directory from the NFS server GENE and clicking OK returns the name to the Network Path drop-down list box.

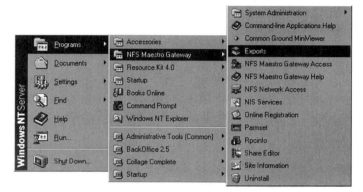

Figure 5.8. *The NFS Gateway menu.*

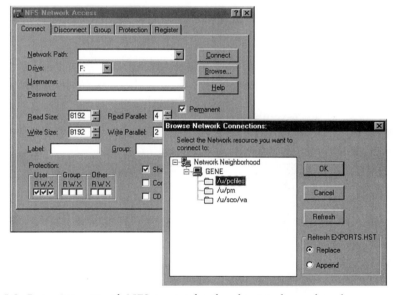

Figure 5.9. *Browsing network NFS servers for the object to be re-shared.*

Once the network path has been determined, a drive letter needs to be assigned. A UNIX user name and password are entered to provide access to the NFS share. By default, the connection is permanent. Click TCP if the connection uses TCP. Set the protection levels in UNIX format. UNIX permissions are covered in Chapter 2, "An Introduction to UNIX."

Figure 15.10 shows a connection for an F drive to a shared resource at \\GENE\u/pcfiles. The path is an interesting combination of Microsoft UNC and UNIX naming conventions. Here is another example of the MPR allowing the appropriate services to find a network resource rather than requiring UNC naming conventions.

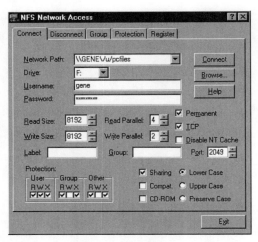

Figure 5.10. *Connecting an NFS resource as the F drive.*

Once NFS resources are mapped to drive letters, they can be viewed as a normal Windows mapped drive and disconnected through the Disconnect tab of the NFS Network Access program (see Figure 5.11). Note the true UNC name as seen by Windows NT in parentheses.

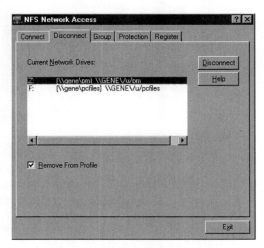

Figure 5.11. *The Disconnect tab for NFS resources.*

Re-sharing Resources to Windows Clients

To share resources out to the Windows clients, the NFS Maestro Gateway Access option is run from the NFS Maestro Gateway menu (see Figure 5.12). From the Setup window, do the following:

1. Enter the share name you want Windows clients to see.

2. Enter the network path to the remote resource.

3. Enter a drive letter. This drive letter will be used by anyone on the local NT server who needs access to the resource entered in step 2. This is the local mapping of the remote data.

4. Click TCP.

5. Set permissions in the lower left corner.

6. Click Add.

After the folder has been shared, you can select the share and change the permissions for Windows users.

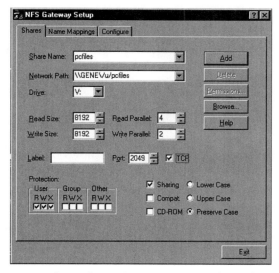

Figure 5.12. *Creating a re-share of a NFS resource to Windows clients.*

To the Windows client who is browsing the NFS gateway, the shares appear as would any Windows share. Figure 5.13 illustrates the NT computer BILBO viewing the shared resources on the NFS Gateway FRODO. There is nothing in the appearance of the share that provides a clue to the fact that the actual data is residing on a UNIX system.

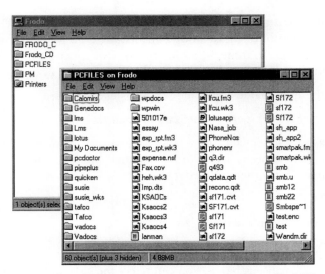

Figure 15.13. *Viewing shared NFS resources from a non-NFS enabled Windows NT computer.*

Hummingbird NFS Maestro Server

Maestro NFS Server provides NFS services to other NFS-enabled computers. Setting up the Server is relatively simple.

The first step is to create the entries for the shared resources in the Exports file. If a default installation was performed, the file will be located in the C:\Program Files\NfsSrvr.nt folder. The syntax of the entries is similar to UNIX. The file can be edited with the user's choice of tools or the Export Editor supplied by Hummingbird. Figure 5.14 shows the Export Editor with two entries.

The folder /c/collage, a UNIX syntax convention, could also be listed as c:\collage. The file comes with a dummy entry to export the C drive, in order to avoid problems of nothing to share at NFS startup. The C drive is exported with restrictions. The default share can be removed once new shares are included. Options to restrict access are shown in the text in the Exports file. In the example, /c/collage grants root access to the computer GENE and /c/COLL-WIN is exported with the normal read/write access.

> **Warning**
>
> *Why did one of the two examples have uppercase letters and the other not? The exporting of folders is case-sensitive. The actual case of the*

folder names is not shown in either Windows Explorer or My Computer. Open a DOS prompt and list the folder with the DIR *command. Use the exact same case for the* exports *line. Failure to check the case will result in the folder not being exported.*

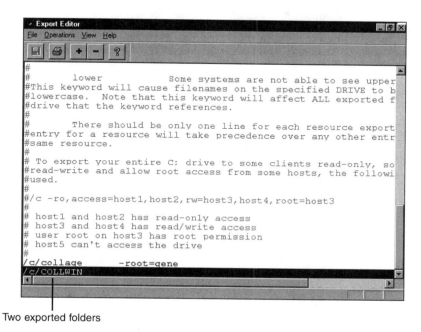

Two exported folders

Figure 5.14. *The NFS Export Editor showing two exported folders.*

The next step is to map Windows NT user and group names to UNIX. Many users may use the same names on both systems. Two that are almost guaranteed to be different are Administrator and root. When mapping names, care must be taken to obtain the correct Windows NT names. Hummingbird includes a command-line utility for this purpose, SHOWPROT.EXE. Figure 5.15 provides a listing of the ownership of the folder c:\collage. The owner is Administrators and the group is Domain Users.

Once the ownership of the file is determined, the correct mappings can be created. To set up the mappings, navigate to Control Panel, NFS Server. Figure 5.16 illustrates name-to-User ID (UID) and Group ID (GID) mapping. The NT username Administrators is mapped to the UNIX UID of 0 (zero) which is the root account. The NT groupname of Domain Users is mapped to the root GID of 3, or sys on an SCO UNIX Openserver system.

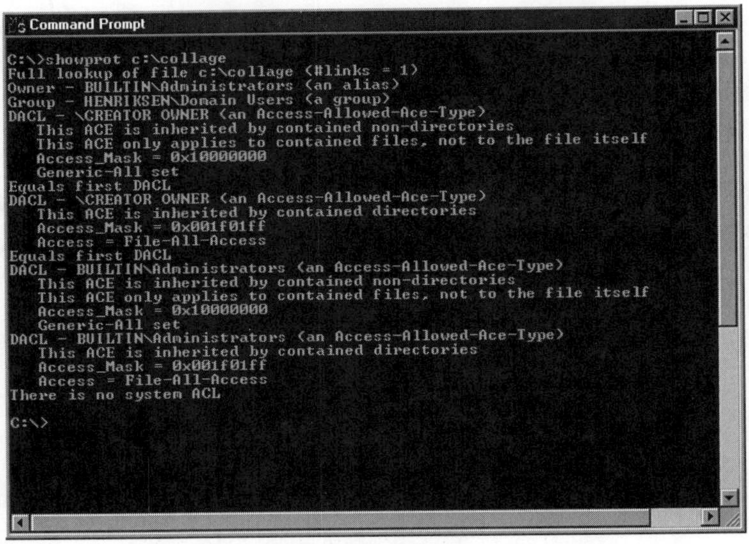

Figure 5.15. *Output of the SHOWPROT.EXE command.*

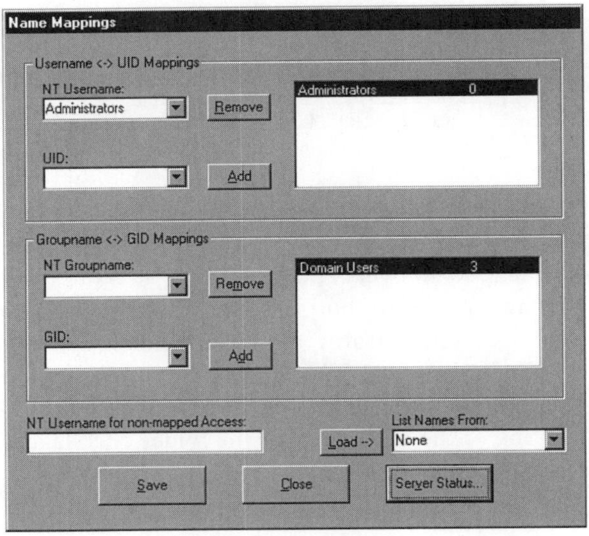

Figure 5.16. *The UNIX UID- and GID-to-NT name and group mapping.*

These mappings allow the proper relationship between the UNIX accounts accessing the NFS share and the NT permissions granted to the NT accounts. Failure to configure the accounts mappings results in denied access.

With the shares defined and the UNIX-to-NT name mappings completed, the next step is to verify that the shares appear as actually having been shared. From the Name Mappings window, select the Server Status button. Figure 5.17 illustrates the NFS Server for Windows NT status window. Select the Exports button to see the shares.

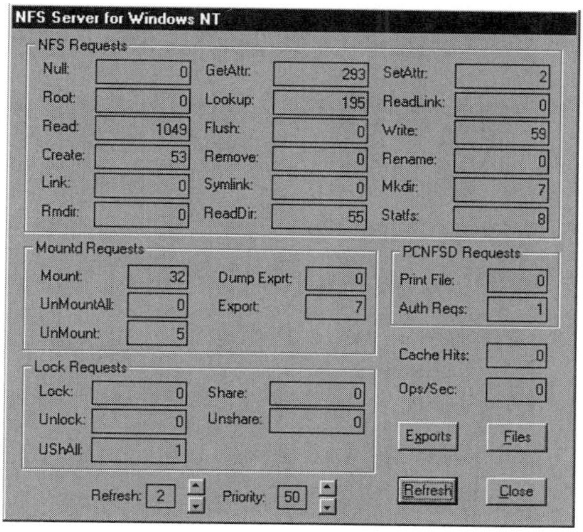

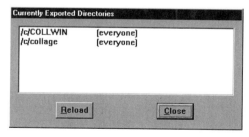

Figure 5.17. *The NFS Server for NT status window.*

In Figure 15.8, the Currently Exported Directories window, the two shares defined in the Exports file appear. This is proof that the export entries were correct. The root assignments do not appear on this display. Limitations, such as read-only or to specific hosts, appear in the displayed information.

Figure 5.18. *The Currently Exported Directories window. If an intended share does not appear here, it will not be available to remote NFS clients.*

Once the share information appears, the next step is to move to a UNIX computer and mount the NFS share onto the UNIX file system. Once this has been done, execute a long listing on the UNIX computer (type **ls -l**) and check the UID and GID of the directory where the data shared folder was mounted. If the UID and/or GID appear as a number such as 65533, then the name mappings are not correct. This number indicates no correlation between the mappings on the NT NFS server and the UNIX user names. Permissions are adversely affected by incorrect name mappings.

Maestro NFS, The Client Software

Maestro NFS is the client version of the Maestro suite. In a manner similar to the Solstice Network Client, the Hummingbird NFS shares are available under Network Neighborhood by clicking Entire Network and selecting Hummingbird NFS as opposed to Microsoft Windows Network.

The install is very simple and, once installed, mapping NFS shares is also simple. Figure 5.10 (earlier in the chapter) illustrates setting up a mapped share. When mapping to a remote share, enter the user name and password for authentication. To map a drive, select NFS Network Access from the shortcut on the desktop or the Start menu.

Once the share is mapped, it appears like any other mapped network drive on My Computer. Maestro NFS includes a number of utilities not included with the Server. Double-click the Maestro NFS shortcut on the desktop and the options appear. There are three sub-windows with additional tools.

Exports displays the NFS exported directories from NFS servers. *Rpcinfo*, or *Remote Procedure Call info*, provides the information necessary to troubleshoot the programs on the remote NFS server. NIS services allow integration with NIS. NIS was previously known as *Yellow Pages*.

The Accessories submenu provides Internet Relay Chat, Gopher, Nslookup, Finger, Talk, Whois, Tar (tape archive) and Network Time. Remote Tools includes REXEC (Remote Execution) and Remote Shell (RSH) along with Remote Copy (RCP), all oriented at the UNIX host.

The Host Access submenu includes FTP, several terminal emulations for telnet, and the NFS printing capability. Network printing with NFS is covered in the Chapter 9, "Windows NT-Based NFS Print Providers."

The System Administration submenu has a graphical Ping and Trace route, programs NT only includes as command-line utilities.

Case Study: NASA

Over the past three years, NASA's chief information officer (CIO) office has pursued an aggressive schedule to reduce the agency's Information Technology (IT) costs, while at the same time increasing its desktop interoperability. NASA's CIO plans to accomplish the savings through standardization, consolidation, and implementing systems that have a high potential for long life cycles.

In December 1995, the NASA Lewis Research Center in Cleveland, Ohio decided to do its part by implementing its Integrated Desktop Environment (IDE) throughout the center. The IDE solution provides Lewis users with MIME e-mail, the Microsoft Office suite, Netscape, access to mainframe systems, server-based file storage, and a variety of other business applications and Internet utilities. The center's Computer Services Division (CSD) was chartered with the responsibility of designing, procuring, and deploying IDE's client/server environment. In eleven months, CSD completed the IDE project by providing centrally administered, interoperable desktop systems to approximately 2,400 Windows, 800 Macintosh, and 800 UNIX users.

NASA-Lewis consolidated its PC X Server software with Hummingbird's Maestro NFS Client software. Before this consolidation, CSD supported two different vendor product lines in order to provide support for both X and NFS on the Windows desktop. This support also enabled the center to standardize on the Microsoft TCP/IP stack, which comes bundled with the Windows 95 and Windows NT operating system. Maestro NFS client integrates well with the eXceed software and has good performance. The following are a few examples of how NASA-Lewis is using the Maestro NFS Client software.

About half of the center's file servers are UNIX systems. These servers are centrally and automatically backed up by the CSD to a mass storage architecture. Various organizations use these servers to augment their local Windows desktop storage. The Maestro NFS client software enables them to connect these servers as another drive letter. Critical documents are stored on these servers with the reassurance of central backup and restoration services. Additionally, the storage capacity of the UNIX file servers offers significantly more space for storing large amounts of data for the engineering groups' CAD drawings. Their Windows workstations work on files that reside on UNIX file servers. Maestro allows a virtual drive connection to the native NFS services found on any UNIX vendor's operating system.

In addition to the client features of Maestro, NASA-Lewis users also find that the product has some useful server capabilities. The FTP server offers six permission levels that can be attached to directories. Windows PCs can be set up as FTP servers to make documents available to other UNIX and Mac users who may not be able to access a shared directory with a NetBIOS connection. These servers also allow sharing files that are too large to send as e-mail attachments. Local users of the Windows workstation notice no performance degradation when remote users access FTP services.

In Lewis's heterogeneous computing environment, it is common for Windows 95 and UNIX users to share an office. The lpd server in Maestro allows users to share local printers between the two different systems. To do this, the printer is connected to the Windows 95 PC and set as the default printer. After the lpd service is configured on the Windows 95 platform, both the UNIX and the Windows 95 workstation can share the local printer. The UNIX user uses the lpr command to print to the Windows workstation.

Maestro offers a telnet server for both Windows 95 and Windows NT. At first glance, it might seem like this would not be very useful, but a few NASA engineers have found a way to put this network service on Windows workstations to good use. Unfortunately, some engineers still only have 80286 Intel PCs to perform DOS-based scientific application programming. Data analysis programs are quite compute-intensive and take a very long time to run on the 286 workstation. Fellow engineers who have high-end Windows NT Pentium workstations run telnet servers on their systems. Users on slow 286 workstations log on to the Windows NT workstations with a telnet session and run their DOS code on the faster computer, thus greatly reducing the execution time. Local users of the Windows NT workstations notice no performance degradation when remote users execute programs on their systems.

The Intergraph NFS Suite

Intergraph has a suite of NFS products that mirror the capabilities of the Hummingbird suite:

- NFS Gateway

- DiskShare

- DiskAccess

Intergraph jumped into the Windows NT market very early and built tools to help other companies in their access and conversion.

NFS products have many similarities, so the following sections provide an overview and a detailed analysis of differences.

Intergraph NFS Gateway

AccessNFS Gateway extends the capabilities of DiskAccess for Windows NT (Intergraphs's NFS client product) by attaching to NFS file and print resources then re-sharing these devices with the Microsoft network as standard Windows networking shares. AccessNFS Gateway was built using the same technology found in DiskAccess. Gateway is ideal for large groups of users who need occasional or infrequent access to NFS file and print resources.

AccessNFS Gateway uses Microsoft's native TCP/IP protocol stack and utilities. Gateway is compatible with all standard NFS server implementations and requires no additional software on the NFS host system. After Gateway is installed, the administrator authenticates Windows users and maps the NFS directory and print resources of one or more systems to equivalent Windows shares. Then when Windows clients browse the Windows NT server, these shares appear as native Windows server resources.

Gateway eliminates the clear-text NFS PC client password schemes, relying instead on the secure, encrypted C2-compliant security native to the Windows network environment. The administrator can limit access to a single NFS system. File access rights are determined by user (UID) and group (GID) identification. The administrator controls which Windows clients have access to the NFS drives on a one-to-one or on a many-to-one basis, allowing Windows users to appear as unique users or many Windows users to appear as a single NFS user account. The authorized client can browse and mount resources as needed.

In addition, an automapping feature links Windows accounts to NFS accounts by automatically associating like names between systems.

Intergraph DiskShare

DiskShare is the NFS server product for Windows NT from Intergraph. DiskShare allows NFS-enabled clients to access data on a Windows NT computer. DiskShare enables file locking to warn application programs when a file is in use by another application. DiskShare allows management of NFS performance by optimizing the number of NFS threads that handle client requests for NFS service.

DiskShare provides tools to monitor NFS operations on the server. Information available includes NFS statistics, RPC statistics, information on RPC calls, information on mounted shares, and information on other NFS servers on the network.

Intergraph DiskAccess

DiskAccess is Intergraph's NFS client product. Installation from the CD is easy. Once the product has been installed, you must reboot. After rebooting, a message appears stating that your NFS login failed and you were logged in with negative UID and GID (see Figure 5.19). If this result is not acceptable, click Yes to create a new login name association.

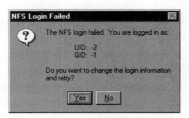

Figure 5.19. *An initial NFS login failure, which occurs on the first login because no UNIX-name-to-NT-name correlation exists.*

When you click Yes on the previous screen, the DiskAccess Properties window appears, enabling you to enter a UNIX user name and password. Authentication may be performed via NIS or a UNIX computer running a PCNFSD daemon. Once a legal name and password have been entered, an NFS Login Successful window is displayed (see Figure 5.20). Future logins by the same NT user are authenticated with the UNIX servers using the data entered here.

The NFS servers appear on a separate network like the other NFS implementations. From Network Neighborhood, an NFS Network entry leads to anther network called *DefaultLAN*; double-clicking this icon lists the NFS servers.

DiskAccess also comes with a DOS-to-UNIX text file conversion tool, ping, an RPCINFO utility, a Show Mount utility, and a DNS query tool.

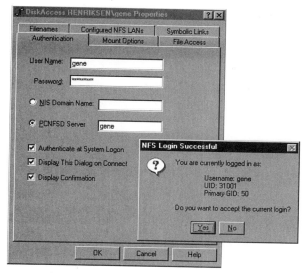

Figure 5.20. *Setting up the login name, password, and means of authentication on a new NFS user.*

Chapter 6

UNIX-Based Solutions

- **AT&T's Advanced Server for UNIX**
  Learn about AT&T's port of Windows NT networking and domain software to UNIX. Learn how to integrate your UNIX computer into an NT domain.

- **Advanced File and Print Server**
  SCO's version of Advanced Server for UNIX is integrated into the GUI administrative interface. Learn how to configure file sharing. See how UNIX users can also be domain users.

- **TotalNet Advanced Server**
  TotalNet Advanced Server supports the NT networking clients as well as Macintosh and NetWare. Learn how to share files and control users.

- **VisionFS**
  SCO's multi-platform server for file and print sharing with NT is easy to configure. See how user's home directories are automatically shared to other users. Set standard permissions for all shares or create unique permissions per share.

- **POWERfusion**
  See how April Systems Design's POWERfusion is managed on UNIX for file sharing. Set up automatic home directory sharing.

- **SAMBA**
  Examine the configuration and use of the free SAMBA software for file sharing. Learn how to configure the control file.

SMB on UNIX

One method that UNIX can use to share data files with Windows NT is to install software on UNIX that supports the SMB protocol. *SMB (Server Message Block)* is a software specification of how data is laid out for transport. It is built around the NetBIOS application programming interface (API). Currently, for a UNIX computer to work with SMB on a network, SMB compatibility must be added to the UNIX system.

For the UNIX administrator, solving the UNIX/NT networking compatibility problem may seem easier if the problem can be solved on familiar territory—UNIX. Unlike the NFS solutions for Windows NT, with UNIX you must find one that works on the UNIX version you are using.

One advantage of SMB on UNIX is the integration of the UNIX computer into the standard Network Neighborhood of the Microsoft Windows Network on the Windows computers. With NFS on Windows, two networks appear on Network Neighborhood: Microsoft Windows Network and the NFS network. Two networks require more work on the part of the user to track down a share. With NFS, it is apparent that the remote computer is not a Microsoft operating system. With SMB on UNIX, the user will not be able to distinguish the UNIX computer from the NT computer on Network Neighborhood.

Mapping of filenames generally follows the same rules throughout all SMB products. Names that are legitimate on one product and not another are truncated to fit the 8.3 DOS specification with characters thrown into the name to keep them unique. One product differs and its method will be explained.

> **Warning**
>
> *When using Windows NT and UNIX on the same network, use caution with tape backup from Windows NT of UNIX data. Select the Windows NT backup that does not set the archive bit. UNIX has no archive bit. When the Windows NT backup attempts to set the archive bit, major changes may occur in the ownership and permissions on files and directories rendering the UNIX data unusable until corrected by an administrator.*

The UNIX-based solutions presented in this chapter will cover a range of UNIX versions. The solutions include the freeware SAMBA, AT&T's Advanced Server for UNIX (ASU) and SCO's implementation of ASU, Syntax' TotalNet marketed by Sun as SunLink PC, SCO's VisionFS, and POWERfusion95.

> **Warning**
>
> *It might be impossible to install multiple SMB products on a single UNIX system. The NetBIOS drivers may not work together. Verify with free downloads before committing your operational computers to such a configuration. SCO's VisionFS NetBIOS drivers and the AT&T (AFPS) NetBIOS will not coexist on a SCO UNIX system.*

The administrator evaluating SMB products for UNIX will want to consider several factors:

- Availability of the product for the specific UNIX version

- Ease of installation

- Ease of management

- Source of technical support

- Access to shared NT resources from UNIX; be aware that most of these are "server" products, not "clients"

Common Internet File System

SMB will eventually give way to the *Common Internet File System (CIFS)*. CIFS is an enhanced SMB definition worked on by a task force of software companies and presented to the Internet Engineering Task Force for consideration as a standard. CIFS is not dependent on NetBIOS. One big advantage of CIFS is that part of a file can be copied rather than the entire file. If a very large file were located on a remote computer, a CIFS-compliant system could request a specific part, such as the last line rather than copying the entire file over the network.

AT&T's Advanced Server for UNIX

AT&T licensed Windows NT source code from Microsoft and ported the code to UNIX. The AT&T software is sold as *Advanced Server for UNIX (ASU)*. You may recall that the original version of Windows NT was named *Advanced Server*; later versions dropped the word *Advanced*. The capabilities this code provides the UNIX computer include SMB and the NetBIOS interface, plus the ability to participate in the Windows NT domain as a domain controller. The software contains the Windows NT domain administration tools:

- Event Viewer

- Help

- User Manager for Domains

- Server Manager

ASU prior to Version 4.0 does not include Windows Internet Naming Service (WINS). Dynamic Host Configuration Protocol (DHCP) is not a part of the SMB protocol. Some versions of UNIX include DHCP as a part of TCP/IP.

Administration of shares and many other Windows network functions may be controlled from the command line with the NET command, which should be very familiar to LAN Manager network administrators.

ASU provides the full range of net command options with the exception of net use. net use is not included because it is a client tool that uses the shares of a remote system. ASU is a server, as the name clearly states. The ASU product is sold by AT&T to various UNIX vendors. Currently ASU is available from NCR, Siemens-Nixdorf, ICL, Digital, Hewlett-Packard, Bull, Olivetti, Data General, and Santa Cruz Operation (SCO).

> ### Warning
>
> *Prior to installing ASU, TCP/IP must be working. If you cannot ping other systems, particularly the Windows NT PDC, do not install ASU until the problem is resolved.*

When installing ASU, the UNIX computer will have to be either a Primary Domain Controller (PDC) or Backup Domain Controller (BDC). If the UNIX system is to become a BDC, it is imperative, just like a Windows NT installation, that the new BDC be able to contact the PDC during installation. In neither case can a BDC be installed if it cannot contact the PDC. This means that both computers need to be running TCP/IP and should be able to find each other with ping.

Permissions to UNIX files by Windows users are controlled at two levels:

- *Windows NT style permissions maintained by ASU.* These may be modified by an NT administrator using the NET PERMS command or through the Administrative tools for NT.

- *UNIX permissions.* A user must have both NT and UNIX permissions to successfully access UNIX resources.

Here's an interesting point with ASU—a Windows NT network can be created with no Windows NT systems on the network! The ASU computers can fulfill the role of the Windows NT computer in the area of domain login and authentication.

Advanced File and Print Server

One implementation of AT&T's ASU is SCO's *Advanced File and Print Server (AFPS)*. SCO has fully integrated AFPS into the normal administrative tools provided with SCO OpenServer. The AFPS CD installation is very smooth.

> ### Tip
>
> *AFPS includes a NetBIOS daemon that will automatically start at boot time. Like Windows NT, SCO will present the console login before all system initialization is complete. This is particularly true with AFPS, which will continue to initialize after your first login attempt. If you log in as **root**, as soon as the login prompt is presented, you will find some of the network facilities are not completely up and working.*

> ### Author's Note
>
> *I have several installations of AFPS with Windows clients and no Windows NT computers on the network. Using AFPS provides the login control, file shares, and printer shares required for the mixed UNIX/Windows environment. Subsequent addition of an NT system requires the new system to be added as a BDC, although it may be promoted to PDC later.*

Administrative Interface

SCO's administrative interface works in both a graphical and character-based mode. Figure 6.1 shows the graphical interface with the AFPS shares listed.

Note that the term Advanced Server appears on the title bar. To access this window, choose System Administration, Filesystems, Filesystem Manager, View. In the View menu, select the Advanced Server shares rather than the NFS shares.

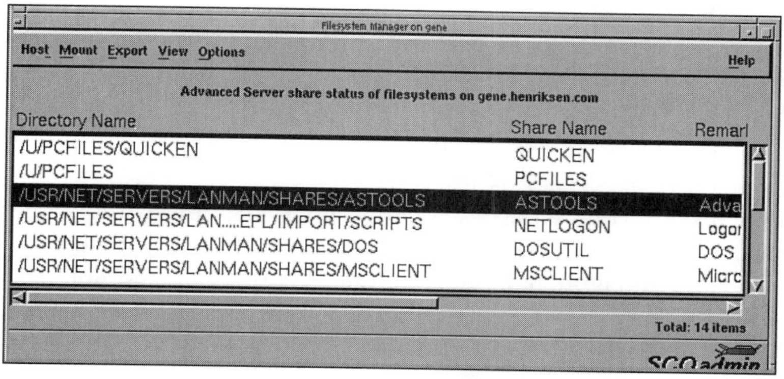

Figure 6.1. *A view of the Advanced Server shares from a SCO UNIX computer.*

Sharing directories to the Windows network can be performed through the SCO administrative tools. Figure 6.2 illustrates the creation of a new share called BUSINESS. The Export menu item enables you to export either NFS or AFPS shares. Access permissions depend on both the Windows NT assigned permissions and the underlying UNIX permissions.

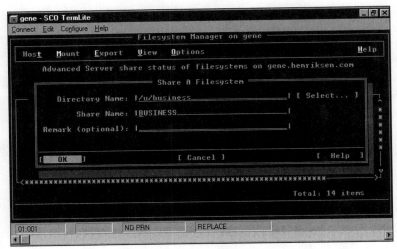

Figure 6.2. *Creating an Advanced Server share from the character-based administration tool of an SCO UNIX computer.*

SCO's administration tool, scoadmin, can be run from an X window, as shown in Figure 6.1; a Telnet session, as shown in Figure 6.2; or from the console on either the native graphical screen or a character-based login.

Figure 6.3 illustrates the list of shares on the SCO UNIX system THOR, as shown from a command prompt window on a Windows NT computer.

Client Share Access

SCO has included LAN Manager Client in the operating system to provide for client access to Windows shares. The networking version of the operating system includes LAN Manager Client. LAN Manager Client is based on older technology than AFPS and restricts shares to the DOS 8.3 name format.

By clicking the Windows Network Neighborhood icon, the SCO AFPS system will appear as just another Windows network server. Figure 6.4 illustrates the same shares seen in Figure 6.3, but from the Network Neighborhood.

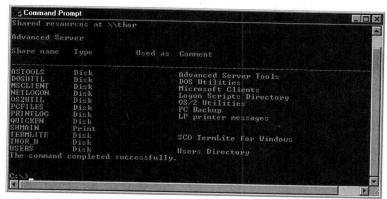

Figure 6.3. *A view of the Advanced Server shares from a Windows NT command prompt.*

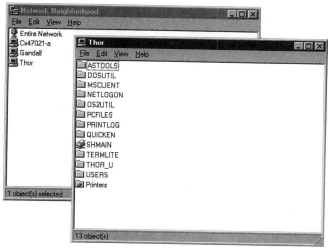

Figure 6.4. *A view of the Advanced Server shares from a Windows NT Network Neighborhood.*

If AFPS includes the domain user name database, how do the domain users integrate with UNIX? Fortunately, the answer is they integrate very well. The mapuname command allows mapping of unlike names between UNIX and AFPS. The lanman.ini file automatically sets the mapping for new users to the same domain and UNIX name. To map unlike names add a mapping:

```
mapuname -a domain:username UNIX_user_name
```

There are three conditions under which a different UNIX user name will be mapped to a domain name automatically:

- Names longer than eight characters (NT supports twenty character user names).

- The new domain user name is a duplicate of a UNIX user name.

- The domain user name contains character illegal in a UNIX user name.

With AFPS, three types of UNIX users can occur:

- UNIX users with no need for Windows network access may have a UNIX only account.

- UNIX users who will log in to the network from an NT computer can have an account that encompasses both UNIX login and Windows network access.

- Windows users that need access to shared UNIX resources but do not need a UNIX login can have a Windows NT account.

Figure 6.5 illustrates how this is accomplished. The option Networked Via controls whether or not the UNIX user has Advanced Server privileges. If the UNIX user account has a login shell of /bin/false, then an attempt to log in via Telnet or at the console will fail.

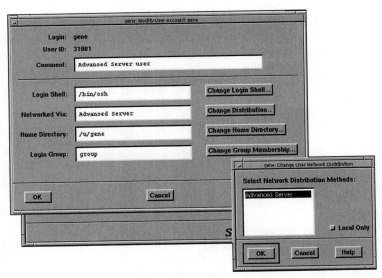

Figure 6.5. *Administering a UNIX account with Windows networking authorization.*

When a new user is created from the SCO system's scoadmin administrative tool, the option exists to provide that user with Windows network access. Conversely, a user created from User Manager for Domains on NT will be entered into the UNIX user database with a login shell of /bin/false. At any time, the UNIX administrator can convert an account to a Windows networked or non-UNIX user.

NT AFPS Management

From a Windows NT computer, the NT components of AFPS can be maintained through Server Manager, Event Viewer, and User Manager for Domains. If the administrator is seated at a Windows PC that is not a Windows NT computer, the administrative tools can be downloaded from the ASTOOLS share from AFPS or from a Windows NT computer.

> **Tip**
>
> *Printers on the SCO AFPS system may be shared for use by Windows clients. See Chapter 10, "UNIX-Based SMB Print Providers," on sharing printers for details.*

Advantages and Disadvantages

The advantages of the Advanced Server implementation from an accounts perspective is the integration of accounts on the UNIX computer into a single database.

> **Warning**
>
> *A windows user can change their Windows networking password but the UNIX password will not be changed, so it is possible to get passwords out of synchronization.*

The limitation of Advanced Server is that it will not coexist with NIS. The Networked Via option allows either NIS or Advanced Server.

AFPS has one nice advantage over Windows NT domains: A domain controller on AFPS can quit one domain and join another without reinstallation of either the operating system or the AFPS software. If your networking environment is undergoing change and you may need flexibility in changing domain structure, AFPS might be a better choice than NT.

Case Study: Peninsula Hospital Services

Peninsula Hospital Services (PHS), Newport News, Virginia, is a central laundry facility supporting several hospitals, nursing home facilities, and doctors' offices. PHS processes approximately 12 million pounds of soiled linen per year.

The software used by PHS to process, deliver, control, and invoice linen runs on SCO UNIX. The office staff has migrated from monochrome terminals to

Windows 95 PCs. The accounting software was upgraded from a single PC to a networked version. Windows NT was added to the network to back up Windows clients and store network-based software.

Data is collected through Kronos timekeeping hardware, and data is dumped to a UNIX share mapped to a Windows computer. Returned soiled linen is counted and entered on machine-readable forms. The forms are scanned and dumped to Windows files on a UNIX share. Periodically, the data is collected, parsed, and error checked by UNIX programs and inserted into a UNIX database.

Initially, the AFPS system was the PDC and there were no Windows NT computers. As the workload for the network grew, a Windows NT system was installed to reduce the load on the SCO system. The UNIX computer now serves as the BDC for the Windows NT domain. After a Windows NT Service Pack overwrote a new disk driver with an older version, the NT PDC crashed frequently and the SCO AFPS computer performed the duties of domain controller.

In this installation, UNIX handles the heavy-duty database manipulation and Windows handles the personal productivity tools. For example, one drive on the UNIX system is used as a backup location for critical files from Windows clients.

TotalNet Advanced Server

TotalNet Advanced Server (TAS) is a product of Syntax, Inc. TAS is not related to AT&T's Advanced Server for UNIX despite the reference to Advanced Server in the names. TAS works with three distinct client types:

- AppleTalk
- NT LAN Manager OS/2
- NetWare

TAS supports the protocols native to each of these realms: AppleTalk, TCP/IP, NetBEUI and IPX/SPX.

TAS is installed on Solaris using the `pkgadd` command. After the command is issued, the install runs with no problems. TAS administration is performed through an HTML-based tool called *TotalAdmin*. Figure 6.6 shows the administration of TAS. In the figure, the LM-NT-OS/2 realm is being configured. The left pane of the window is the menu for TAS. By clicking the large arrows, you can expand the display to include all options under a heading. This is very handy for navigating the menus.

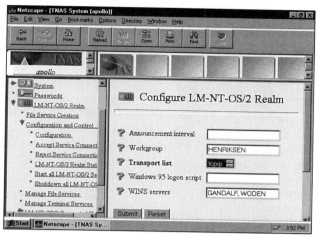

Figure 6.6. *Configuring TAS.*

TAS includes the capability for Macintosh clients to store files on a UNIX server while saving all the normal Macintosh file system attributes. File names are maintained in their native format and can be mapped for cross-platform access. A DOS client accessing a Macintosh file will see the name in the DOS 8.3 format.

TAS Handling of Filenames and Attributes

TAS also includes the Japanese and Unicode character sets. Any client accessing a file will have the filename translated as legibly as possible to meet their requirements. TAS handles all the hidden attributes and non-UNIX file characteristics by creating shadow files and directories on the UNIX computer to maintain the data. When filename translation results in names colliding, TAS inserts a hexadecimal number to ensure name uniqueness.

Delayed Authentication to Improve Speed

To improve network access times, authentication for a particular network path is delayed until the path is accessed. Since TAS can access NFS mounts to share with clients, an NFS server that is down will not cause a delay until actual access is attempted. NFS automounts are not resolved until accessed, further improving performance.

Browsing and WINS

Windows NT integration with TAS includes browsing. TAS can be set to attempt to become a Master Browser. Tunable parameters allow the administrator to adjust how hard a TAS server will work to become the master browser in an election.

In Figure 6.6, shown earlier in this section, two WINS servers were listed in the NT-LM-OS/2 Realm. If using a WINS server, make sure TAS is aware of the WINS server. List the WINS servers (comma separated) in the Configure screen.

Authenticating Clients

TAS can serve as a Windows 95 logon server, storing password authentication data on the UNIX host. TAS does not operate as either a PDC or BDC, but serves as a proxy authenticator. TAS can also store login scripts for Windows 95 clients. Proxy authentication is performed on behalf of a domain controller. TAS maintains the user names and passwords in a cache to provide this capability. To aid TAS in locating the PDC and BDCs, do either of the following:

- Enter the domain controllers in the /etc/hosts file on the TAS server.

- Enter a static NetBIOS name to IP address mapping, as shown in Figure 6.7.

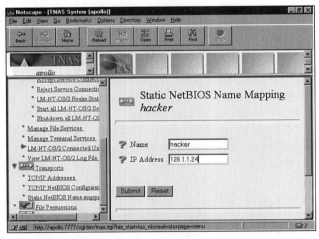

Figure 6.7. *Creating static NetBIOS to IP address mapping.*

User names longer than allowed in UNIX can be mapped to UNIX user names. TotalAdmin handles this process to reduce client administration. If UNIX passwords contain uppercase letters, the TAS system requires a tilde (˜) before each uppercase letter as the password is entered.

Checking the Status

To keep check on the status of your TAS server, use the System at a Glance option. Figure 6.8 reports the services available and the number of users connected. The status will update every two minutes automatically.

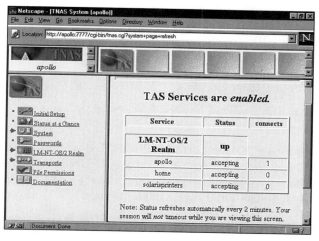

Figure 6.8. *System at a Glance.*

TAS is available through Syntax for IBM's AIX, Sun's Solaris on both SPARC and X86, Hewlett-Packard's HP-UX, and Silicon Graphics' IRIX. Support for NetBEUI only is available on Sequent, SunOS, and HP 9.x. TAS can be purchased as SunLink PC from Sun Microsystems.

VisionFS

SCO offers a family of connectivity products called *Vision*. VisionFS is the file system member of the family, providing Windows clients the opportunity to access shared directories from a UNIX file system.

VisionFS differs from AFPS in one major way: VisionFS does not become involved in domain administration in an NT domain. VisionFS acts more like a member server in the domain.

The capability to configure the VisionFS server as a WINS server is a nice feature of VisionFS.

VisionFS will run on the following and later UNIX versions:

- SCO OpenServer 5
- SCO OpenDeskTop 3
- SCO UnixWare 2.1
- Sun SPARC SunOS 4.1.2
- Sun Solaris 2.3
- HP UX 9 and 10

- IBM AIX 3.2.5

- Digital UNIX 3.0

- ICL DRS/NX Version 7

- Silicon Graphics IRIX 5.3

The client systems can be Windows NT 3.5*x*, NT 4.0, Windows 95, and Windows 3.1*x*.

If you are a seasoned SCO administrator, VisionFS does not install through the normal SCO methodology. To install on a SCO UNIX system, mount the CD-ROM (mount -r /dev/cd0 /mnt), change to the CD-ROM directory (cd /mnt), and execute the setup command: ./SETUP.

With SCO OpenServer 5.0.4, VisionFS is licensed for as many users as the operating system. On systems prior to SCO OpenServer 5.0.4 or other platforms, a license must be purchased for the number of users desired. Installation mainly consists of pressing the Enter key to accept the installation defaults.

VisionFS Administration

Administration of VisionFS on UNIX is very limited. Most of the administration is done from a Windows system with the Profile Editor included in the visiontools share from the UNIX system. Figure 6.9 illustrates the contents of the visiontools share, the visionfs folder of that share, and the Profile Editor.

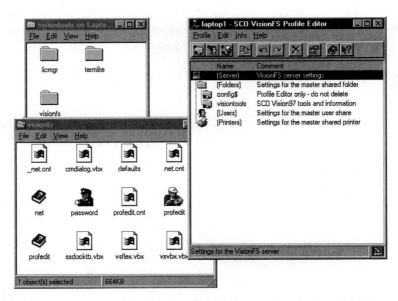

Figure 6.9. *The VisionFS Profile Editor with the visiontools and visionfs folders.*

The Profile Editor contains three icons with the names Folders, Users, and Printers. These contain the settings for the default conditions for each of these objects and are referred to as the *masters*:

- Master shared folder contains the default settings for all folder shares.

- Master user share contains the default settings for all user home directories.

- Master shared printer contains the defaults for shared printers.

Any shared folder you create can be linked to the master shared folders default settings, or a unique set of share properties can be defined for the share.

The visiontools folder also includes a lightweight terminal emulator for SCO Ansi emulation—termlite. termlite can be installed from the visiontools share.

The Profile Editor

Each VisionFS system has a profile editor that controls the settings for that specific computer. If multiple VisionFS servers exist, it is not possible to edit the profile on one machine with the profile editor that is running on a second machine. Each UNIX computer's Profile Editor will work only on the profile local to it.

The Server Properties dialog box of the Profile Editor includes the capability of VisionFS to become a WINS server and to register itself with a WINS server. Encrypted passwords can be enabled between the Windows computer and the VisionFS server.

Figure 6.10 illustrates the Users tab of the Server Properties dialog box. Broadcasts can be restricted to specific protocols. Server access can be limited to one workgroup, or left available to all. VisionFS servers can be set to exchange information with other VisionFS servers creating Internet workgroups.

> **Tip**
>
> *VisionFS is designed to run with Windows NT and Windows 95/3.1x. Passwords in NT are case sensitive. The passwords sent to VisionFS over the network from other Windows versions may not be case sensitive. VisionFS will attempt to log you in to the VisionFS UNIX server with upper and lowercase variations. If the password is foo, VisionFS will try foo, foO, fOo, fOO, Foo, FoO, FOo, and FOO. By default, it will attempt swapping up to eight characters.*
>
> *If your passwords exceed eight characters, change the value of the Swap Case Up To field to 16 in the Server Properties Passwords tab. If you do not do this, the initial login attempt will fail and you will be prompted for a password.*

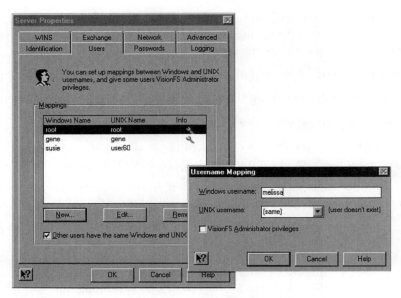

Figure 6.10. *Creating a new Windows to UNIX name mapping.*

Mapping UNIX and NT User Names

If all Windows users have the same names as their UNIX accounts, the only required entries are for VisionFS administrators. In Figure 6.10, users root and gene are both administrators. User susie is mapped to the UNIX user60 account. A new user name mapping for Windows user melissa is being created. When a Windows user name is entered, the option (same) is the default for the UNIX user name and to the right of that is the warning (user doesn't exist). A drop-down list of UNIX users is available for selection. Adding an administrator requires clicking the VisionFS Administrator Privileges box.

User Share Access

The default for all share permissions are located in the master shared folder. VisionFS automatically provides access to each user's UNIX home directory as a share. If you do not want the UNIX home directory to be used as a Windows share, go to the Master User Share Properties dialog box by clicking on the Settings for the master shared folder in the Profile Editor. Select Custom and enter a new location, such as **/u/windows/(*user-name*)**. Create directories for each VisionFS user in the /u/windows directory.

Additional shares can be created by the administrator. In Figure 6.11, a new share named va_phoenix is being created with the UNIX directory /u/va.phx.

The Availability area in the va_phoenix Properties window has two options for Active and Browsable. The Active option can be used to temporarily disable a share. The Browsable option determines if the share is hidden from Network Neighborhood. The Link check boxes to the right will link these functions to those of the master share.

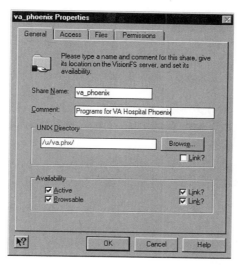

Figure 6.11. *Creation of a new share named va_phoenix.*

The Access tab allows setting the share to Read-Only for all users or restricting access by UNIX name or UNIX group. Other Access options include setting Actions on directories and files, such as create, delete, rename, open, read, and write. All of these options are linked to settings for the master share by default.

Under the Files tab, settings for following symbolic links and various locking options are presented. All options presented here are linked to the master share by default.

The Permissions tab allows setting the UNIX permissions on files and directories created in the share. The standard Read, Write, and Execute permissions for owner, group, and others are settable for both files and directories. Once again, these are linked to the master share by default.

The VisionFS server can be a master browser and appears in the Network Neighborhood as a Windows server.

Case Study: VisionFS at Raytheon

Rayetheon Systems Company, formerly Hughes Defense Communications, uses VisionFS in its network of SCO, Solaris, and Windows NT.

Rayetheon also uses SCO's XVision X terminal software to run its development system (see Chapter 12, "Telnet and Application Enhancement," for more information on XVision). Currently, the group is developing field artillery systems and tactical Internet systems for the Army. Before purchasing the Vision products, it downloaded evaluation copies to test their usability.

Rayetheon combines VisionFS on SCO OpenServer with SAMBA on Sun to provide total visibility throughout the system for files and printers. Its three Sun Ultra Enterprise 3000s, each with 6 processors, contain a 400 gigabyte storage system. Six SCO UNIX systems run on HP Vectras. The remainder of the servers are Windows NT.

To allow unencrypted passwords between Window NT and other SMB systems, follow these steps—when editing the Registry, all the usual warnings apply (this information is from Microsoft Knowledge Base article Q166730):

1. Run the Registry Editor (Regedt32.exe).

2. From the HKEY_LOCAL_MACHINE subtree, go to the following key:

   `\system\currentcontrolset\services\rdr\parameters`

3. Click Add Value on the Edit menu.

4. Add the following:

   ```
   Value Name: EnablePlainTextPassword
   Data Type: REG_DWORD
   Data: 1
   ```

5. Click OK and then quit the Registry Editor.

6. Shut down and restart Windows NT.

POWERfusion95

POWERfusion95 is an SMB product from April System Design in Sweden. Installation is simple with only three questions asked—node name, workgroup or domain name, and license number. Configuration is through a character-based interface.

Currently POWERfusion95 runs on the following:

- AIX
- SCO UNIX

- Generic Intel-based System V Release 4 (includes UnixWare, Solaris, DG/UX, and ICL)

- Sun SPARC Solaris

- Digital UNIX (DEC OSF/1)

- Motorola 88K

- HP-UX version 9 and 10

- Data General AviiON DG/UX

Check the Web site for the most current listing.

In Figure 6.12, a POWERfusion95 shared disk resource is listed in change mode. The options for the file server are to view, add, change, and delete shared resources.

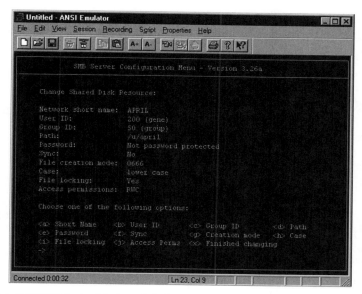

Figure 6.12. *POWERfusion95 shared disk resources in Change mode.*

Tip

When using user-level security, it is possible to make the server share the home directories of users automatically. This makes configuration of the server shared resources much easier.

Use the homeshare option to enable this feature and to specify the name of the shared resource in the /usr/fusion95/cfg/pcserve.ini. If you specify homeshare=HOME$, then use the following command line to access it:

```
NET USE H: \\FUSION95\HOME$
```

If you want to restrict the range of users who have shared disks, set the homeminuid and homemaxuid to the minimum and maximum user IDs that are allowed access to their home drives.

SAMBA

SAMBA is an SMB freeware product. SAMBA is a suite of programs that work together to enable clients to access a server's shared disk space and printers via the SMB protocol. While SAMBA was originally written for UNIX, it has been ported to other operating systems.

Clients for SAMBA include LAN Manager, Windows for Workgroups, Windows NT, OS/2, and Linux. SAMBA provides the ability for UNIX computers to behave much like a Windows NT server from the client's perspective.

SAMBA is available for the following systems with Makefile support ready to compile from source code:

- A/UX 3.0
- AIX
- Altos Series 386/1000
- Amiga
- Apollo Domain/OS sr10.3
- BSDI
- B.O.S. (Bull Operating System)
- Cray, Unicos 8.0
- Convex
- DGUX
- DNIX
- FreeBSD
- HP-UX
- Intergraph
- Linux with/without shadow passwords and quota
- Lynx 2.3.0
- MachTen (a UNIX-like system for Macintoshes)
- Motorola 88xxx/9xx range of machines
- NetBSD
- NeXTSTEP Release 2.X, 3.0 and greater (including OpenStep for Mach)
- OS/2 using EMX 0.9b
- OSF1
- QNX 4.22
- RiscIX
- RISCOs 5.0B

- Sequent
- SCO (including: 3.2v2, European dist., OpenServer 5)
- SGI.
- SMP_DC.OSx v1.1-94c079 on Pyramid S series
- SONY NEWS, NEWS-OS (4.2.x and 6.1.x)
- SunOS 4
- SunOS 5.2, 5.3, and 5.4 (Solaris 2.2, 2.3, and 2.4 and later)

- Sunsoft ISC SVR3V4
- SVR4
- System V with some Berkely extensions (Motorola 88k R32V3.2).
- Ultrix
- UnixWare
- UXP/DS

SAMBA is used by many organizations. Browsing the SAMBA Web site yielded the information that Bank of America has 1,200 SAMBA hosts and 15,000 SAMBA clients. SAMBA is used by Cisco and companies ranging from 3Com to Xerox.

Often, freeware lacks support. The SAMBA Web site lists companies by state and by country that provide SAMBA support. The developers do not offer support.

To use SAMBA, download it from the SAMBA site and read the instructions. SAMBA also comes on CD with some products, such as Caldera Linux. Newsgroups and bug reports appear on the Web site and should provide plenty of help for the beginning SAMBA user.

Chapter 7

Thin Server Technologies

- **Thin Servers Explained**
  Learn what thin servers are and how can they solve UNIX/NT file sharing problems. The operation and management of three thin servers are examined.

- **Implementing Thin Servers**
  NationsBanc-CRT tells what thin servers have done for them.

Thin Servers Explained

Thin servers are a new category of computer hardware that provide simultaneous sharing of data through NFS and CIFS/SMB. If you need additional file storage that must be accessible to both Windows NT and UNIX, thin servers may be the answer to your problems.

High-end file servers have been around for some time. Large NFS servers are available from companies like Auspex, which is implementing the AT&T Advanced Server for UNIX to provide Windows NT access to data. Other major computer companies such as Unisys have recently released new file server systems. Systems attached to the network for purposes of filesharing are collectively called *Network Attached Storage (NAS)*.

While fat servers have been around for some time, they have required NFS to be added to NT for file access. As Auspex and other large server companies add dual-file access protocols for native UNIX and NT access, the fat servers will provide the same file access as the thin servers. When these become available, the network manager will need to evaluate both fat and thin servers based on cost effectiveness.

A *thin server* is a network device designed solely for the purpose of file sharing. Thin servers exist for both CD-ROM and hard disk sharing. The thin servers discussed here are those that provide access to more than one network protocol. The advantages of these thin servers lie in two areas:

- They support both the SMB and the NFS file sharing methods so no additional software is necessary on the client or the server.

- They are less expensive and less difficult to configure than the standard full-service operating systems.

Thin servers generally have from 25 to 40 commands total in their operating system vocabulary. Since thin servers only perform one job, there is no additional overhead either in disk space or in memory for unrelated tasks. Using NT or UNIX to run a file server includes the mostly unused overhead of email, printing, routing, and executing user programs and network services such as WINS, DHCP, DNS or Remote Access Service (RAS).

One major cost advantage of thin servers is the lack of requirement for client licenses. When you buy a new server with UNIX or NT, you face the prospect of buying user licenses for the number of clients who need to connect simultaneously. The thin server permits as many clients as need servicing for one purchase price. Another cost factor is the lack of need for a monitor, keyboard and other accessories required for the normal server since they are managed and configured over the network with browser-based software.

The thin server is optimized for network file access, some providing 5 ms response times, faster than many disk drives. Plugged in to the network where they are needed, traffic on the network backbone is reduced. With the demand for data storage escalating rapidly, thin servers represent an inexpensive, scaleable way to provide the required storage.

Author's Note

One vendor went so far as to say the server operating system is obsolete, and that the era of the thin server is here. Several companies offer thin servers and plan to expand the thin server concept to other areas. With thin CD-ROM servers already available, perhaps thin tape backup servers are on the way.

AutoNet from Network Power and Light

Network Power and Light (NP&L) is a division of Mylex Corporation, a major manufacturer of disk controllers and arrays. AutoNet is a Plug and Play thin file server sold by NP&L to other manufacturers for inclusion in their products. While you will not see NP&L's name on the front panel, their hardware may be beneath the covers. The AutoNet unit will support access by both Windows NT and UNIX clients simultaneously. Using a RISC processor, AutoNet is designed to move data quickly from disk to network.

The AutoNet unit can contain up to 128 MB of RAM with a 2 MB RAM Flash memory that holds the operating system. The unit fits in a 3.5 inch, full-height disk drive slot. External LEDs provide status information on power, Ethernet speed, Ethernet link, Ethernet activity, and SCSI activity.

AutoNet uses an operating system from Wind River embedded as firmware. The network operating system is both multi-tasking and multi-threaded with an enhanced 32 bit FAT file system. Because of its design, AutoNet can execute multiple reads and writes simultaneously, even when the requests are from different network protocols.

The AutoNet unit supports up to seven hot-swappable, Ultra-Wide SCSI devices using a Symbios 53C875 SCSI controller. The network connection supports TCP/IP over 100Base-TX (100 Mbit Ethernet) and 10Base-T (10 Mbit Ethernet) with automatic speed selection. An RJ-45 connector is required. Both SMB and NFS Version 2 and above are supported. Network management via SNMP is included.

Device management is performed through Netscape Navigator 4.*x* or Internet Explorer 4.*x* and above. The Java applet that provides device management is stored on the device and downloaded to the client.

To upgrade the embedded operating system requires downloading over the Internet and updating the Flash memory—much quicker than upgrading either UNIX or Windows NT. To increase storage, the unit is powered down and a new hard drive is added. On power up, the AutoNet unit senses the new drive and automatically configures, partitions, and formats it, based on default settings that are user modifiable (see Figure 7.1). The additional capacity is then made available to the network.

Access control is through the Filesystems tab of the Java applet. For UNIX, standard NFS controls are used to allow or disallow individual hosts (see Figure 7.2). ReadWrite can be set for all hosts or for a specified list of hosts. ReadOnly can be set for all or a specified list of hosts.

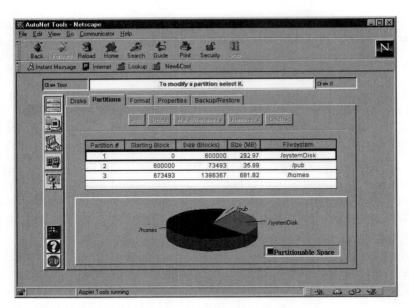

Figure 7.1. *The Disk Partition tab showing three disk partitions.*

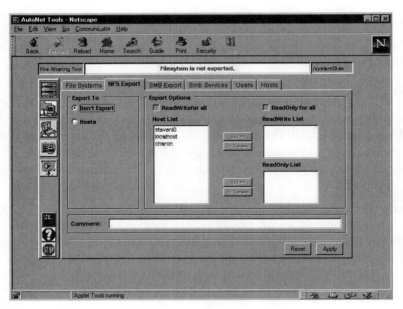

Figure 7.2. *The NFS configuration preparing to export the /systemDisk to hosts.*

A hosts file is maintained on the AutoNet controller. The hosts file is configured through the Hosts tab of the File Sharing Tool as shown in Figure 7.3.

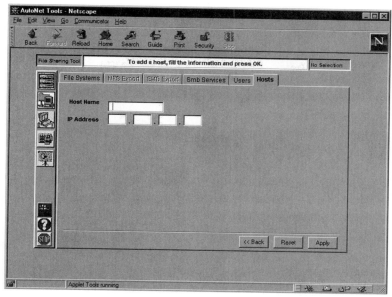

Figure 7.3. *The Hosts configuration for NFS.*

SMB access is controlled through the SMB tab illustrated in Figure 7.4. Shared filesystems permissions can be set by host or by user. As with NFS, resources can be declared ReadOnly or ReadWrite for all or specified users and hosts. Share names to be shown via Network Neighborhood are assigned to each share.

Micronet's Impact

Impact is another vendor of thin servers. Impact provides versatility of storage media by supporting CD-ROM, Jaz, and SCSI hard drives. Up to 22 SCSI devices (7 narrow and 15 wide) can be attached to an Impact appliance. Built-in RAID 1 (mirroring) provides fault tolerance.

Installation of an Impact system is simple—unpack, plug into the network, plug into power, and turn it on. Enter the IP address of the Impact unit in your Web browser, and follow the administrative instructions (which take a much shorter time to perform than those for a UNIX or NT server). Figure 7.5 shows the interface for setup.

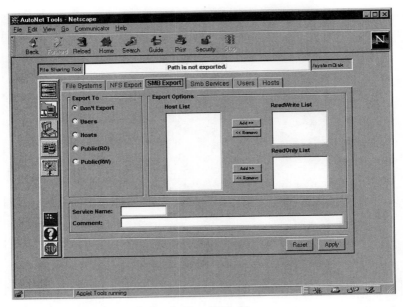

Figure 7.4. *The SMB Export tab for sharing SMB files.*

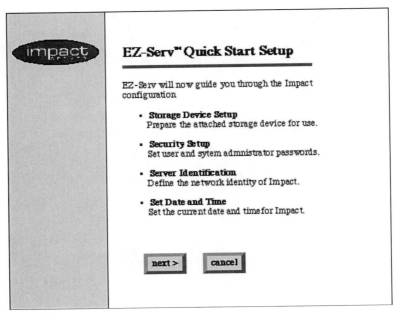

Figure 7.5. *The EZ-Serv Quick Start Setup display.*

Security is based on the Windows 95 peer network (share access) controls with user-level security to be added in the first quarter of 1998.

The system uses a Pentium processor with up to 128 MB of RAM. The Impact unit without disk drives costs about the same as the average desktop PC.

Figure 7.6 illustrates the EZ-Serv Server administration capability for sending email notification to an administrator.

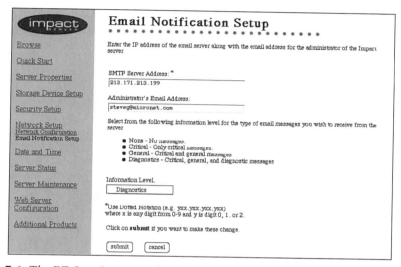

Figure 7.6. *The EZ-Serv Server configuration for email notification of the status of an Impact unit.*

Network Appliance's NetApp Filer

Network Appliance's thin server is the *NetApp Filer*, capable of NFS/CIFS simulateous access. NetApp Filer uses a thin operating system, ONTAP, to manage the hardware and data. ONTAP is tightly integrated with RAID data protection to ensure faster performance and better reliability than add-on RAID systems. The ONTAP RAID Manager automatically senses a disk drive malfunction and immediately starts rebuilding the data on any available hot spare. Further data protection is afforded through battery-backed non-volatile write cache. The battery-backed cache protects against loss of data when the system crashes due to a power outage.

NetApp hardware is available with redundant power supplies, providing higher reliability in the event a power supply dies. All hardware is rack-mountable.

The serviceable hardware is mounted in a drawer that can be accessed without unmounting the hardware from the rack. Adding memory or a new network card requires halting the system, adding the new component, and rebooting.

Adding new disk storage is even easier than upgrading memory. A new SCSI drive can be plugged in without bringing the system to a halt, disrupting service, or having to rebuild the disk array. Current models range from a maximum storage capacity of 52 GB to 439 GB with RAM capacity up to 512 MB. Network attachment can be via twisted pair, up to 100 MB, or fiber (FDDI) with multiple network attachments.

ONTAP software allows access by Windows NT or UNIX through NFS, CIFS or HTTP. Figure 7.7 illustrates a NetApp Filer attached to a heterogeneous network.

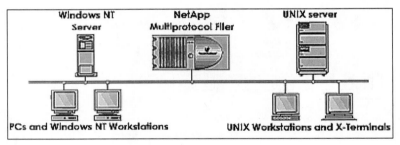

Figure 7.7. *A typical NetApp network scenario.*

WAFL Technology

ONTAP uses a file system called the *Write Anywhere File Layout (WAFL)*, a log structured file system. WAFL accumulates a number of write operations in the battery-backed write cache before simultaneously writing them to disk. The WAFL technology allows striping data across all disks with a single parity update. Average response time is under 5 milliseconds.

The ONTAP operating system is designed to handle large directories efficiently. While most operating systems slow down in large directories, ONTAP delivers performance up to 20 times faster on large directories.

WAFL supports both UNIX and Windows style file attributes to eliminate problems with compatibility and file locking. Both UNIX and Windows data can be backed up with a single backup solution.

Snapshot Technology

A part of the WAFL design is the *snapshot*, allowing up to 20 read-only versions of the operating system to exist. Snapshots allow backup to be performed even while files are being updated. A snapshot is a "frozen" picture of the pointers to data blocks in use at the time the snapshot was made. When a user updates a file after a snapshot is taken, only the changed block is affected. The changed data is written to a new block and given a new pointer.

Figure 7.8 illustrates the idea of snapshots with the snapshot and *root inode*, or current data. After the snapshot, changes made to data in block D are written to a new disk block. Snapshots can be made in seconds for a 200 GB file system.

> **Tip**
>
> *Backing up from snapshots guarantees a good backup without forcing users to close all files and avoid using data during the backup.*

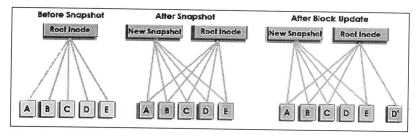

Figure 7.8. *The snapshot system, tracking changes to files.*

Snapshots are a parallel file system with hidden directories in each existing directory. The snapshots are logged into the directories by names such as hourly.1, hourly.2, and so on. The snapshots themselves are directories allowing users to restore a previous copy of a file without resorting to a tape restore.

Snapshots are configured by the administrator to be captured as desired or on demand. Figure 7.9 shows the Configuration Manager window for snapshots. When a snapshot is captured, updates are made to the hidden directories to record the information.

Figure 7.10 shows the G:\lab directory, a listing of the ~snapshot subdirectory of the G:\lab directory, and a listing of the hourly.0 directory with the ~snapshot directory. A user can restore a file to a previous condition by retrieving it from a ~snapshot directory. This retrieval pulls together the disk blocks that contained the file at the time the snapshot was taken.

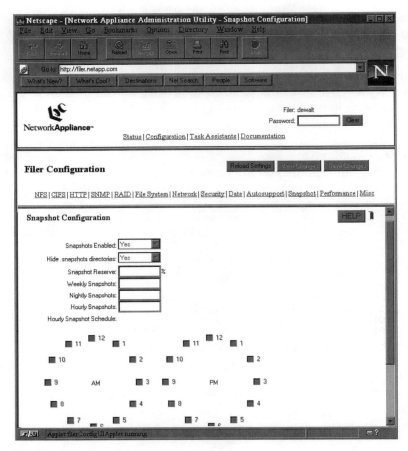

Figure 7.9. *The Snapshot Configuration window.*

NetApp Filer Administration

All administration of a NetApp Filer is performed by pointing a browser at the Filer and running HTML/Java administration scripts. The Filer may be monitored in real time by applets on the administrator's desktop computer.

In a Windows NT environment, the NetApp Filer becomes a member of a domain. Windows users using NT and domains are authenticated through the domain controller. NFS allows sharing of files through the standard /etc/exports. NFS users are always authenticated by the host that has permission to mount the share.

The NetApp Filer can be used as a server on both an internal network and on the Internet. Figure 7.11 illustrates a server with two network connections: one for the Internet using HTTP with read-only permissions and the second connection on the internal side with NFS, CIFS, and HTTP interfaces.

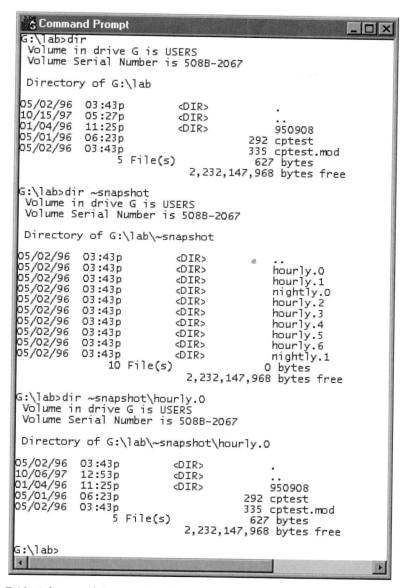

```
Command Prompt                                              _  □  X
G:\lab>dir
 Volume in drive G is USERS
 Volume Serial Number is 508B-2067

 Directory of G:\lab

05/02/96  03:43p        <DIR>          .
10/15/97  05:27p        <DIR>          ..
01/04/96  11:25p        <DIR>          950908
05/01/96  06:23p                   292 cptest
05/02/96  03:43p                   335 cptest.mod
              5 File(s)             627 bytes
                        2,232,147,968 bytes free

G:\lab>dir ~snapshot
 Volume in drive G is USERS
 Volume Serial Number is 508B-2067

 Directory of G:\lab\~snapshot

05/02/96  03:43p        <DIR>          ..
05/02/96  03:43p        <DIR>          hourly.0
05/02/96  03:43p        <DIR>          hourly.1
05/02/96  03:43p        <DIR>          nightly.0
05/02/96  03:43p        <DIR>          hourly.2
05/02/96  03:43p        <DIR>          hourly.3
05/02/96  03:43p        <DIR>          hourly.4
05/02/96  03:43p        <DIR>          hourly.5
05/02/96  03:43p        <DIR>          hourly.6
05/02/96  03:43p        <DIR>          nightly.1
             10 File(s)              0 bytes
                        2,232,147,968 bytes free

G:\lab>dir ~snapshot\hourly.0
 Volume in drive G is USERS
 Volume Serial Number is 508B-2067

 Directory of G:\lab\~snapshot\hourly.0

05/02/96  03:43p        <DIR>          .
10/06/97  12:53p        <DIR>          ..
01/04/96  11:25p        <DIR>          950908
05/01/96  06:23p                   292 cptest
05/02/96  03:43p                   335 cptest.mod
              5 File(s)             627 bytes
                        2,232,147,968 bytes free

G:\lab>
```

Figure 7.10. *A listing of the snapshot directory showing the files that could be retrieved.*

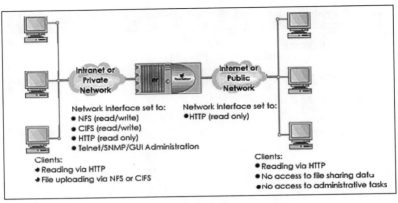

Figure 7.11. *A NetApp Filer used on both the Internet and an intranet.*

Case Study: Implementing Thin Servers

NationsBanc-CRT, a wholly owned subsidiary of NationsBank NA, provides derivative products and foreign exchange services to worldwide markets. NationsBanc-CRT develops its own proprietary trading applications while also employing third-party applications. NationsBanc-CRT bought its first NetApp server (Filer) in the fall of 1993 and now has more than 30 filers installed at its Chicago world headquarters and in multiple sites worldwide. These sites form the base of a very large UNIX wide area network spanning three continents.

With non-stop trading activity at exchange centers around the world and a high demand for instantaneous information, NationsBanc-CRT requires system reliability and performance. The firm runs the risk of a substantial revenue loss in the event of even the slightest system failure. That's why it chose the Network Appliance NetApp Filer with integrated RAID 4 technology.

Paul Canning, vice president of network services for NationsBanc-CRT, says, "We literally pulled the plug out of the wall and this machine barely took notice. Within 45 seconds, we were back online with no disruption to our daily business. And we pulled disks out of the rack and it kept running. Our NetApp server does one critical thing and it does it very well—it keeps our worldwide offices operational around the clock."

The 33 staff members in the Chicago-based Network Services group are responsible for supporting 1,100 users and maintaining operations in offices throughout the U.S., as well as London, Frankfurt, Singapore, Hong Kong, Paris, and Tokyo.

Faced with increasing performance and reliability issues with their existing HP server platform, Canning and his staff began benchmarking a variety of systems. They were convinced that an open systems environment was the right answer. One of the first systems they evaluated was unable to meet all of the company's demands. "In addition to the lack of scalability, it was not able to demonstrate reliable recoverability," says Canning.

When it came time to benchmark the NetApp Filer, Canning was quickly impressed. "I was immediately won over by this machine. It's a low-maintenance system with a clearly faster response time. Our users can't wait for system support. They're in a time-critical environment and this server is virtually self-maintained. During our analysis, NetApp proved better, cheaper, and faster than anything else we tested."

Competitors tried to convince NationsBanc-CRT that there was less disk space available and that more time and attention would be required to maintain the operating system with a NetApp Filer. Canning found no basis to either claim. "The disk space is abundant and we have only one person assigned to maintain the OS," states Canning, "which is more than adequate."

NationsBanc-CRT has exploited NetApp's snapshot feature as well. To help ensure that data is not lost or destroyed, this feature provides NationsBanc-CRT users with an online, read-only copy of the entire file system, allowing backups of the system without interruption and enabling users to save space and recover corrupted or deleted files.

Canning points out how the NetApp Filers combine high levels of reliability with exceptional performance. "NFS performance is critical to our business operations," he says. "Network Appliance is succeeding in delivering both reliability and performance in its product family. As far as NationsBanc-CRT is concerned, every claim that Network Appliance makes for performance, speed, and reliability is proven through real results."

# Part III

Printing Between UNIX and NT

Chapter **8**

LPR/LPD

- **The Basics of LPR/LPD**
  The /etc/printcap (printers.conf on Solaris) is explained, as well as UNIX System V versus BSD printing.

- **LPR/LPD Setup on UNIX**
  Configure Solaris, Linux, and SCO printers for LPR/LPD printing.

- **LPR/LPD Setup on Windows NT**
  Configure a new port for TCP/IP printing. Also, learn how to print to UNIX printers.

- **Using LPR/LPD as a Gateway**
  Print to UNIX printers from Windows clients through a Windows NT LPR/LPD gateway.

The Basics of LPR/LPD

LPR *(Line Printer Remote)* is the UNIX command for submitting print jobs and is the client side of UNIX remote printing. LPD (Line Printer Daemon) is the server half of the service. LPQ is the command to list the status of a remote print queue.

There are two major systems of UNIX printing:

- Berkeley Systems Division (BSD, which originated at the University of California Berkeley)

- System V, the AT&T version

System V includes Solaris, HP-UX, IRIX, and SCO UNIX. System V printing can be distinguished by the use of the lp, lpstat, cancel and lpmove commands. The directory /var/spool/lp contains most of the printing subsystem except the actual commands that are stored in /usr/bin or /usr/sbin. The System V printing commands do not support LPR/LPD capability.

BSD systems use the LPR/LPD system as their native print method, and a print definition file named /etc/printcap. BSD systems will work with Windows NT as they are set up. Caldera Linux uses the LPR/LPD print method.

Solaris has an additional package that supports BSD printing. The package SUNWscplp is named the SunSoft Print–Source Compatibility (Usr). Adding this package to a Solaris system creates a /usr/ucb (University of California Berkeley) directory. Within the /usr/ucb directory are the BSD commands, several of which are links to the print commands in /usr/bin.

SCO UNIX contains the LPR/LPD capability. The default installation uses System V printing. The SCO command, mkdev rlp, will copy the standard System V commands to the /usr/lpd/remote directory. The commands in /usr/bin will then be replaced by the BSD commands. Both lp and lpr are linked to the same program after this change is made. When a print command is issued, the job is passed to the scheduler, lpsched. The scheduler determines whether the print job is to be sent to a local or remote printer. If the job is destined for a local printer, the commands in /usr/lpd/remote are called. If the print destination is a remote printer, then the commands in /usr/bin are used to send the print job to the remote system.

To work with Windows NT, therefore, the UNIX version being used must support the LPR/LPD capability.

Tip

A quick way to print without the LPR/LPD setup is to use the remote command execution capability. This requires trusted access; see Chapter 4, "UNIX TCP/IP," for details.

Assume that you want to print to a UNIX computer, Thor, from an NT computer or another UNIX computer. The file to be printed is named unattend.txt. The command to execute on NT is

```
TYPE UNATTEND.TXT|REXEC THOR "lp -d main"
```

The rexec could be replaced by rsh if trusted host/user access is configured. Use rexec if you do not have trusted access and have an account name and password. The same setup will work between two UNIX systems if the type command is replaced with cat.

As an interesting side note, you would think the UNIX command would have to be in lowercase letters, typical UNIX style. It works fine for me in uppercase as well.

When setting up remote printing, follow these steps:

1. Print to the printer locally. Prove that the printer works for local use before attempting Remote use.

2. Ping the remote host by name. Prove connectivity and name-to-address resolution.

3. Run a remote command with REXEC. Check trusted access configuration.

If the printer works locally, the printer host is reachable by pinging, and the trusted access is working. Any problems with remote printing are most likely confined to the remote printer setup.

Chapter 4 includes a discussion of trusted access. If trusted host or trusted user access is not desired for security reasons, the /etc/hosts.lpd file can be used. To provide print permission, edit the /etc/hosts.lpd file and include the name of the remote host. The format for the hosts.lpd file is one system name per line:

```
Peanuts
Apollo
```

The host names must be resolvable by either the /etc/hosts file or DNS.

Author's Note

Windows NT terminology redefines the standard printing terminology. In UNIX, a printer is a device with paper, toner or a ribbon that produces printed output. That same device is called a print device in Windows NT. The NT use of the term printer refers to software drivers. A thorough discussion of Windows NT printing can be found in the Windows NT Workstation Resource Kit. To set up UNIX printers, refer to your UNIX documentation.

LPR/LPD Setup on UNIX

The configuration file for LPR printing is /etc/printcap. All three of the UNIX variants in this book will automatically configure the printcap file from entries in the adminstrative GUI. A printcap file is shown as follows:

```
1. # Remote Line Printer (BSD format)
2. main:\
3.     :lp=/dev/tty2a:ex:sd=/usr/spool/lpd/main:
```

The printer, main, is attached to the second serial port, /dev/tty2a, known in

the DOS/Windows world as *COM2*. The spooler directory is
/usr/spool/lpd/main.

To provide additional security, an `:rs:` entry in the printcap limits printer
access to accounts that have a same name account on the system with the
printer.

For serial printers, the serial parameters need to be included in the printcap
entry. A serial printer on a 9600 baud line would have `:br#9600:` in the printcap definition.

Other serial considerations are parity/no parity, XON/XOFF and the conversion of newlines to carriage return/newline. If the printer uses no parity, needs
translation of newlines, and uses XON/XOFF for flow control, the definition
would appear as

```
:ms=-parity,onlcr,ixon:
```

The `-parity` turns off parity, the `onlcr` means on output turn newlines into carriage return/newlines and the `ixon` instructs the system to use XON/XOFF in
the flow control. Parameters in the `ms` option are the same as those used in the
/etc/termcap file. Our expanded definition may look like this:

```
1. # Remote Line Printer (BSD format)
2. main:\
3. :lp=/dev/tty2a:ex:sd=/usr/spool/lpd/main:\
4.     :rs:br9600:ms=-parity,onlcr,ixon:
```

The backslashes at the end of lines are a continuation indicator. The backslash
should be typed and immediately followed by pressing the Enter key. The backslash is a UNIX convention that takes away the special meaning of the following character. In this usage, the backslash allows the Enter key to perform a
carriage return without being considered as an end of line. In essence, the
entire printer definition is on one line.

Other options in the printcap file include suppressing the print header, suppressing form feeds, setting page width, setting page length and restricting the
number of copies.

Troubleshooting Tip

*The `onlcr` is necessary for printers used by both UNIX and Windows for
text printing. UNIX text lines end with a linefeed, whereas DOS lines
end in a carriage return/linefeed. Printers configured for DOS/Windows
text printing will not print correctly with UNIX text. The first line will
print, the print head will drop to the next line and print the second line
without performing a carriage return. This produces a stairstep printout.*

LPR on Solaris

Solaris does not use the standard file name /etc/printcap. Instead, the Solaris file is called /etc/printers.conf. The format of printers.conf is similar to printcap:

```
01. #    If you hand edit this file, comments and structure may change.
02. #    The preferred method of modifying this file is through the use of
03. #    lpset(1M) or fncreate_printer(1M)
04. #
05. apollo1:\
06.      :bsdaddr=apollo,apollo1:
07. main:\
08.      :bsdaddr=thor,main:\
09.      :description=standard parallel:
10. hp:\
11.      :bsdaddr=gandalf,hp:\
12.      :description=HP Laser III:
```

The bsdaddr provides the server name and printer name, which are comma separated. In the above example, there are three printers named apollo1, main and hp. The printers are located on apollo, thor, and gandalf.

Solaris printers are configured through the Admintool. From a shelltool or cmdtool window run the Admintool. Choose Browse, then Printers. Figure 8.1 illustrates adding the remote printer on Gandalf named HP. The result of applying this is the hp: entry in the /etc/printers.conf.

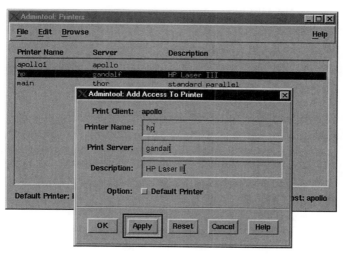

Figure 8.1. *Adding a remote NT printer in Solaris.*

LPR on Linux

Since Linux uses BSD printing as its default, no workarounds are necessary to get started on LPR printing. Figure 8.2 illustrates adding a remote printer on Caldera Linux.

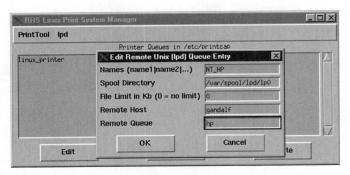

Figure 8.2. *Adding a remote NT printer in Linux.*

After adding the printer, the /etc/printcap file will resemble the one below. Note the warning in the file header.

```
01. # /etc/printcap
02. #
03. # Please don't edit this file directly unless you know what you are doing!
04. # Be warned that the control-panel printtool requires a very strict format!
05. # Look at the printcap(5) man page for more info.
06. #
07. # This file can be edited with the printtool in the control-panel.
08. ##PRINTTOOL## LOCAL epson 300x300 letter {}
09. linux_printer:\
10.     :sd=/var/spool/lpd/lp:\
11.     :mx#0:\
12.     :lp=/dev/lp0:\
13.     :if=/var/spool/lpd/lp/filter:
14. ##PRINTTOOL## REMOTE
15. NT_HP:\
16.     :sd=/var/spool/lpd/lp0:\
17.     :mx#0:\
18.     :rm=gandalf:\
19. :rp=hp:
```

LPR on SCO

SCO UNIX has the capability to use both the BSD and the System V print systems. During the initial setup, the System V lpsched system is installed. The BSD capability is loaded on the system waiting for the administrator to request it. Figure 8.3 illustrates the Printer Control window for a SCO UNIX printer.

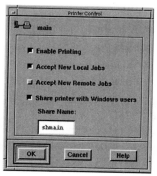

Figure 8.3. *Setting up an SCO printer for LPD receipt of new remote print jobs.*

Tip

Remember that names are case sensitive in UNIX.

The Printer Control window regulates the availability of the printer. If the printer is not accepting new local jobs, local UNIX users receive an error when attempting to submit print requests. If the printer is accepting jobs but is not enabled, print jobs are accepted, but are held in the queue and not sent to the printer. In this case, the default on the computer is to allow print sharing to Windows systems (refer to Chapter 10, "UNIX-Based SMB Print Providers," for more information).

The first time the Accept New Remote Jobs option is selected, SCO converts the system to using LPR/LPD. Selecting the option and clicking OK results in a message box, as shown in Figure 8.4. Clicking OK automatically configures the LPR/LPD system and creates the /etc/printcap file.

Figure 8.4. *The message box asking to configure remote printing.*

The /etc/printcap file is automatically configured for printer main. Having completed these steps, a remote UNIX system or Windows NT system can print to printer main on this system.

UNIX-to-NT Configuration

Configuring a UNIX computer to print to an NT server's printer via LPR/LPD is just as easy. Figure 8.5 illustrates adding an NT printer as a remote printer to an SCO UNIX system. Again, the /etc/printcap file is automatically updated. We had previously configured the LPR/LPD remote service in allowing remote print jobs to be sent to another server, so we do not get the message box a second time.

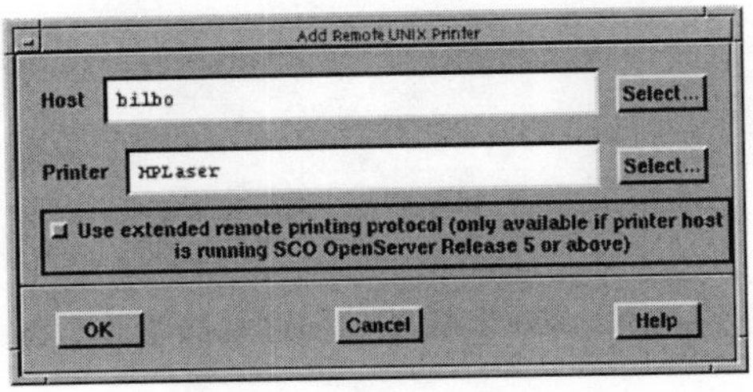

Figure 8.5. *Creating a printer on UNIX to send output to a remote LPD service.*

The /etc/printcap file now has an entry for the remote HPLaser printer on BILBO as well as the original line for main. The HPLaser line points to BILBO as the remote machine (rm=BILBO), the remote printer name HPLaser (rp=HPLaser), and the local spool directory of /usr/spool/lpd/HPLaser:

```
# Remote Line Printer (BSD format)
main:\
    :lp=/dev/tty2a:ex:sd=/usr/spool/lpd/main:
HPLaser:\
    :lp=:rm=BILBO:rp=HPLaser:sd=/usr/spool/lpd/HPLaser:
```

For SCO UNIX, the lpstat command is used regardless of whether the remote line printing is installed. Running the lpstat -t command will display information about the remote and local printers. The command will take longer when remote printers are configured as it sends out queries for status information.

The remote line printing may be configured manually by executing mkdev rlp. The /etc/printcap file can be edited with a text editor. SCO, like Solaris and Linux, has made the manual configuration unnecessary in most cases.

Warning

When printing from a UNIX application that produces finished output ready for the printer, such as graphics or WordPerfect for UNIX, include the -o raw *option in the print command.*

```
lp -d main -o raw printfile
```

This option instructs the receiving system to pass the raw output straight to the printer. The same holds true when sending print files to a UNIX printer from a Windows program.

LPQ on UNIX

The UNIX lpq command will list the status of printers in the /etc/printcap on Linux or /etc/printers.conf on Solaris. SCO does not use lpq, maintaining its lpstat command for the same purpose.

Linux provides slightly different options to lpq than Solaris:

- Both support the -P *<printername>* and -1 for a long listing

- Both support requesting a specific print job ID

- Both offer the capability to refresh the information at intervals

- Solaris offers the *username* option to retrieve information on all print jobs belonging to a single user

- Linux offers a debug option

Information from lpq can be used to remove a remote print job with lprm.

LPR/LPD Setup on Windows NT

Windows NT does not install TCP/IP printing by default. The printing portion must be added later by choosing the Network applet in the Control Panel, clicking the Services tab and finally clicking Add. After the list is built, click Microsoft TCP/IP Printing as shown in Figure 8.6. You will then have to reboot to get the services working.

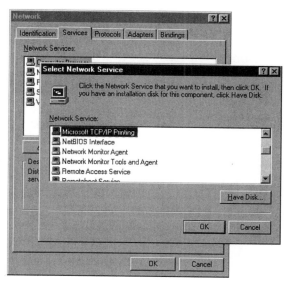

Figure 8.6. *Adding Microsoft TCP/IP printing to a Windows NT computer.*

The LPD Service

Once installed, the TCP/IP Print Server service does not start automatically. To use the NT computer as an LPD server, the LPDSVC service must be running. To get this started automatically, choose Control Panel, Services and change the Startup parameters of TCP/IP Print Server to Automatic.

> **Tip**
>
> *The service will not start if no printers are configured. Make sure a printer exists before starting the service.*

The print system is now configured to receive print jobs from a UNIX computer.

Printing to Remote UNIX Systems via LPR

A printer may exist on a UNIX system that is required for printing by a Windows NT client. Microsoft permits printing to a remote UNIX printer by way of LPR. One method of using LPR is from the command line. Although this probably will not be the normal method of execution, the following syntax will work:

```
LPR -S<ip_address> -P<printer_name> <filename>
```

The -o option to the LPR command includes output directives. The most common of these is -o raw instructing the receiving system to pass the data through to the printer without further rendering.

The normal method of using LPR is to set up a Windows NT printer to use LPR as its protocol:

1. Click on Add Printer. The Add Printer Wizard appears.

2. Click on New Port. The Printer Ports window opens with a list of available ports. LPR will appear on the list if you added TCP/IP printing.

3. Select LPR, and the Add LPR Compatible Printer window opens.

4. Enter the IP address or host name and the name of the printer on the remote system.

5. Click OK, then click Close. A new port appears above LPT1 with the host name or IP address you entered.

Figure 8.7 illustrates adding an LPR port.

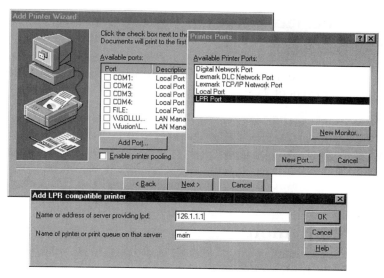

Figure 8.7. *Creating an LPR port for a printer.*

Once the printer has been created, right-click the printer and select Properties. The Ports tab will appear as in Figure 8.8, showing the new port: Printer MAIN on IP address 126.1.1.1.

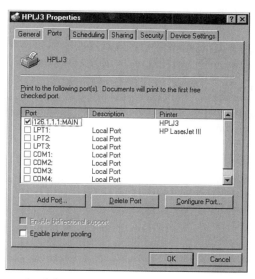

Figure 8.8. *The Ports tab of the LPR Printer.*

The Line Printer Queue (LPQ) Command

With LPR printing, there is not an icon that can be double-clicked to check the status of the remote print queue. The LPQ command is used to check the status of the remote print queue. The LPQ command displays information on the printer queue. The syntax is

```
LPQ -S<ipaddress> -P<printername> -l
```

Most Windows commands are not case sensitive. The LPQ command is. The S and P options must be in uppercase. The l option must be lowercase. The -l option provides verbose output. There is no NT equivalent of the UNIX lprm command. Print jobs that need to be remove from a remote LPD queue will have to be removed at the remote host.

Using LPR/LPD as a Gateway

When Windows NT is on a network, often the clients are Windows 95 or Windows 3.1x. Windows NT can be set up to print to a TCP/IP-based printer, such as one on a UNIX system, or a network printer device, such as an HP with a JetDirect card. The NT computer can then share the printer to other Windows clients. In this manner, Windows clients may print to any LPR/LPD printers on the network for which they have permission without the overhead of the additional LPR/LPD software.

To configure a gateway to a UNIX printer:

1. Create a Windows NT printer as described in the "Printing to Remote UNIX Systems via LPR" section earlier in this chapter.

2. Double-check that printing works between the Windows NT system and the UNIX printer. If this is not working, setting up the next phase will lead to frustration.

3. Double-click on the Windows NT printer to start the print queue window.

4. Share the Windows NT printer to Windows clients on the network.

5. From a Windows client computer, create a new network printer.

6. Select the shared Windows NT printer.

7. Print a test page.

8. Watch the print queue on the Windows NT printer. Your print job should appear and then disappear as the print job is sent to UNIX.

9. Check the UNIX print queue or the UNIX printer.

You should now have a Windows client printing through a Windows NT gateway to UNIX.

Another use of this methodology is to accept, through LPD, print requests from any LPR-enabled computer and pass them on to any printer on the network that is visible to Windows NT. This is a reverse of the previous scenario.

Use of LPR/LPD on Windows NT can provide many cross-platform printing benefits. There are some problems with this printing methodology, though. Windows clients will not get messages back from UNIX if the printer runs out of paper. Windows computers cannot manage the print queue on the UNIX computer. However, the benefits outweigh the problems.

Chapter 9

Windows NT-Based NFS
Print Providers

- **NFS Printing from Windows NT**
  What is NFS printing? How do we set it up on the UNIX side? What is pcnfsd and what if you can't find a copy?

- **The Solstice Network Client**
  Learn how to set up printers and get NT users authorized to print on them.

- **Hummingbird**
  Use Hummingbird's RPCINFO command to aid in setting up pcnfsd printing and in connecting to a UNIX printer.

- **Intergraph Disk Access**
  Disk Access is Intergraph's entry into the pcnfsd scene.

NFS Printing from Windows NT

If you have chosen NFS as your filesharing technology between UNIX and Windows NT, then you will have NFS printing available. But why would you print with NFS rather than the LPR/LPD method provided as part of the Windows NT and UNIX operating systems? Because printers on UNIX that are available for LPR printing from Windows NT do not show up in a browse list.

If your workstations are Windows NT, then users will be able to browse the NFS Network Neighborhood and find printers. This will lessen the management overhead of adding the LPR protocol to NT and creating the NT printers. If users need to change from one printer to another, NFS printing will make that task simpler.

pcnfsd: What It Is and How to Get It

NFS printing from Windows to UNIX requires the UNIX pcnfsd (PC Network Filesystem Daemon). pcnfsd supports a printing model based on the use of NFS to transfer the actual print data from the client to the server. The client issues a print initialization request to the server and the server returns the path to a spool directory the client may use.

NFS printing requires setup on both the UNIX and NT sides of the network equation. The first step is to prepare the UNIX printer to receive the print request from the NT client. A PCNFS daemon must be running on the UNIX server. Verify that the PCNFS daemon is running on SCO by running

```
rpcinfo -p <systemname> ¦ grep pcnfsd
```

and on Solaris by running

```
rpcinfo ¦ grep pcnfsd
```

The list resulting from this command should include pcnfsd or rpc.pcnfsd, depending on the version of UNIX being run. The rpc.pcnfsd entry indicates Solaris.

pcnfsd on SCO

Santa Cruz Operation (SCO) provides pcnfsd as a default part of the networking operating system and is found in the /etc directory. It is started by the /etc/nfs script that checks for its existence and, if found, starts it as shown in the following code.

```
1.      [ -x /etc/pcnfsd ] && {
2.              echo " pcnfsd\c"
3.              pcnfsd &
```

pcnfsd on Solaris

Solaris includes pcnfsd in the SUNWpcnfd package. The package is available on a CD that also provides PCNFS for Windows NT and Windows 95. The CD is part of the Solaris Server Intranet Extension. To install this package, insert the CD in the CD-ROM and type:

```
cd /cdrom/cdrom0
cd nfsc
```

Use the ls command to list the contents of the directory. Both a SPARC and an i386 directory should appear. The cd command takes you to the directory matching your computer architecture.

An `ls` should show the SUNWpcnfd file. Use the `pkgadd` command to load the software:

```
pkgadd -d `pwd`
```

The term `` `pwd` `` causes the `pwd` command to be executed and the path to replace the term. In effect, it is the same as

```
pkgadd -d /cdrom/cdrom0/nfsc/i386
```

At boot time, the /etc/rc3.d/S32pcnfs script is executed by the operating system executing the `rpc.pcnfsd` daemon.

Troubleshooting Tip

Caldera Linux does not come with pcnfsd, although it does support NFS. For Linux and other UNIX versions that may not have a pcnfsd available, the FTP software company (another NFS vendor) has a download site for pcnfsd source code. To obtain the software, ftp to `ftp.ftp.com`.

To get the PCNFSD source code, download the file pcnfsd2.tar from the anonymous FTP site in the directory /support/pub/unix. The file is a UNIX-format TAR archive containing sources and makefiles, and builds information for many of the most popular UNIX flavors. Pick the version that fits and compile it. This requires that you have a C compiler.

Once compiled, start pcnfsd from a script file with the other boot processes. The script should look like this:

```
1. if [ -f /usr/etc/rpc.pcnfsd]; then
2.      /usr/etc/rpc.pcnfsd
3.      echo -n ' rpc.pcnfsd started'
4. fi
```

Note that the /usr/etc directory may not be your choice of directories. You may select any directory you choose.

Tip

The most current version of pcnfsd is version 2. If you discover your version is prior to version 2, upgrade it for enhanced user authentication and printing.

To determine the version that is running, use the `rpcinfo` *command. The second column of the listing is the version, the fifth column is the program name.*

pcnfsd Setup

The spool directory must be exported by NFS on the UNIX server. For SCO OpenServer UNIX systems, the spool directory is /usr/spool/pcnfs. The spool directory may be changed by making an entry in the /etc/pcnfsd.conf file such as:

```
spooldir path
```

Add the /usr/spool/pcnfs directory to the /etc/exports file to ensure that it is exported at boot time.

The client system must be authenticated by a UNIX NFS server. This authentication requires the client to have a UNIX account. Authentication failure will result in the client being unable to access NFS shares. Depending on the NFS client on Windows NT, the method of setting up the UNIX account login will vary. In Chapter 5, "Windows NT-Based Solutions," several major NFS products and authentication methods were examined. In some cases, all NT users can be authenticated as a single user on UNIX by name mapping.

PCNFS prints to UNIX printer names. To configure different names or functionality with the lp command, use the /etc/pcnfsd.conf file for configuration. Here's an example:

```
dummy printer1 - lp -dprinter1 -oraw $FILE
```

Print input destined for dummy to printer1. The -oraw option instructs the printer script not to do any processing on the data to be printed.

The pcnfsd.conf file is a list of configuration changes for pcnfsd. In addition to the printer statement above, user authentication logging can be turned off by adding

```
wtmp off
```

to the file.

> **Tip**
>
> *For permission to use a PCNFS printer, the remote client must be authorized through an entry in either the /etc/hosts.equiv or /etc/hosts.lpd file.*
>
> *Authorizing a remote host through /etc/hosts.equiv has security ramifications. If you are not familiar with the trusted hosts concepts, use the /etc/hosts.lpd file for authorization. Both files use the same format and are a list of host names.*

When printing to a PCNFS server, the normal Windows NT printer document management will not work. Once the print jobs have been submitted to UNIX, Windows NT has no control over them.

Solstice Network Client

The Solstice Network Client supplies PCNFSD support for Windows NT. There is no server component supplied; NT can print to a UNIX PCNFS host but not receive print jobs from UNIX. Support for LPD on non-NT Windows clients is provided to enable LPR/LPD printing. See Chapter 8 for more information on LPR/LPD printing.

When the Solstice Network Client is installed, check the Services applet in the Control Panel to ensure that the Solstice NFS services are set for automatic startup.

In Figure 9.1, the printer UX_HP is visible as being shared by laptop1. By double-clicking on the desired printer, a warning appears that the printer must be set up before it can be used. This printer is identified as a PCNFS printer by the pcnfsd prepended to the name of the printer, as shown in Figure 9.2.

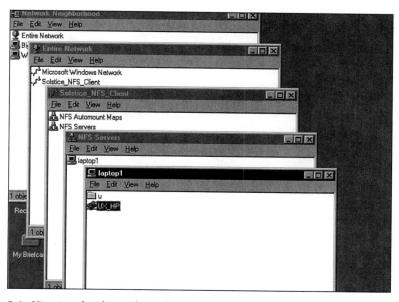

Figure 9.1. *Viewing the shares from the UNIX system laptop1 on the Solstice_NFS_Client network.*

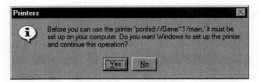

Figure 9.2. *The warning to set up the printer before attempting to use it. Note the* pcn-fsd *prepended to the name of the printer.*

The next step is to click the Yes button and set up the printer in NT. NT will not be able to use the drivers on the UNIX computer, so a warning window announces the fact and offers the opportunity to install a driver on the local machine. When printing from one NT computer to another, the computer with the printer can download appropriate drivers to the client computer.

If the drivers for the particular printer are not available on the local computer, you are prompted to insert the NT Installation CD or to select a network site for the drivers. Insert the CD or select a network site where the I386 directory (if an Intel computer) can be found. Once installed, the properties of the printer reveal the port to be a pcnfsd port (see Figure 9.3). The printer can be shared to other Windows users.

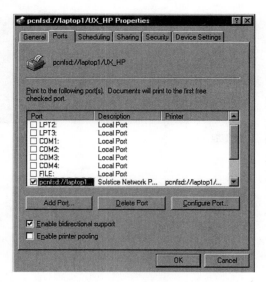

Figure 9.3. *The Ports display after the printer has been set up showing the PCNFSD port for printing.*

> **Warning**
>
> *The UNIX computer sharing UX_HP has not shared the spool directory for the printer. A printer may be created using this shared printer without an error at creation. When attempting to print to the newly acquired printer share, an error will occur when the pcnfsd daemon on the UNIX host cannot return a share name for the spool directory. The error message is shown in Figure 9.4.*

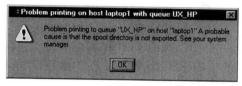

Figure 9.4. *The error message displayed when no spool directory is shared from the UNIX host.*

Installing a PCNFSD Printer

To install a Solstice Network Client PCNFSD printer on Windows NT without browsing the Network Neighborhood's Solstice Network, follow these instructions:

1. Click the Start button, point to Settings and then click Printers.

2. Double-click the Add Printers icon.

3. Select My Computer, then click Next.

4. Click Add Port.

5. Select the Sun PCNFSD port and then click New Port.

6. Enter the printer queue name from the UNIX computer. The name may be in one of several formats including:

   ```
   server:printername
   pcnfsd:\\server\printername
   pcnfsd://server/printername
   pcnfs:\\server\printername
   pcnfs://server/printername
   //server/printername
   \\server\printername
   ```

   `123.45.67.89:printername` (where `123.45.67.89` is the IP address of the UNIX host)

7. Click OK, then Close.

8. Click the box next to the PCNFSD port you specified.

9. Select the printer manufacturer and then the model from the list.

10. Enter a printer name if the default is not acceptable.

11. Click Not Shared, then Next.

12. Click to print a test page and then Finish.

Hummingbird

Hummingbird is one of the industry leaders in third-party NFS. In Chapter 5, you can find a discussion of its NFS products: Maestro NFS, NFS Server and NFS Gateway. Its NFS printing product installs as part of the regular NFS product. The Hummingbird package supports both NFS and LPR/LPD printing. The Hummingbird LPR/LPD creates a new port similar to printing to an HP JetDirect printer.

To determine if the PCNFSD daemons are running on the UNIX host, use the RPCINFO application, shown in Figure 9.5. RPCINFO indicates which PCN-FSD daemons are running on the selected host, the port numbers used, the number (used by all UNIX vendors), the version (it is normal to have multiple versions running), and the protocol (TCP or UDP). Here we have both versions 1 and 2 of PCNFSD running over both TCP and UDP. This provides support for any PCNFS client.

To ease your burden, use the NFS Network Access to set up a login name and password combination for NFS to use when you connect to the PCNFSD print server. Figure 9.6 illustrates that my login on NT will result in logging into the UNIX computer as root for printing purposes.

> ### Tip
>
> *Using root as your normal login would not be a good idea. Root privileges should not be abused. When installing software on UNIX, you are usually logged in as root. When installing software on NT, you are often logged in as Administrator. For test purposes, you can test as root and Administrator. Some products transmit passwords as plain text on networks. That may or may not be a consideration on your network.*

Creating an NT printer to send print jobs to the UNIX PCNFSD printer is simple:

1. Click the Start button, point to Settings, click Printers.

2. Double-click Add Printer.

3. Select the button for Network Printers and click Next. (Note this is opposite from the Solstice method).

4. Enter the network path and queue name in the \\server\printer_queue format or click on the Hummingbird NFS entry in the Entire Network and browse for the printer as shown in Figure 9.7.

5. After the printer is selected, you are prompted to select a manufacturer and model and finish out the same steps as listed in the Solstice instructions.

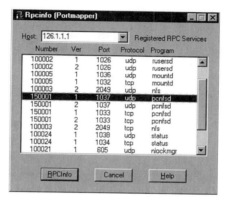

Figure 9.5. *The RPCINFO application showing the Remote Procedure Call daemons running on the UNIX host.*

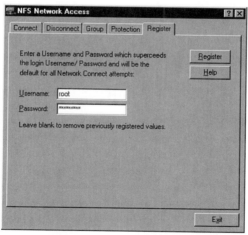

Figure 9.6. *The NFS Network Access setup for a username and password for the UNIX host.*

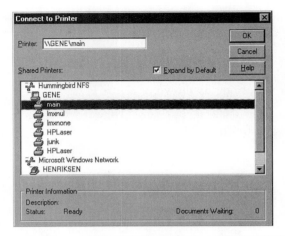

Figure 9.7. *Browsing the Hummingbird NFS neighborhood for PCNFSD printers on a UNIX host.*

After clicking the Finish button, you are not prompted to print a test page. Right click on the newly created printer's icon and select Properties. If you check the Ports tab, there is no port listed for the printer. Figure 9.8 is an example of how it should look. Unfortunately, every attempt to exit without a port being checked yields an error message stating you must select a port. Click Cancel to escape this.

Figure 9.8. *The Ports tab of the Printer Properties lists no port for the printer.*

Once the printer has been created, print a test page. It should work the first time, if you have followed the instructions. If the PCNFSD directory is not shared by UNIX, you will get an error at this point rather than during the adding a printer phase. Figure 9.9 shows the error message.

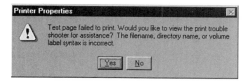

Figure 9.9. *The error from not having the PCNFSD directory shared on the UNIX host.*

Intergraph DiskAccess

Intergraph includes an NFS print client in its suite. Configuration of a printer through Intergraph NFS is similar to the instructions for Hummingbird. The main difference is the name of the NFS Network Neighborhood entry. For Hummingbird, the NFS network name is Hummingbird NFS, while the Intergraph entry in Network Neighborhood is NFS Network.

When NFS Network is double-clicked, the DefaultLAN window appears. Double-clicking DefaultLAN yields a list of NFS servers. When traversing the Add Printer windows, the Intergraph NFS entry appears as Intergraph Disk Access Network rather than as NFS Network. Figure 9.10 illustrates the process of locating a PCNFSD printer.

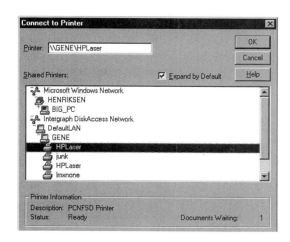

Figure 9.10. *The Network Neighborhood window in Add Printer with Intergraph NFS installed.*

With all PCNFSD printing, there is no report from the UNIX host computer to Windows NT reporting on the status of the printer. The printer may be incorrectly configured, disabled, not accepting new requests, out of paper, or not working correctly. The first step should always be to verify the configuration on the UNIX computer.

Chapter 10

UNIX-Based SMB Print Providers

- **Advanced Server for UNIX**
  AT&T's ASU comes in many flavors; we will look at one in particular—SCO's AFPS.

- **Advanced File and Print Server**
  AFPS provides a nicely integrated SMB print service in the SCO administrative program. SMB printers are created as easily as local UNIX printers.

- **TotalNet Advanced Server**
  TAS offers a different approach to management—with a browser. Sharing printers is no problem through the administrative tools, but there are a few tricks to be learned.

- **VisionFS**
  Another SCO entry, VisionFS allows printing from Windows to UNIX, and from UNIX to Windows printers. You learn how to configure the same printer for different options for different users.

- **Fusion95**
  The Swedish entry provides a maximum of 1,000 Windows printers available to a single UNIX computer. See how to print to a Windows printer via three different ways.

- **SAMBA**
  The freeware SAMBA is configured on a Linux system. Find out how to share printers to the Windows clients.

Printing with SMB Between UNIX and Windows NT

With a suitable Server Message Block (SMB) server product, UNIX can provide printers to Windows clients that appear in the Network Neighborhood and use these printers on Windows computers for UNIX printing. In some cases, UNIX can browse for Windows printers that appear in the Network Neighborhood.

The products described in this chapter are all SMB enablers for UNIX. SMB is the file sharing protocol used by Microsoft in Windows NT. As an administrator, you must choose the product that provides the capabilities you need.

UNIX does not return printer error codes to Windows clients. Be aware that, for example, you will not receive error messages indicating the printer is out of paper.

> ### Warning
>
> *Checking Properties on a remote UNIX printer provides some default information regardless of whether or not a printer is actually attached to the UNIX computer. Do not count on the Properties capability.*
>
> *For example, a UNIX printer can be created with no physical printer attached to the computer. An NT printer can be created to print to the UNIX printer. In my test, I created an HP Laser III. Right-click the NT printer, and choose Properties. The amount of printer memory in this non-existent printer is shown as 2048 KB. The upper tray was shown with letter sized paper. In actuality, the printer does not exist.*

When choosing an SMB print server for UNIX, you should keep in mind several considerations.

- Who will provide support?

- Will it work with my version of UNIX?

- How is it configured and maintained? Do I want a GUI or can I work with configuration files?

- When the print jobs have been submitted to the server, does my client still have control over the print queue?

> **Tip**
>
> *When printing text files from both Windows and UNIX to a dot-matrix printer, the characters used to terminate a line become a problem. Some dot-matrix printers have a setting for automatic line feed at the end of a line. If the printer prints correctly from one operating system and either double spaces lines or does not perform line feeds, then set the printer to work properly with Windows. Edit the UNIX printer script to convert newlines to carriage-return newlines.*

With shared printers, the problem of deciding where the rendering of print data for the printer will occur is important. Most Windows software will process the output for the printer. If the output is then passed to a UNIX printer that assumes the print job needs rendering for the printer, the result becomes a few graphical characters and often many pages of blank output.

> **Tip**
>
> *If you have problems printing to a UNIX printer, print the report to a file. Copy the file to a UNIX shared folder and then experiment with various UNIX print options until you get the desired output.*

Creating a Windows printer to use a shared UNIX printer involves the normal setup using the Add Printer Wizard. Figure 10.1 illustrates adding a printer from the UNIX computer Gollum.

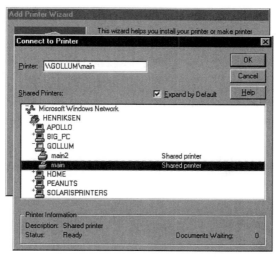

Figure 10.1. *Creating a Windows printer using a printer shared from UNIX.*

Advanced Server for UNIX

In Chapter 6, AT&T's Advanced Server for UNIX was discussed for file sharing. In the section following, SCO's implementation of ASU will be used to illustrate the print sharing capabilities of ASU.

When NT servers use printers from other NT servers, the print server can maintain the printer drivers. When the server maintains the drivers, clients get the latest copy of the drivers automatically. This currently is not a feature in any of the SMB printers covered. As a result, whenever a printer is created on an NT system to print to a non-NT SMB server, the printer drivers will have to be installed locally. AT&T's ASU has added this feature to version 4. SCO will add the feature in their implementation of ASU. Check with your vendor to see if it will be available on your vendor's implementation.

Advanced File and Print Server

SCO has successfully incorporated AT&T's ASU into *Advanced File and Print Server (AFPS)*. ASU, being a UNIX port of Windows NT software, shares printers through an implementation of the LAN Manager NET SHARE command. SCO has integrated the sharing capability into the SCOadmin administration facility. The SCOadmin tool has two faces: one for XWindows servers and the other for character-based administration.

Printer Setup

In Figure 10.2, a UNIX printer spooler is being configured to use a Windows shared printing device. The UNIX printer will use a printer model called *passthrough* for printer processing. The passthrough model does not process the output, instead sending it on to the host computer for rendering.

In Figure 10.2, beside the Windows printer Share Name option is a Select box. Tab over to the Select box and press Enter to browse the Windows computer's printer shares. Printers shared from Windows may be restricted with a password for access.

AFPS includes the capability to share printers with Windows. In Figure 10.3, a UNIX printer, main, is shared with Windows clients as SHMAIN.

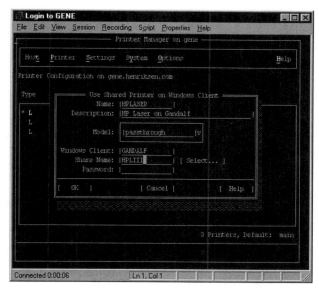

Figure 10.2. *Creating a UNIX printer, HPLASER, to print to a printer named HPLIII on a Windows NT host computer named GANDALF.*

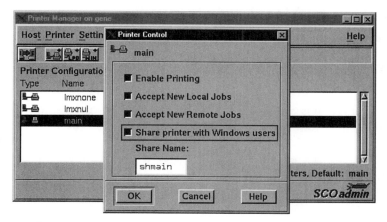

Figure 10.3. *Sharing a UNIX printer to Windows clients through SCO's GUI admin interface.*

Printer Driver Scripts

Normally, on an SCO system, the printer driver scripts are located in the /usr/spool/lp/admins/lp/interfaces directory. A script named for the printer exists in the directory for every printer on the system. All print driver scripts are ASCII text files that can be edited with a suitable text editor.

For AFPS printers attached to a Windows computer, the script in the interfaces directory redirects the print job to the AFPS printer directory. The script in the interface checks for a `raw output` option for the print job. The `raw output` option informs the receiving computer to print the data as received. If `raw` is not present, it maps newlines to carriage-return plus newlines, an appropriate mapping to convert a UNIX text print job to a DOS text print job.

The printer scripts for AFPS are stored in a different directory from the standard UNIX printer scripts: /var/opt/K/SCO/asusrv/3.5.2n/clipr. If your version of AFPS is not 3.5.2n, then change that portion of the path to your version.

The clipr directory contains two files for each remote Windows printer. The files are named <printer> and <printer>.cfg. The file with the printer name is the UNIX interface script. For instance, to delete the extra form feed at the end, comment out the line that has

```
echo "\f\c"
```

To comment out a line, insert a # in front of the line. The .cfg file contains the name of the local printer, the local printer model (interface script), the remote system name, and the remote printer name.

TotalNet Advanced Server

TotalNet Advanced Server (TAS) provides printing services to Windows NT systems to use UNIX printers. TAS is also available through Sun with Solaris 2.6. TAS is installed on the UNIX computer from the command line and managed from a Java-enabled browser.

All documentation is available through the browser. To run the management software, point your browser to `http://computername:7777` (in my case, I used `http://apollo:7777`). Make sure your Windows computer can find the UNIX system. This may be accomplished through DNS or hosts files. It is not necessary to configure the TAS system for the 7777 port.

Managing TAS

My Windows NT 4.0 came with Internet Explorer for Windows NT version 2.0 and would not run the TAS management software. The error message `Javascript not enabled or supported` appeared when attempting to run the software. Upgrading to IE 3.02, available on the Service Pack's CD in Microsoft's TechNet, solved the problem. Netscape Navigator 3.0 also worked well.

An interesting point is how TAS shares appear in Network Neighborhood. In most cases, computer names appear and double-clicking the computer reveals the shared objects. With TAS, each service created appears as a separate item in the computer list. This could be a slick way to hide actual computer names from browsing users. It can also be used to create specific share sets for different users.

Printer Setup

Figure 10.4 illustrates the first step in setting up a printer for sharing. UNIX printers have to be defined to the TAS system before they can be shared.

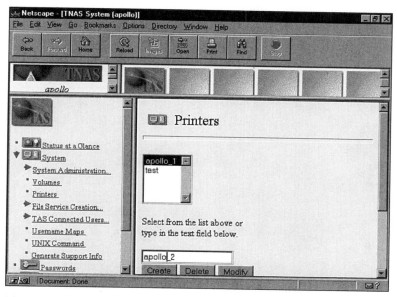

Figure 10.4. *Starting the setup of a printer for sharing.*

Figure 10.5 shows how the printer share name is linked to the UNIX printer. Here a UNIX printer queue named apollo_2 is being set up as a shared printer, apollo_2. When a printer share name is input, the UNIX printer queue name defaults to the share name. A print option of raw causes UNIX to send the request straight to the printer untouched. The permissions are user level, not share level, so no share level password is used.

Tip

While it is not documented anywhere and no warnings will notify you of a potential problem, printer and other share names are limited to eight characters.

Warning

Creating shares with longer names will be frustrating because you will try to determine the cause of the missing share. I successfully proved that it was not possible to use a share name over eight characters by creating a shared printer named apollo_printer. apollo_printer was not visible on the network.

TAS does not use the NT level of LAN Manager support and cannot use longer names. This will be fixed in a future version. The eight character name problem is common to all older LAN Manager versions.

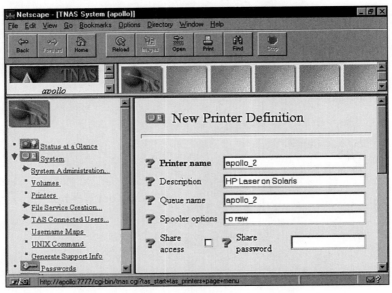

Figure 10.5. *Setting the parameters for the apollo_2 shared printer.*

Tip

One of the biggest problems reported by Syntax tech support—probably 90% of calls—is forgetting to scroll to the bottom of the form. When creating a new printer or folder share, scroll to the bottom of the window on the right. The desired service that the object will be part of must be selected. See Figure 10.6.

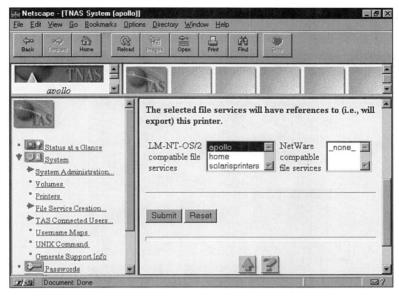

Figure 10.6. *Selecting the service that will contain the new printer.*

Print to Windows From UNIX with TAS

The `ruprint` command can be used to print to an SMB remote printer from the UNIX system with TAS. You can find `ruprint` in the TotalNet home directory under the bin subdirectory.

```
ruprint -u username -p password filename //server/printer
```

I attempted to leave out *username* and *password* in hopes of being prompted for a login name and password. Leaving out *username* or *username* and *password* resulted in an error message returned from the server.

Once the print job has been sent to the remote printer, the user no longer has any management or control of the print job.

VisionFS

VisionFS printers can be shared and controlled much like directory shares. The *Master Printer Share* is the repository of the default settings for shared objects. With any printer, linking the properties to the Master Share is another way of taking the default settings. These can be overridden as desired on individual shares.

Configuring User Requirements

To allow configuration of the print command, VisionFS includes the Commands tab on the Master Shared Printer Properties screen, shown in Figure 10.7.

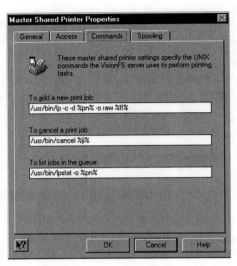

Figure 10.7. *Shared printer properties for detailing the printer commands.*

In the To Add a New Print Job text box, notice the option -o raw. If different users require different capabilities, create separate printer shares with the required capabilities. Options might be required for portrait versus landscape, changing paper bins, and changing lines per inch or characters per inch. These separate printer shares will point to the same UNIX printer, but have different capabilities.

When VisionFS starts, it scans for UNIX printers and automatically shares them. This feature can be turned off by removing the check from the Active box on the General tab of the Master Printer Share.

> ### Warning
>
> *When the Active box for the Master Printer Share is unchecked, all print-ers with the Active box linked to the Master Printer Share are unshared. Uncheck the Link for Active box on the individual shares to allow them to appear.*

Printing to Windows Printers from UNIX with VisionFS

Printing to a Windows printer from VisionFS 2.0 requires configuring a script file to use the /etc/printcap file on BSD style printing. See Chapter 8 for more information on the printcap file. The instructions given here are for Solaris. VisionFS prints to NT via a limited SMB client program, vfscprint. Version 3.0 of VisionFS will include a more expanded SMB client.

The setup of a Windows printer is a two-step process:

- Install a printer script

- Configure an entry in the printcap file

Install the script in a suitable directory, such as the bin directory for VisionFS. You can find out where that is from /etc/vision.conf. Call the script by a suitable name—for example, you might call the following script smbdocprint or gandalf_print. Change the file permission so it is readable and executable by everyone, but not writeable by anyone (such as `chmod a-w+rx` *filename*).

```
################################################################
#!/bin/sh
# These are the two important variables. Set visionfs to the
# path of your visionfs executable,
# and set smbprint to the name
# (i.e. //server/printername) of the printer you are adding
visionfs=/s/vision/bin/visionfs
smbprinter=//thor/doc
PATH=$PATH:/usr/ucb # The directory that the command 'tail' is in
export PATH       # must be included in path because visionfs uses
                  #'tail'.
$visionfs print $smbprinter - --user guest --password
################################################################
```

The second step is to let the printer services know how to access the script. You do this by creating an entry in the printcap file (/etc/printcap).

Create an entry similar to the following one.

```
################################################################
smbdoc:\
    :lp=/dev/null:mx#0:\
    :sd=/var/spool/smbdoc:\
    :lf=/var/adm/smbdoc-log:\
    :if=/s/vision/bin/smbdocprint:
################################################################
```

The lp option declares the printer device—in this case, /dev/null—because there is no device associated with the printer.

mx is the maximum file size; 0 means no limit.

sd is the spool directory. You will have to create this directory yourself, just create it in /var/spool and call it after the name you are using for the printer.

lf is the logging file. Make sure you create this file when you set up the printer; put it in /var/adm and call it after the printer name with a -log on the end (such as touch /var/adm/smbdoc-log).

if is the input filter; this should be the script that was created earlier, so put the path of the script in here.

After creating the entry in the printcap file, the printer should be ready to print. If it doesn't seem to work, then check that all the path names for everything are correct and that all file permissions are correct. Also check the error logging file (lf option in the printcap file), which may be of some help.

Once setup is completed, you should be able to print with lpr -P*printer_name*:

```
lpr -Psmbdoc filename
```

Since this method uses LPR/LPD, refer to Chapter 8, "LPR/LPD," for LPR/LPD commands.

Fusion95

Fusion95 has a character-based interface as the only management tool. There is no client based management tool. Fusion95 allows a maximum of 1,000 SMB client printers, which is enough for most users. When print jobs are submitted to a Fusion95 server, Windows clients have no control over the queue.

Capabilities

Fusion95 installed in a network provides two methods of network printer usage:

- A PC user can print on any UNIX printer
- A UNIX user can print on any PC printer

A smbprtup program is used to implement SMB printer clients. Data directed to this smbprtup will be sent to a Fusion95-configured SMB print server on the network.

Configuration files reside in the /usr/fusion95/cfg catalog and are named lprt00 to 999. The configuration files handle any required translation of line feed to carriage return/line feed and national characters.

Configuring an SMB Client Printer

To configure the printer client, run the smbprt.sh program and select which printer to configure:

```
/usr/fusion95/smbprt.sh
```

This program can also be started by running the /usr/fusion95/fusion95 menu shell and selecting Printer Client, Printer Configuration.

Figure 10.8 illustrates the main menu of the Fusion95 menu shell.

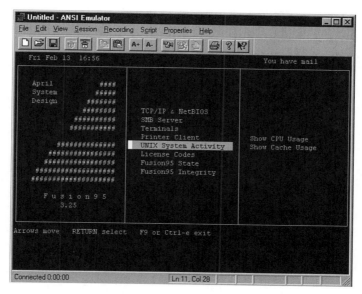

Figure 10.8. *The main menu for the Fusion95 menu shell.*

Tip

When using the menu shell, the arrow key moves up and down the main topics. The submenus appear to the right as each main topic is highlighted. The Enter key will not work at this point. Use the right arrow key to move over to the submenu of choice. Press the Enter key to get the submenu.

The following is a configuration dialog:

```
SMB printer client configuration
=================================
Which printer config file do you want to setup (0-999): 03
Configuration options for SMB printer client '/usr/fusion95/cfg/lprt03.cfg'
```

```
1. Show printer set up
2. Set up printer
3. Remove printer set up
4. Print a test page
5. Choose a different printer client
x. Exit
--> 2
Enter the print server/spooler name:  SERVER1
Printer name on node SERVER1:  HPLASER
Password or * for no password :  *
Username or * for no username :  KEITH
Should insertion of CR before a LF be turned on or off:  on
Should character translation be turned on or off:  off
```

Once the script is completed, the printer is now ready for use. Figure 10.9 shows the Printer Configuration menu displaying a printer.

Figure 10.9. *Displaying a print client setup.*

Three Methods of Printing to SMB Clients

Fusion95 provides three methods for printing to a PC printer from UNIX:

- Named pipe devices

- lp spooler system

- Using the `smbprtup` command

Named Pipes

At installation, Fusion95 will automatically set up eight named pipes:
/dev/lprt00 through /dev/lprt07. These pipes will direct print output via the
smbprtup printer client program to their respective network printers. For applications that need to send data directly to a device rather than through a print
spooler, this will provide a way to get data to a networked printer.

Author's Note

*I have used the same technique for software that did not print to a spool-
er. In such instances, network printers cannot normally be used. A simple
named pipe can be created and used by a shell script that checks the size
of the data in the pipe. When data is found, the shell sends the data to
the print spooler responsible for getting it delivered to a remote printer.*

*In the following script, a named pipe, /dev/oki, is the device for the print-
er. The* cat *command copies the data in the pipe to the file /u/oki.prt. The
size of oki.prt is tested using the -s operator. If the file /u/oki.prt has a
non-zero file size, then the file, oki.prt, is printed to the printer named
oki.*

```
(while true
do
cat >/u/oki.prt < /dev/oki
if [ -s /u/oki.prt ]
then
    lp -d oki /u/oki.prt
fi
sleep 1
done )
```

lp Spooler System

The standard UNIX lp command can be used to send print requests to SMB
clients. At installation, eight printers are set up, lprt00 through lprt07. These
will direct output through the smbprtup program. These printers are administered as normal UNIX printers.

The smbprtup Command

The third option is to use the smbprtup command directly:

```
cat filename ¦ smbprtup -c/usr/fusion95/cfg/lprt03
```

The -c option instructs smbprtup to use the lprt03 configuration file for printing. Running the smbprtup command with the -h option will provide a help listing of other options.

Sharing UNIX Printers

By comparison to printing to Windows printers, sharing a UNIX printer is rather simple. From the Fusion95 menu shell, highlight SMB Server. Press the right arrow key next to Configure Server. Press Enter to get into the Configure Server options. Select <f> for Printer Server Parameters. The options now include View, Add, Delete or Change shared printer resources. Select Add, which is the <b> option, not the <a> option.

The first data required is the resource short name. There are no help options here. This prompt is asking for the UNIX printer name. Later it is redisplayed for confirmation as a network short name. The other prompts are for a password to protect the resource, a spooler program, and print options. Figure 10.10 illustrates this process at the point of entering the options to the print process.

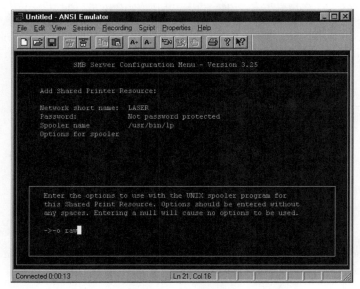

Figure 10.10. *Creating a shared UNIX printer for Windows clients.*

SAMBA

SAMBA, the freeware SMB software for UNIX, provides bi-directional printing capabilities for UNIX and NT. SAMBA will pass UNIX print requests to an SMB printer out on the network and will accept incoming requests to a UNIX system and put them in the print queue for a UNIX printer.

There is no graphical interface for configuring SAMBA. Everything is set up through configuration files. Because SAMBA is a freeware product ported to many UNIX variants, you should be sure to look for information on the specific UNIX version you will use. The information here is based on SAMBA on Caldera Linux.

Printing to UNIX from Windows

The simplest setup is printing to a UNIX printer from Windows. The first step is to create a UNIX printer. In this example, I created a printer named linux_printer using the Caldera Looking Glass graphical window administration tools.

When printing to a UNIX printer, the Windows print queue management is able to manage the documents sent to UNIX, if they haven't been printed. The SAMBA software uses the LPR/LPR capabilities of the LPQ command to retrieve information.

The printcap File

The /etc/printcap file is essential to SAMBA printing. printcap is a printer capability file that provides information on where the printer is located and other information. The printcap file is used by all UNIX BSD printing. The printcap from my Linux machine follows; it was created automatically when I created the printer:

```
# /etc/printcap
#
# Please don't edit this file directly unless you know what you are doing!
# Be warned that the control-panel printtool requires a very strict format!
# Look at the printcap(5) man page for more info.
#
# This file can be edited with the printtool in the control-panel.
##PRINTTOOL## LOCAL epson 300x300 letter {}
linux_printer:\
    :sd=/var/spool/lpd/lp:\
    :mx#0:\
    :lp=/dev/lp0:\
    :if=/var/spool/lpd/lp/filter:
```

While all this looks a bit unreadable, it is patterned after the /etc/termcap file, an old standby in UNIX systems. The sd term defines the spool directory. The mx defines the maximum size of the print job, with 0 meaning unlimited. The lp term is the printer device, in this case parallel port 0 or LPT1 in DOS terms. The if term defines the input filter command.

If the printer were on a remote computer configured for LPR printing, the lines would look like this:

```
:sd=/var/spool/lpd/lp:\
:lp=\
:rm=server1\
:rp=main:
```

The rp is the remote printer name, and rm is the remote server name. There are other options that may appear; check the man pages on printcap for more information.

The smb.conf File

Next you need to update the information in the main SAMBA configuration file, /etc/smb.conf. The following listing is an extract of the file that came with Linux after a few modifications:

```
workgroup = HENRIKSEN
;
[global]
    printing = bsd
    printcap name = /etc/printcap
    load printers = yes
    guest account = guests
;
[linux_pr]
    comment = Genes Printer
    valid users = gene
    path = /home/gene
    printer = linux_printer
    public = no
    writable = no
    printable = yes
```

SAMBA was written for many versions of UNIX, so it is necessary to define the printing type: Berkeley UNIX (bsd), System V UNIX (sysv), Hewlett-Packard HP-UX (hp), or IBM UNIX (aix). The printcap name does not have to be /etc/printcap. If it is, don't change it. If it isn't, define it here. There is nothing worse that cleaning up behind an administrator who customized the system beyond all recognition.

For the printer, linux_pr, the only valid user is gene. The path for spool data is /home/gene. The local printer name is linux_printer. It is printable by gene. It is not a public printer.

Once the smb.conf file configuration has been established, the printer is available for browsing and printer creation from a Windows system. For more information on smb.conf, see the man pages.

Printing to Windows from UNIX

Printing from UNIX to a Windows NT printer is a bit more complex. You cannot go to the UNIX print utility to create a remote SAMBA printer. You also cannot fake it by creating a remote printer and giving it an NT system name. The Linux print tool will create an entry in the /etc/printcap for an LPR print to an LPD service. Instead, you must create an entry in the printcap file yourself.

> **Warning**
>
> *You may have noticed the warnings in the printcap lines that you should not edit the printcap directly unless you know what you are doing. Read and heed!*

If you have questions about SAMBA printing, find the smbprint or smbprint.sysv scripts and read them closely. On Caldera Linux, these were located in /usr/doc/samba1.9.16p7-1/examples/printing. The numbers following samba in the path name will change with different versions. The printcap entry illustrates the necessary lines to create a printer entry for a remote Windows printer:

```
hplaser:\
  :cm=HP Laser on Gandalf:\
  :sd=/var/spool/lpd/hplaser:\
  :if=/usr/local/etc/smbprint:\
  :mx=0:\
  :lp=/dev/null:
```

You can see a few new entries here. The second line identifies the printer.

> **Tip**
>
> *The input filter is the smbprint script located in the /usr/local/etc directory. You may have to copy it there or change the path. It is not put there by default in Linux.*

The configuration file is the last part to create. Looking back at what you have done, the only place you defined the server was in a comment. You need to create a file in the spool directory for the printer: /var/spool/lpd/hplaser/.config.

The .config file needs the following format:

```
server=Gandalf
service=HPLaser
password="password"
```

In the smbprint script is a line to create a debugging file:

```
logfile=/tmp/smb-print.log
```

This may be required during testing. To reduce log file growth once the system is tested, change the logfile destination to /**dev**/**null**. /dev/null is the *bit bucket*, the bottomless pit that devours unwanted output.

One final note on printing to a Windows client: For automatic CR/LF translation when printing, uncomment the following line:

```
#        echo translate
```

It was not as easy as printing to UNIX, but it can be done.

Part IV

Application Integration

Chapter 11

Application Brokers

- **Access to Heterogeneous Server Applications Through a Single Login**
  Learn how to access applications from a mixed server environment through a single login.

- **SCO's Tarantella**
  Tarantella is the only entry in the Application Broker field. Find out how application brokers can be configured and used.

- **Case Study: Tarantella in a Multinational Organization**
  This case study investigates an implementation of Tarantella in Europe.

Access to Heterogeneous Server Applications Through a Single Login

The basic function of an Application Broker is to deliver immediate access to any type of application from any client, without the need for any client installation. The broker does this by occupying a middle-tier position—independent of applications and clients.

This quote from SCO's "An Application Broker for Network Computing" white paper is the focus of Application Brokers.

An *Application Broker* serves as a central publisher of applications from many servers of different types. The applications may be X Windows, Microsoft Windows, character-based UNIX, or mainframe. Windows NT servers must be multi-user, such as Network Computing Device's WinCenter.

With the variety of clients and applications in organizations today, IS management must be careful to ensure that each client will work with all the applications required. The problem becomes one of client system management leading to a high cost of operation.

For an organization with Windows NT, UNIX, AS400, and mainframe servers, client systems need to have the necessary terminal emulators to deal with various applications. For an organization with Macintosh, Windows 3.*x*, Windows 95, Personal Digital Assistants (PDAs), handheld PCs with Windows CE, and Windows 98 due on the market in mid 1998, the range of client software to handle applications is astounding.

Total Cost of Ownership

Most everyone in the information management business has heard the *TCO* acronym by now. *Total Cost of Ownership* is a major concern for organizations with desktop PCs. Anyone with experience in the Windows environment has probably known the frustration of installing a new application only to find out that the behavior of a seemingly unrelated piece of software has now changed. Loading "fat" clients with new software does not reduce the TCO—it increases it. Problems occurring at this level result in lost time for the worker and all those who attempt to help.

In a large organization, roll-out of new applications or emulator software that lets you use server applications is time consuming and expensive. When you get your copy depends on where you are in the list to be installed. With an Application Broker, the software that lets you use the application is installed on the server and is instantly available to all authorized users.

A few years back, client/server was touted as the solution to network and productivity problems. Client/server has lost its luster as costs have climbed beyond the perceived benefits. The next step was a call to rewrite the applications in Java. The rewriting of code in Java is a sideways step that leaves the "fat" client still bloated with software. What is needed is a simpler method of getting applications to the user.

The Application Broker's Role

The solution to the problem is the Application Broker. The application broker sits between the client and server. The server sends displays to the broker, which is masquerading as the client. The broker transforms the displayed information into Java `display` and `input` statements and forwards it to the real client. The Java-based client software displays the information without knowledge of the broker's role.

Loading a complete Java environment could lead to a fat client. In this case, the display is done by Java applets downloaded from the broker and weighing in at about 200K, a rather small package. The Java applets work with a Java enabled browser. How does all of this work? Let's look at the only entry into the new category of Application Broker.

SCO's Tarantella

Santa Cruz Operation (SCO) has been a vendor of UNIX and XENIX since the early 1980s. As network computing became more prevalent, SCO has added new software. Advanced File and Print Server allows SCO UNIX to participate in an NT domain. VisionFS allows SCO UNIX to look like a Windows server.

Based on its background with the Vision family of Windows to UNIX connectivity software, SCO created Tarantella. Tarantella is a totally new concept for network computing.

Tarantella currently runs on Solaris and UnixWare. Future releases will include NT and SCO OpenServer.

Warning

The Solaris version runs only on SPARC Solaris. Attempting to install on the Intel version of Solaris will result in an error when the ttaserv program is executed.

Installation is from a CD. The install options include *Base* and *Full*. The Full install includes additional fonts. If the Base package is installed, additional fonts may be added later. Once installed, a Netscape Web server must be created and configured for Tarantella sessions in the Netscape Administration window. Configuration consists of pointing the Netscape Server to the appropriate Tarantella directories for content and programs. After this is done, clients should be able to connect to servername/tarantella. Tarantella is started at bootup by the script /etc/rc3.d/S90Tarantella

Tip

If installing on UnixWare, the default temporary directory is /var/tmp. This may be too small. To overcome this problem, unmount /var/tmp:

```
umount /var/tmp
```

or set the TMPDIR *environment variable to a filesystem with more space:*

```
TMPDIR=/home;export TMPDIR
```

Tarantella is the middle tier of a three-level network model. Figure 11.1 illustrates Tarantella's position in the network. The servers Mainframe, NT and UNIX sit on the application server third tier. Tarantella occupies the middle. Clients are the first tier. In the case of Tarantella, the client can be Windows PCs, palmtop computers running Windows CE or other Java client, Java network computers (NCs), or kiosks with a Java-enabled Web browser. Ultimately, even a cell phone with Web capability can be a client. All that is required for a client is a Java-enabled browser.

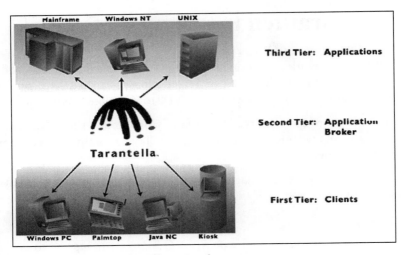

Figure 11.1. *The three-tier Tarantella network.*

The Tarantella approach to network computing is decidedly thin client. Tarantella's server-based middle tier is masquerading as the client that the server applications expect to be dealing with. The Tarantella broker sends down thin, transient Java `display` and `input` statements to let the user see and use the application. This works for all types of applications: legacy mainframe and UNIX applications and client/server NT applications.

Ways do exist to download new applications to clients from servers automatically, but that still leaves a fat client.

Terminal emulators can talk directly to legacy applications without Tarantella. Again, this requires installation at the client, another fat client solution.

Tarantella isn't just a large terminal emulator for server-based applications. Tarantella's architecture provides additional benefits.

Suspend and Resume

One useful feature is *Suspend and Resume*, best illustrated with an example. A technician gets a call from a customer about a problem. In order to research the problems, he logs into the Tarantella server, and starts a database search for the problem. Without waiting for the response, he suspends his login and drives to the client site. At the client site, with a handheld unit, he logs back into the server and resumes the session to pick up the answer. Without this feature of Tarantella, the technician would at best need to wait by his own machine and at worst be unable to get to the application at all when he reached the client site.

Suspend and Resume also works when a client computer freezes or crashes. For example, a worker is running a critical application on a server through Tarantella from her desktop computer. Part of the way through the process, smoke begins to pour from her computer. She is smart enough not to call the computer room and ask if the server is burning because she is getting smoke from a networked computer. She turns off her computer and logs in from her cell phone or from another worker's PC, and the display now reflects the current state of the process. In the fat client model, she would need to contact IS, and potentially wait days for her PC to be "cloned" before being able to use the application, let alone restarting the process.

How could this happen? How can a user leave one workstation, log into another workstation, perhaps of a different type, and continue with the process? As long as the client has a Java-enabled browser, Tarantella sends display updates to all clients, so switching client platforms has no effect on the display.

Adaptive Internet Protocol

Another feature of Tarantella is *Adaptive Internet Protocol (AIP)*. The operative word here is *adaptive*. The primary function of AIP is to adapt to the client device capabilities, network bandwidth, and network load. AIP makes no assumptions about the network, instead it intelligently figures out the network capabilities.

If the client has little or no local processing power or the network traffic is high, AIP sends data in small efficient packets with the broker doing much of the work. If the client is capable and network traffic is low, AIP pushes more data and work onto the client. This adaptation is accomplished by monitoring the client and the network, and adjusting the internal model on which AIP bases its decisions.

AIP checks the round trip time to determine the speed of the connection and the amount of data that can be transmitted in a period of time to determine the available capacity. Based on calculations, it determines the appropriate compression to compensate for the network speed.

For each type of application that can be run on the client, there exists a Protocol Engine and a Display Engine. For instance, when running an X application on the client, the X Protocol Engine on the Tarantella server would intercept the data stream from the X application. After massaging the information, the Protocol Engine sends data to the X Display Engine that was downloaded to the client.

A number of optimizations can be made by the Protocol Engine before passing the data onto the network:

- X sends display commands one at a time while Java works better drawing a single image. The Protocol Engine merges the commands one by one into an image before sending it.

- If the application sends a display request that will not execute or will execute slowly in Java, the Protocol Engine converts the request to a more efficient form.

- The Protocol Engine can request the Display Engine cache data such as fonts, files and pixmaps that are used frequently to reduce network traffic.

- Finally, the Protocol Engine will compress data based on the network load. Compression uses CPU cycle, but may be a good trade off if the network is near capacity. Because the Protocol Engine and Display Engine work as a pair, the variable compression is understood at both ends.

> **Tip**
>
> *The administrator can enable or disable parts of AIP on a per-application basis through the Tarantella Control Center.*

The User Interface (Webtop)

Tarantella gathers all the objects (applications, documents, and so on) associated with a user and dynamically creates a Web page representing this information. The user interface is called a *webtop*. Figure 11.2 pictures the user's webtop after logging on to the Tarantella server. Available objects are located on the left side of the webtop; the right side is for application space.

Once users log in, they begin executing applications. Applications may be windowed or full screen. Figure 11.3 shows a user's view of the webtop in use.

Programs from UNIX, NT, and the Web can be executed by the user from the webtop. The user does not need to know the source of the application or select the correct terminal emulator. The mechanism for performing this sleight of hand is that the icons are all Java applets, built with the Tarantella Control Center. When the user clicks on these applets, a request is sent to the application broker to invoke the application or view the document. Through Tarantella's server engines, session engines and data-store engines, the whole process is transparent to the user. Applications are delivered to the user from NT or from UNIX without regard to the source of the application as far as the client is concerned.

Figure 11.2. *The user's webtop interface after logging on to the Tarantella server.*

Microsoft Word document   Tarantella home page

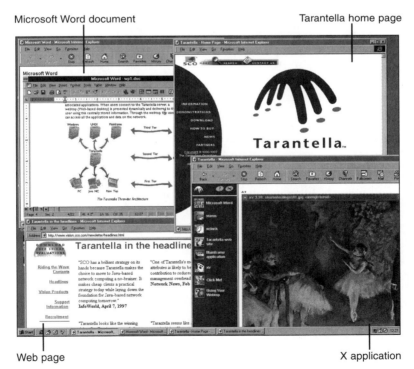

Web page   X application

Figure 11.3. *Viewing applications in the user's webtop interface.*

Administration and Management

Administration of Tarantella begins with designing the distribution of applications to users. The process is a top-down, organizational structure method:

1. Starting at the top, select the applications that will be available to all organizational users, perhaps a UNIX corporate application and Microsoft Word. Assign those applications to the top level.

2. Move down the organizational structure to the desired point. Figure 11.4 illustrates the starting point for the process. Create new departments as required. Assign users to departments. Select applications and assign to department levels or to users.

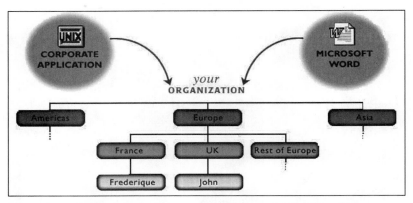

Figure 11.4. *Assigning two applications to the top organizational level.*

After you assign applications, users can log into the system. Tarantella works up the tree assembling a list of objects the user is authorized to access and builds the user's webtop. Adding a new person to the accounting department automatically provides that person a webtop with access to all objects authorized for the department. Remember, the webtop definition is 100% held on the server and can be changed and instantly implemented by the administrator.

3. To publish a new application, select the level(s) that will need access to the application and add it to the tree. Instantly, all authorized users have access.

Figure 11.5 illustrates the Control Center Assistant for Tarantella. From the Control Center, an administrator can view which users are logged on, what applications a user is running, customize a user's webtop, and add a new user. Users can be moved from one department to another by marking the users, selecting the new department, and choosing to move them there.

In addition, from the Control Center an administrator can add a new application or document to Tarantella's vocabulary. Administrators can set server settings to control login and diagnostic settings, authentication mechanisms, and file locations.

> **TIP**
>
> *Tarantella uses the UNIX password file or NIS to provide a user list for administration and login authentication. Passwords are transmitted over the network in an encoded form.*

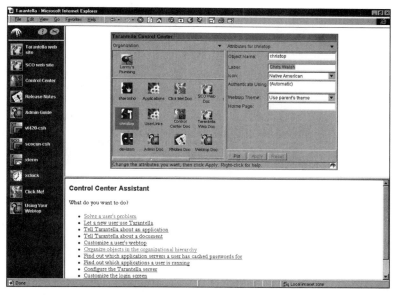

Figure 11.5. *The Control Center—the management console for Tarantella.*

Implementation

With each paradigm shift in computing, a large cost has been associated with implementation. In contrast, Tarantella works with the existing environment. There is no need to rewrite applications for Java, or abandon mainframe or client/server and move to a new method. Tarantella takes existing applications and publishes them to the users without them having to be concerned with the proper terminal emulator or X server.

In a smaller environment, Tarantella can reside on the same server as the applications or on a separate server.

Case Study: Tarantella in a Multinational Organization

"Saved from an IT nightmare" are the words of one of the first implementers of SCO's Tarantella. After carrying out a live-environment pilot project with Tarantella, this corporation found the cost of implementation was cut by 40% and network performance improved by 90%. This was achieved by applying the Tarantella solution to an existing client/server system comprised of Windows PCs connected via a WAN to an Oracle database on the UNIX server.

With more than 1000 offices in 66 countries, the corporation works on a large volume and slim profit margin, driving the requirement for a low-cost structure. The problem it faced was deploying business-critical applications to users at remote sites fast and inexpensively. With no IT expertise at remote sites, a skilled person had to visit each site to install the software necessary to access the Oracle database. Once installed, performance over the WAN was poor and affected users' productivity.

Initially, an attempt was made to improve the application to produce optimized WAN performance. After optimization, performance was still too poor. They considered four options for improvement:

- Run database servers at remote sites on Novell servers. Database management would have proved difficult, and Novell was not an Oracle-preferred server.

- Put UNIX servers in remote offices to overcome the database management issues. This failed on two counts: lack of UNIX expertise in the remote sites and additional investment in hardware and software.

- Install Citrix WinFrame, the multi-user version of NT. A trial of this solution solved some of the performance issues, but still required local installation of the WinFrame client software at the remote sites.

- Install Tarantella. A trial was set up using a beta version of Tarantella. Excellent productivity resulted from this option, due to the AIP used by Tarantella that optimizes data flow over the network. Since there is no client component, no additional expertise or support was required at the remote sites.

The organization therefore implemented Tarantella based on not having to provide additional on-site software and hardware. It should be noted that Citrix WinFrame has an average network load of approximately 15 to 20 Kbps for each user, a very low figure compared to client/server computing.

Chapter 12

Telnet and Application Enhancement

- **X Windows**
  This chapter discusses two X Windows systems and points out some of the differences and advantages of each. For basic X window usage, either system will do. Look at the differences to determine which one you need.

- **Telnet**
  Many telnet versions are available. This chapter highlights two and introduces you to application face lifting and application rejuvenation. Revamping those UNIX character-based applications may not be as difficult as you thought.

X Windows

The X Windows standard has been around for several years. UNIX workstations use X Windows for graphical work, and most UNIX systems have an administration tool that uses an X Windows interface.

The Microsoft or Macintosh Windows user is accustomed to a single window for each application that may create input windows or dialog boxes; however, these windows are not independent of the main application. Microsoft Windows can display windows only on the host that is running the application.

In the X Windows system, the application has a display output stream that may be directed to any X server. The application and display may be on the same machine or on two different machines. For instance, an X application can be started on a UNIX host with the display pointed to a Windows computer running a PC X server. Some X applications can write to many screens at once.

When Windows NT workstations need to run an X Windows application from a UNIX server, the application will not run in the Windows mode. The workstations must have an X Windows software package called a *PC X Server*. An *X Windows server* is the system on which the display is running. The X Windows server is not necessarily the system on which the application is stored.

Two major vendors of PC X servers are SCO and Hummingbird. SCO's XVision and Hummingbird's Exceed illustrate the major points of PC X servers. The following sections provide you with the features available.

XVision Eclipse

One member of SCO's Vision family is *XVision*. XVision runs on Windows NT or Windows 95 and displays an X session from a UNIX system. SCO provides a number of controls that can be configured on the Windows NT host relating to the display and the particular UNIX client.

Remember that the terms *host* and *client* seem reversed on X Windows. Figure 12.1 illustrates a login on an X Windows "server" (a Windows NT system) into a UNIX computer.

Figure 12.1. *An SCO login X Windows display on Windows NT. Note that there is no Windows frame at the top.*

Single Window X Login

XVision can be configured to allow the a single X window, as opposed to the normal multiple window scenario. For example, the SCO login shown in Figure 12.1 will only run in a single window display. If multiple windows are used, the administration programs can be executed from an X window.

To configure the XVision for a single window, use the properties sheet. Figure 12.2 illustrates the properties for XVision. To start the properties sheet, right-click on the **xv** icon on the right side of the taskbar while XVision is running.

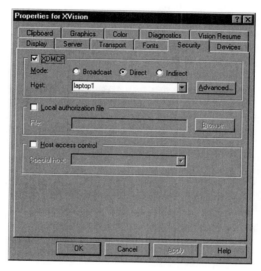

Figure 12.2. *Properties for XVision.*

The instructions for setting up a single window follow:

1. In the Display tab, select Single Window.

2. Click the Advanced tab next to Single Window.

3. To eliminate the Windows title bar, click Full Screen Mode.

4. Click the Security tab.

5. Select XDMCP.

6. To ensure that only one UNIX X system will respond, select Direct and enter the desired host's name.

7. Click Advanced and select One Session.

When a session starts, XVision contacts the desired UNIX system and starts the login. The advantage of the method described here is to provide a SCO login that looks exactly like the SCO graphical console login. In the next sequence of events, you will set up a multiple windows environment to get to the SCO administration program, scoadmin.

Using the UNIX Application Wizard

XVision provides a UNIX Application Wizard in the New UNIX Program setup selection of the Start menu. You will use the Application Wizard to configure an X program to be run on demand. When starting a UNIX application, users feel like they're starting a Windows application.

The first question from the wizard is the UNIX host name. Figure 12.3 illustrates this step in the wizard.

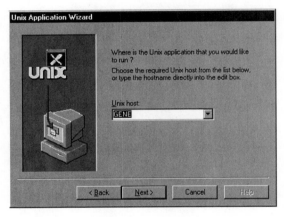

Figure 12.3. *The first step in the UNIX Application Wizard—entering the host name.*

The next item is the program to be run, with a browse capability on the remote UNIX host. The browser uses the UNIX Neighborhood application, which resembles the Microsoft Network Neighborhood. Figure 12.4 illustrates browsing for the scoadmin command to be run on the X server.

Third, select the type of application: X application. Other choices are used for applying this method to starting character applications. Provide a name for the program. The name appears in the Start menu under UNIX Programs when the wizard is completed.

The result is an icon that appears in the Start menu that the user double-clicks to start the X application. This icon can be turned into a Windows 95 Shortcut icon by dragging and dropping from Windows Explorer onto the Windows desktop.

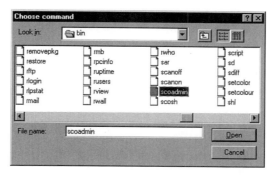

Figure 12.4. *Browsing a UNIX machine to find the X application.*

Fourth, you are offered the opportunity to try the program before committing to an entry in the menu.

Author's Note

I highly recommend running the program before completing the wizard. Picking the wrong UNIX program can be easily corrected here. Sometimes it may take some experimentation to find the correct program to run. For instance, on Solaris you may choose admintool for user administration and cmdtool for a command line. On Caldera Linux, the administrative GUI is lg, an acronym for Looking Glass. I found that for Caldera Linux, it worked best when I started an xterm-color program and then manually started lg from the xterm. For SCO OpenServer 5, the admin program is scoadmin.

Zones

You only have a limited amount of space on your monitor screen. Whether you suffer through a 14 inch, have a 15, 17, or 19 inch, or have the good fortune to have a 21 inch monitor, you still will never have enough viewing area. Through the XVision Zone capability, you can assign programs to zones and switch from zone to zone to see the running applications.

Zones are groupings of programs that can be switched onto the screen as desired without closing and reopening or iconifying them. Zones allow assigning an application to separate window overlays.

Figure 12.5 illustrates the Zone Control window, listing the applications in the four default zones. In this instance, Zone 1 is active. Notice the zonebar at the top of the screen. Zone 1 contains the Sun Admintool showing the users' information. Zones 2 and 3 are in virtual display space ready to be front-and-center with a click of the mouse. The normal Windows NT backdrop and icons appear in all zones. Only the active programs assigned to zones can be switched in and out on demand.

Windows programs can also be part of a zone; you are not limited to X programs in zones. Notice in Figure 12.5 that the Zone 1 list includes Collage Capture, a Windows program running on the NT computer from which the screen capture was made.

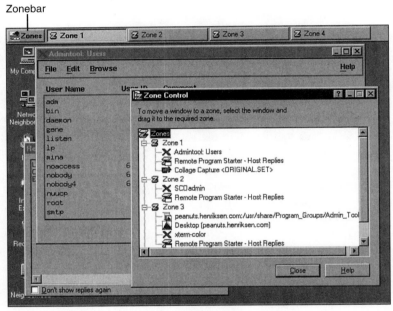

Figure 12.5. *Using zones to control the display on the console screen.*

Zones can be renamed with useful names. The system administrator sitting at an NT computer could have a different zone for each remote UNIX computer being managed. In addition, Windows programs can be clustered into zones for ease of access.

A single program can have a display in multiple zones. This useful feature allows viewing output of an application in multiple zones. Closing the application in one zone closes all displays for that application. Multiple displays in multiple zones do not equate to multiple copies of an application, only one copy with multiple displays. Running programs can be dragged into different zones.

Starting a second copy of a program in another zone will bring forth the Zone Police, a warning that the application is running elsewhere. The Zone Police can be disabled in the Zone Properties' General tab.

Suspend and Resume

An advanced feature is *suspend and resume*. This feature appears in SCO's Tarantella product and allows an X session to be suspended from the PC and resumed later. Vision Resume requires a UNIX proxy server to maintain the application's status after a suspend operation. The user can then resume the session from the same or another X Windows server. The advantage of suspend and resume to the user is twofold:

- A running application can be suspended and resumed later without having to restart the application.

- A system crash on the user's PC does not terminate the UNIX application and the user can reboot and resume the application.

For more information on SCO's Tarantella product, see Chapter 11, "Application Brokers."

Tips and Security

With any software product, tips and detailed information are important time-savers. XVision includes a 17-chapter, 7-appendix manual. One appendix is devoted to tips on using XVision with various UNIX variants.

Security is always a concern in administering a network. Passwords are necessary for access control. Multiple passwords become confusing and hinder users in performing their work. Thus, passwords need to be protected from compromise.

With XVision, passwords can be handled in three ways:

- The user may be prompted for a password whenever an object is accessed.

- A password may be stored with an object, in which case the stored password is used upon first access and, if not valid, the user is prompted for a password.

- Passwords may be stored in a password list file.

Hummingbird Exceed

Hummingbird, the makers of the NFS products previously covered, have two versions of X: regular Exceed and Exceed 3D. The 3D version supports OpenGL. The Exceed product comes with a supply of manuals whose total thickness is about the same as the XVision manual. The Exceed manuals include *Getting Started*, *Basic User's Guide*, *Application Guide*, and a *Windows 95/NT Applications Guide*.

As with most computer techies, I load first and read documents later. Getting Exceed up and running was very easy. There is a nice menu that includes much more than you would expect from an X application: FTP, LPR, LPD, telnet, host explorer (telnet), and print explorer to name a few.

Exceed's Setup Wizard

My favorite tool for starting new programs is always the wizard, and Exceed has one. Client Wizard walks you through your first connection with ease. In the first wizard dialog box, I provided the host name and operating system. The list of operating systems included: BSD, DEC UNIX, DEC VMS, HP UNIX, IBM AIX, SCO, SGI IRIX, Sun, and a generic UNIX entry. The Next button brings up the dialog box shown in Figure 12.6.

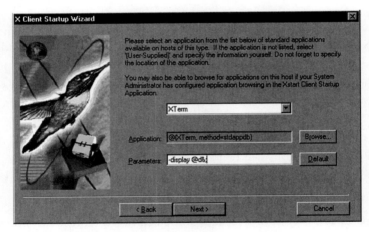

Figure 12.6. *Client Wizard for Hummingbird.*

It is not unusual to have problems connecting the X terminal session for the first time. In Figure 12.7, a Run button appears to test the application. If the expected results do not appear, check the Display Host Replies box and click the Run button again. In this instance, I received an error box stating the login is incorrect because the password entered is wrong. You may find that some UNIX systems will not allow a root login from other than the console without some additional configuration.

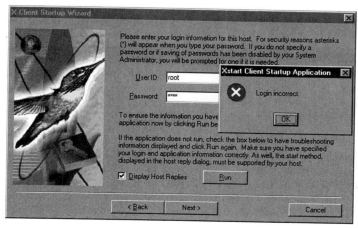

Figure 12.7. An error message resulting from an invalid login attempt.

Fortunately, the Back button allows you to return to the previous setup window and change information. I found that SCO OpenServer did not want to run with the default Parameter line. Once I removed the trailing semi-colon, it worked properly. The Display Host Replies check box indicates the source of the problem with a message stating the host had found an unexpected semi-colon.

Once the Xterm login was working, I completed the wizard. One of the options is to create a shortcut. Dragging the shortcut to the desktop gave me quick access. Logging into the UNIX computer now requires a double click on the icon. From the resultant Xterm, I can enter any program I want to run and am authorized to run. Figure 12.8 shows the results of creating Xterms to run on two UNIX systems. The Solaris Admintool, SCOAdmin and an X calculator are all running.

Exceed 3D

Exceed 3D provides all the tools for developing local OpenGL X applications in three dimensions. Demos of three-dimensional local X applications are included.

Figure 12.9 shows the Insect demo.

Tip

In using 3D, if two different color systems are used simultaneously, the colors may not display correctly. Upon executing a 3D demo, my entire screen turned the same color as the background of the demo until I clicked in the background.

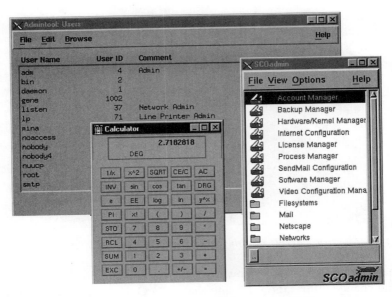

Figure 12.8. *Three graphical X windows running from two UNIX systems.*

Figure 12.9. *A 3D demo from Exceed 3D.*

The dynamic link libraries included with the 3D product can be used in new product development, and no royalties need to be paid to Hummingbird for their use. Using Motif libraries will result in royalties due to the OSF.

Telnet

Telnet is an old TCP/IP application for terminal emulation over a network. There are many telnet versions available, including the one that comes with Windows NT.

Several telnet versions include the ability to customize the display from a monochrome, Courier 10-pitch display to more eye-pleasing displays. These changes are referred to as *face lifting* and *application rejuvenation.*

The standard-issue telnet client from Windows NT is shown in Figure 12.10. Options are scarce; if you do not like VT-52 or VT-100/ANSI, then you need to look elsewhere. Why they chose to emulate long extinct hardware, I don't know. This telnet is a bare minimum. It may fill your needs if you have no requirement for additional features.

Figure 12.10. *The Microsoft Windows NT telnet client.*

SCO includes *Termlite,* a telnet client, with Advanced File and Print Server and VisionFS which is bundled free with OpenServer 5.0.4 and above. Termlite is a likable implementation of SCO Ansi console emulation. While TermLite is a good telnet client for SCO systems, you may want a product with more capabilities. Termlite does not provide many extensions. As the name implies, it is a lightweight terminal emulator.

Many other companies offer telnet as a part of their communications package. Century Software has sold TinyTerm for many years. Other vendors are listed in Appendix A.

Multiview 2000

JSB Corporation has produced terminal software for several years. Its original Multiview product was designed to provide multiple character-based windows on dumb terminals and offer the capability to run multiple programs on a single terminal in full-screen mode, switching between programs with keystroke combinations such as Esc+F1.

Multiview 2000 is a heavyweight terminal emulator. Multiview has a script recorder to log scripts for playback. Perhaps its prime reason for consideration is application face lifting. This process uses properties of character based displays converted into more distinctive form.

Figures 12.11 and 12.12 illustrate a before and after sequence of a character application. Display attributes such as underline, bold, blink, and reverse can be mapped to colors and raised boxes.

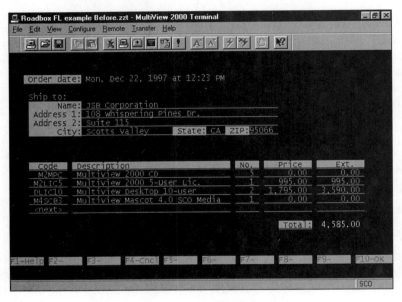

Figure 12.11. *A character-based display before face lifting.*

Author's Note

While reading the book, you might find that these figures may not appear as dramatic improvements in black and white. It looks much better in color than on the printed page. This holds true for the figures shown previously and ones that appear later in this chapter.

TermVision

TermVision, a heavy-duty telnet client, is one member of SCO's Vision family and has additional configuration capabilities. When any of the Vision family products are installed, an analysis is run on the network to verify the products can run without errors.

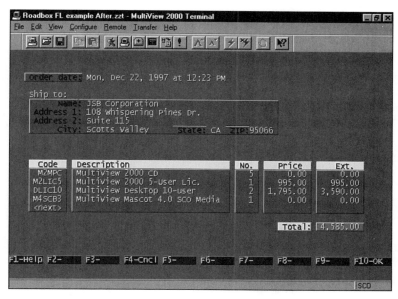

Figure 12.12. *A character-based display after face lifting.*

One utility included with TermVision (and XVision) is the *Host Explorer*, the UNIX equivalent of Windows Explorer. Files may be copied from one UNIX computer to another or between UNIX and Windows NT hosts. Files on a remote host can be deleted, created, or copied, and data transfer may be performed in text, binary, or automatic mode. Entire directories may be transferred via drag and drop.

TermVision has more than one stage of face lifting. The final stage is called *application rejuvenation*. Starting with a character-based display on TermVision, seen in Figure 12.13, it moves through two stages of improvements.

TermVision has 12 tabs in the Emulator Configuration dialog box as shown in Figure 12.14. Features can be defined and saved in a configuration file to be used whenever the terminal emulator is used. The Attributes tab is shown with options to set colors and box style attributes.

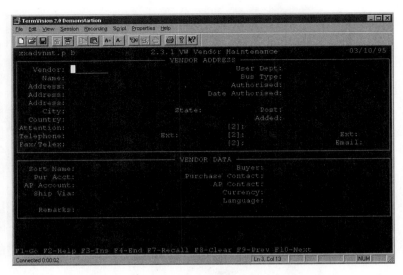

Figure 12.13. *An unadorned character-based application displayed on TermVision.*

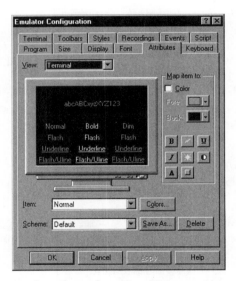

Figure 12.14. *Setting visual attributes for a TermVision session.*

Applying various attributes can turn a very dull display into a colorful one that begins to resemble a graphical output. Figure 12.15 is a rework of Figure 12.13 using only the Attributes settings in TermVision.

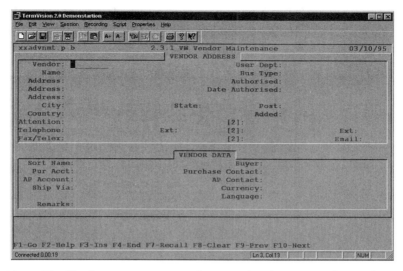

Figure 12.15. *The Vendor Maintenance application after dressing up the attributes.*

Application Rejuvenation using OLE

The object-oriented design of TermVision accommodates OLE Automation. OLE objects "expose" certain "methods" or functions to other programs. *OLE (Object Linking and Embedding)* is a means for transferring data between programs.

Another program can be written to call these exposed methods, effectively driving the object. In the case of the emulator modules in TermVision, methods have been exposed which enable the development of a front-ending program. The front-end sits between the user and the legacy application so that the user sees a true Windows interface while the legacy application remains unchanged. The benefits of running a tried-and-trusted application on a reliable UNIX server are retained, while the user benefits from an easy and potentially more efficient user interface.

More importantly, the development cost of a front end is far less than that of re-engineering a legacy application. The system can even be enhanced by including some logic in the front end to verify data entry or perform other functions. Development tools supporting OLE Automation include Microsoft Visual Basic 4, Visual C++, and Borland Delphi.

The advantage of OLE and visual programming is to provide a true graphical front end for the user interface. A small Visual Basic program can be developed for each application that hides the terminal emulator and effectively "scrapes" the data from the emulator and displays it according to the rules of visual programming. Figure 12.16 shows the Vendor Maintenance application after a Visual Basic program has been written to front-end it.

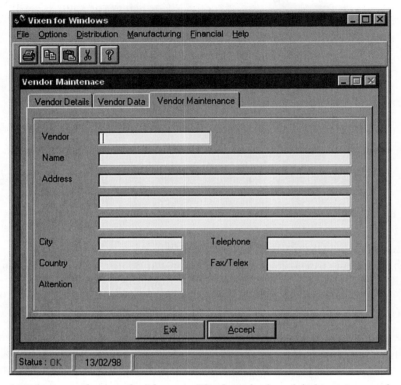

Figure 12.16. *A new front end with a true Windows look and feel running on the PC while the original application is untouched.*

Based on conversations with the SCO programmers who developed TermVision, once the core Visual Basic program has been written, it takes five to ten minutes per screen to write the new interface. Approximately 10 to 12 Visual Basic commands are involved in the process.

Author's Note

While writing this section, I spoke with David Wight, a trainer and contact person for the Vision services division of SCO in Leeds, England. I convinced him more people would be likely to use this technology if they knew where to start, and if they had a sample program to use. He offered to make available the source code for the Visual Basic demo program they use for application rejuvenation along with some help information for programmers.

If you are interested in implementing application rejuvenation, download information from SCO's Web site and email David for source code. The consultancy email address alias for his office is `cipros@sco.com`.

TermVision is available on the following systems:

- SCO OpenServer Release 3 and 5
- SCO UnixWare 2+
- Sun SPARC SunOS 4.1.3+
- Sun SPARC Solaris 2.4+
- IBM RS/6000 AIX 3.2.5+
- Hewlett-Packard HP-UX 9 and 10
- Digital UNIX 2.0+
- DG AViiON DG/UX 5.4
- Siemens Nixdorf SINIX 5.42
- Sequent DYNIX/ptx 2.1.6
- ICL DRS 6000 DRS/NX 6 and 7
- Generic Intel System V Release 4

Case Study: Dibb, Lupton, and Broomhead Legal Office

Forget the stereotypical solicitor's office with a well-used typewriter and towering piles of briefs; here's a solicitor's practice that is definitely in the 1990s.

With its headquarters in Sheffield, England, Dibb, Lupton, and Broomhead also has offices in five other major cities. Its IT strategy puts PCs running Microsoft Windows 95 on every employee's desk and links them to a Digital Alpha 4100 UNIX server via a fiber-optic backbone.

Over 1,500 staff members have access to the Arista accounting and client billing information running on the UNIX server. The Arista application is supplied by Axia, and at the heart of this system is an Informix database engine. Each PC user views the practice's key application via SCO TermVision, a 32-bit terminal emulator that gives seamless access to the UNIX application from the Windows 95 interface.

Dibb, Lupton, and Broomhead's IT strategy is to move away from Novell to Microsoft's Windows 95 and Windows NT at the workgroup level and carry on using UNIX for mission-critical applications. Although currently using Novell servers for file sharing, it plans to replace these with Windows NT servers.

SCO TermVision was chosen because this 32-bit terminal emulator is tightly integrated with the Windows 95 interface and can multi-task with other Windows applications running on the PC. It operates concurrent licensing so even though it is installed on 1500 PCs, Dibb, Lupton, and Broomhead only pays for the number of licenses required. It was also impressed by the ease with which it was configured into the Windows environment. When a new setup is installed on a PC, TermVision installs it alongside the other Windows applications in one easy step.

Part V

Windows NT and UNIX Tools

Chapter 13

Microsoft Tools: The Resource Kit and TechNet

- **The "Other Half" of Windows NT**
  There are two resource tools available from Microsoft: the Resource Kit and TechNet.

- **The Resource Kit**
  The Resource Kit is a collection of books and utility programs that provide far more information on NT than the management utilities and documentation provided with the operating system. In this chapter, you look at some of the many utilities.

- **TechNet**
  Need the latest Service Pack? Looking for a way to resolve a problem? Cannot locate information on an error message? TechNet is a collection of CDs with a wealth of information. Don't operate NT without it.

The "Other Half" of Windows NT

Windows NT is not truly complete without two add-ons: the Resource Kit and TechNet. Actually, there are two Resource Kits, and TechNet is a monthly subscription. Tech support calls to Microsoft on NT cost about $200 per incident. For the price of two or three tech support calls, you can have a wealth of Microsoft's own database available.

As an instructor, I often find students who own but have never looked at the Resource Kit. The utilities available in the Resource Kits make them indispensable to the administrator of Windows NT.

The Resource Kit

Two major versions of the Windows NT operating system are sold: Server and Workstation. There are also two resource kits: Server and Workstation. Both kits currently list for $69.95, although they can be found discounted in many places.

Workstation Versus Server

According to the Resource Kit cover materials, the Workstation version is "The official companion to Microsoft Windows NT Workstation version 4.0." The Server version's cover states "For Windows NT Server Version 4.0." The subject matter of the two volumes is very different. If you are running NT Server, you need both kits.

An example of the differences in the two kits can be found in a comparison of the CDs provided with each. The Workstation version contains 348 MB versus 292 MB of files for Server. Workstation still includes information on the MIPS and PowerPC versions on NT. Looking at individual subjects, the Workstation kit contains 18 objects on the Registry compared to 14 in the Server kit. The Server kit is more loaded toward the desktop tools (15 objects plus the PowerToys folder) compared to Workstation's 10 and no PowerToys.

The Workstation kit covers information about the installation and management of the individual computer. The section on Optimization including performance monitoring, and detecting bottlenecks in the CPU, disk, cache, and memory, plus a rundown of all the performance monitoring tools, is not repeated in the Server kit. There is a single reference in the Server kit to Performance Monitor and that is a reference to the Workstation kit.

The Workstation kit also covers reliability and recovery in depth, as well as over 100 pages on the management of the Registry. The Workstation kit consists of a single book of 1350 pages and a CD. The Server kit is a boxed set of 3 books and a CD. The books are *Resource Guide, Internet Guide,* and *Networking Guide.*

The Server kit is oriented toward networking, although the Workstation kit covers the subject briefly. The Server books also cover reliability and recovery with emphasis on fault tolerant disk configurations and recovery from hardware failure.

The Server kit includes information on domain planning and network security. As could be expected, the *Networking Guide* includes detailed information on WINS, DHCP, DNS, browsing, and other features of NT networking.

In addition to the Workstation and Server kits, two supplements have been published for the Server kit. Supplement One is a 300-page book primarily concerned with Internet Information Server. A section on Directory Service Manager for NetWare is included, along with several pages of corrections for the Server and Workstation kits. Supplement Two is an updated CD-ROM.

Warning

There are two errors I have found in the Networking Guide and confirmed with Microsoft. Pages 551 and 566 both refer to the hosts file as being case-sensitive. This is incorrect. The hosts file was case-sensitive in Version 3.1, the original NT version, but was fixed in 3.5. The documentation has not kept up. The course materials for the TCP/IP class correctly state that the file is not case-sensitive, but show an example implying case sensitivity. The hosts file is used for IP address-to-hostname resolution.

In the upcoming sections, you look at specific utilities in the resource kits and discuss their usage. When troubleshooting NT, your best bet is often a resource kit utility.

The Diagnostics Menu

Many of the utilities for program status and performance monitoring were demonstrated in Chapter 1. From the Start menu, choose Programs, Resource Kit 4.0. Figure 13.1 illustrates the options available.

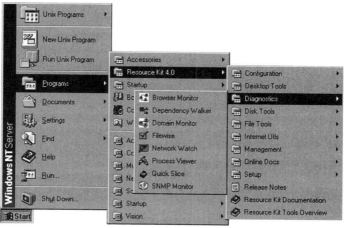

Figure 13.1. *The NT Server Resource Kit menu.*

The Browser Monitor

In the Diagnostics menu of the Server Resource Kit is the *Browser Monitor*. Browsing is a major factor in Microsoft networking and it is sometimes important to determine the computers that are serving as browsers. The Browse service allows computers and resources to appear in Network Neighborhood. The Browser Monitor displays browse information as shown in Figure 13.2. This tool is not available in the Workstation kit. Highlighting a browser with a single click provides a list of the domains and servers listed on the browser.

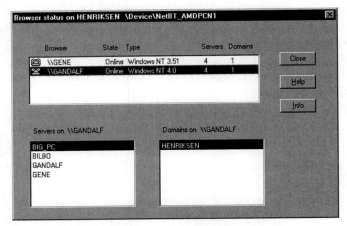

Figure 13.2. *The Browser status on domain HENRIKSEN.*

Double-clicking a browser will provide additional information as shown in Figure 13.3. For tracking down browse problems, the information provided here is crucial. From the window, you learn the services available from the browser. In the information listed in the Browser Info window, you can learn that GANDALF is serving as a backup domain controller and has Server, Workstation, Print Queue Server, and Dial In Server services. GANDALF is an NT computer serving as a backup browser.

Further details are available on types of packets received, such as election packets and server announcements. Elections are held to determine the Master Browser on a subnet. Since the statistics collection began, there were 90 server announcements. From this information, a network administrator can put together a picture of the browser traffic load on the domain. For more detailed information on browsing, see Chapter 3, "Microsoft TCP/IP on Windows NT 4.0."

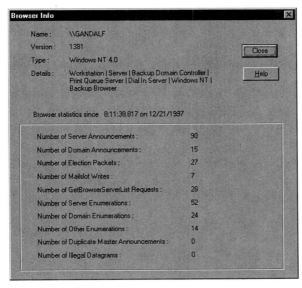

Figure 13.3. *The Browser Info window of the Browser Monitor.*

The Domain Monitor

With a large Microsoft network consisting of multiple domains, a tool is needed to check the status of primary domain controllers and the trusted domain link status. The *Domain Monitor*, located in the Diagnostics menu of the Server Resource Kit, does the job. This is another tool not available in the Workstation kit.

Figure 13.4 illustrates the Domain Monitor. The primary problem associated with trust relationships is the loss of a trust connection. Without the Domain Monitor, you have no direct way of checking the connection.

Net Watch

For an administrator's view of what is shared and who is using it, Net Watch is more informative than Server Manager. As you know, Server Manager displays the sharename, number of users, pathname of the share, and any attached users. While Server Manager displays the entire pathname for long paths, the display box may not be wide enough to allow a full display. It is not possible to scroll the display to the end of the path.

Net Watch provides additional information: the computer name, date and time of the connection, and the number of files open. Net Watch options include showing open files, hidden shares, and shares in use. Net Watch also permits management of shares including disconnecting users and creating new shares.

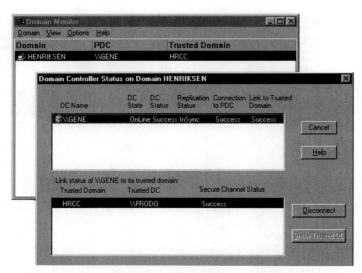

Figure 13.4. *The Domain Monitor reports on PDCs and trust relationships.*

Figure 13.5 illustrates the shares and connections on GANDALF and part of BILBO. From the connection option, computers may be added to and removed from the displayed information. The default display is for the local computer. The Workstation version does not include this utility. To access Net Watch, choose Resource Kit, Diagnostics (where it is referred to as Network Watch).

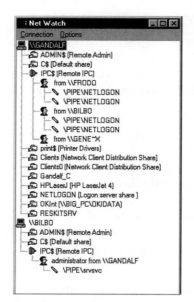

Figure 13.5. *Net Watch displays shares and connections.*

FileWise

Also in the Diagnostics menu is *FileWise*. The purpose of FileWise is to collect data about files and folders and save them to a tab-delimited file. The data can then be loaded into a database for comparisons.

An administrator could use this tool to track sizes of database files to get an estimate of growth rate. Another use is to track critical system files to make sure that no one has replaced legitimate files with hacked versions for their own purposes, such as compromising system security. A database of file information could be used as the basis for a program to compare the data to the current condition of the files.

Figure 13.6 illustrates the user interface to FileWise. FileWise is included in both kits.

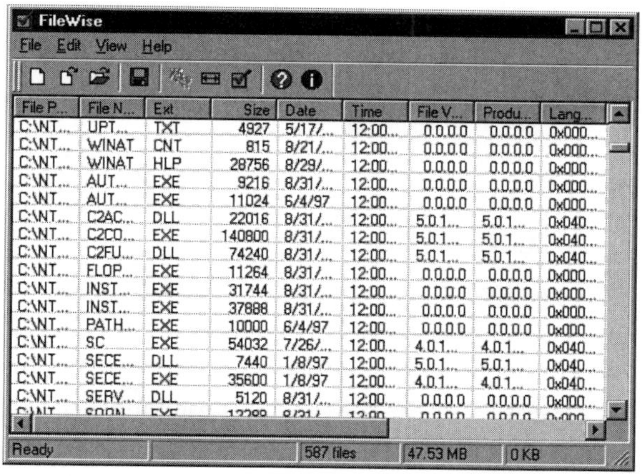

Figure 13.6. *The FileWise file data utility.*

Text Viewer

You can find the TextViewer, as shown in Figure 13.7, in the File Tools menu of the Resource Kit. TextViewer allows you to view various text files. In Figure 13.7, the file is an .HTM file for the Internet Information Server root WWW display. The drop-down text box above the text allows filtering files to be displayed in the left side of the window. TextViewer is available in both kits.

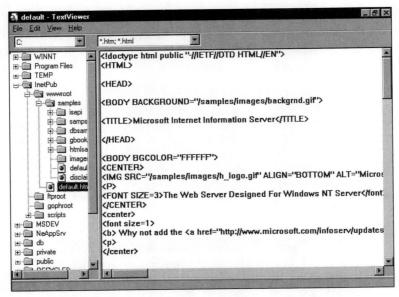

Figure 13.7. *TextViewer enables you to view text files of different types.*

IP Configuration

The IPCONFIG command line utility is included in the base operating system and is a command line only version. The Resource Kit version can be run by choosing Resource Kit, Internet Utls.

The Resource Kit version can be run from the command line, WNTIPCFG, and is similar to the Windows 95 version, WINIPCFG.EXE. If the Resource Kit installation directory is part of your path, type in the name at the command prompt or change the directory to the Resource Kit directory and execute it.

The initial display shows only the upper half; full detail is obtained when you click the More button (see Figure 13.8). The IP Configuration utility is included in both resource kits.

When using DHCP for assignment of IP addresses, the buttons across the bottom allow release and renewal of IP addresses for the selected adapter or all adapters. The equivalent command line syntax would be IPCONFIG /RELEASE and IPCONFIG /RENEW. This is useful when an option value has changed on the DHCP scope that is supplying the IP addresses to this machine. Releasing the current information and forcing a renewal of the IP lease will result in all new options being acquired by a computer.

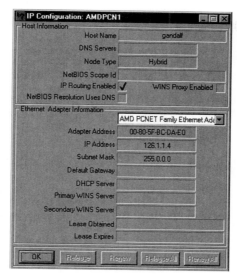

Figure 13.8. *IP Configuration provides a graphical replacement of the* IPCONFIG *command line.*

Shutdown Workstation

With UNIX computers, it is no problem to shut down or reboot another computer. You remotely log in and issue a shutdown command. The Shutdown Workstation option in the Resource Kit Management menu will shut down a remote computer, given the correct user authority. A text message of up to 127 characters can be sent to the targeted computer with an option to kill applications without saving data and an option to reboot.

Figure 13.9 demonstrates how to select a remote computer for shutdown. The Abort option enables you to retrieve an errant shutdown command if the affected user screams too loudly.

Figure 13.10 illustrates the message on the receiving end of a shutdown command. When the command is run with no parameters, the graphical interface appears. It is possible to run the command from a command line to shut down a remote computer. The command line capability provides batch file possibilities for rebooting computers.

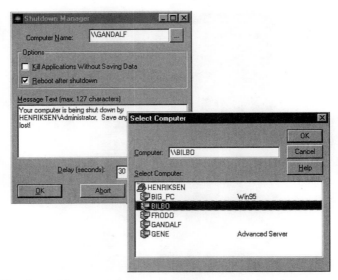

Figure 13.9. *Shutdown Manager selecting a remote computer to reboot.*

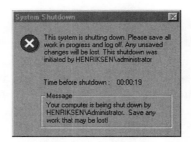

Figure 13.10. *Your system is shutting down.*

The Setup Manager

Windows NT provides unattended install functionality. When rolling out a number of NT computers that will have identical setups, files can be prepared to answer questions in the setup dialog box. These automated installation files are called *answer files*. With an answer file, an installation can be automated and run with

```
Winnt /u:answer_file
```

Answer files have several sections that specify settings for the network, modem, user data, SCSI drivers, and other settings. For full details, see the NT Workstation Resource Kit Appendix A, "Answer Files and UDFs."

Rather than hand build these files, the Windows NT Setup Manager, available in the Setup menu item of the Server Resource Kit, provides an easy way to configure the files (see Figure 13.11). The following is a sample of the output.

```
[Unattended]
OemPreinstall = no
ConfirmHardware = no
NtUpgrade = no
Win31Upgrade = no
TargetPath = *
OverwriteOemFilesOnUpgrade = no

[Display]
ConfigureAtLogon = 0
BitsPerPel = 8
XResolution = 640
YResolution = 480
VRefresh = 60
AutoConfirm = 1

[Network]
DetectAdapters = ""
InstallProtocols = ProtocolsSection
InstallServices = ServicesSection

[ProtocolsSection]
TC = TCParamSection

[TCParamSection]

[ServicesSection]
RAS = RASParamSection
SNMP = SNMPParamSection
```

More Command-Line Tools

In addition to the tools illustrated so far in this chapter, there are many more command-line tools. The Server Resource Kit box lists 190 tools and utilities, 30 more than in the Workstation kit. Command-line tools, such as ADDUSERS, allow batch file addition of new users or migration of user lists.

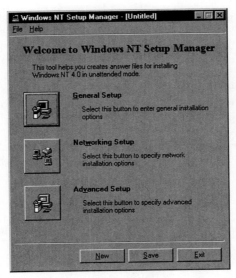

Figure 13.11. *The Setup Manager for unattended installs.*

ADDUSERS was designed to allow users to be added, listed, and removed from a domain by a batchfile or command line. When setting up a domain, user's names and global and local groups can be placed in a file and added as a batch.

When changing domain models, it is necessary to add users to a new domain and delete them from the old domain. ADDUSERS can simply the process:

1. Create a list of all users in the domain:

   ```
   ADDUSERS /D domainlist.txt
   ```

2. Edit the file and delete users and groups that will not be transferred.

3. Copy the file to the new domain PDC. Add the users and groups to the domain with the C option to ADDUSERS.

   ```
   ADDUSERS /C domainlist.txt
   ```

4. On the original domain, use the user list to remove the users from the old domain.

   ```
   ADDUSER /E domainlist.txt
   ```

Other handy utilities include those detailed in the following list:

Utility	Description
SHOWGRPS	Shows groups of which the current user is a member
SHOWMBRS grp	Shows members of a group
USRTOGRP	Adds users to a group
CACLS	Displays or modifies access control lists
PERMS	Displays users permissions to file or directories
FIXACLS	Resets ACLS for system directories to install settings (NTFS only)
TELNET daemon	Allows command line access to NT
PERL	Scripting language
REXX	Scripting language
POSIX	UNIX utilities for POSIX subsystem

Online documentation contains the same manuals that are included with the kit. The usual Index and Find options come with the documentation. A separate menu Help option provides help with the tools and utilities. Many of the utilities have help files on disk, so as you browse the installation directory the help file often appears with the executable. Double-click the help file and check it out before you execute. The icon for a help file is a book with a question mark on the cover.

TechNet

With the overall complexity of Windows NT, purchasing TechNet should be a requirement for any organization that supports Windows NT. If the printed documents of the resource kits are not required, the online documentation in TechNet should suffice. I buy the resource kits because I haven't found a CD reader as handy as a book. I carry my TechNet set with me in the field because, at some customer sites, I cannot get access to the Web to research problems.

Author's Note

Unlike the resource kits, TechNet is not a book with a CD you buy once. TechNet is a subscription to a service. Updated CDs are delivered monthly. The service, as of February 1998, costs $329/year for a single user copy and $759/year for an unlimited license version.

If you work with Windows NT and other products in the BackOffice suite, you need TechNet. With support calls costing approximately $200 per incident, it doesn't take many calls to equal or exceed the amount of TechNet. The original shipment includes a ring binder with 10 or more CDs including service packs for all business products (NT, Office, Windows 95, BackOffice), Resource Kit utilities for the business products, and client and server utilities. Each issue of TechNet includes more than 4,000 updated articles with the support information database.

Figure 13.12 illustrates the home page of TechNet. The left-hand side of the window is a document list. The right-hand side displays text documents.

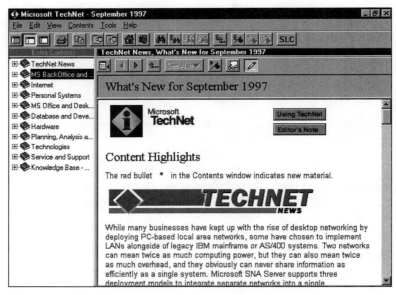

Figure 13.12. *The TechNet home page.*

Figure 13.13 illustrates the information (referred to as *books*) available for Windows NT Server. MS Windows NT Workstation is highlighted at the bottom left, but not expanded. Note the documents include the NT Server Manuals, Hardware Compatibility List, resource kits, and additional information.

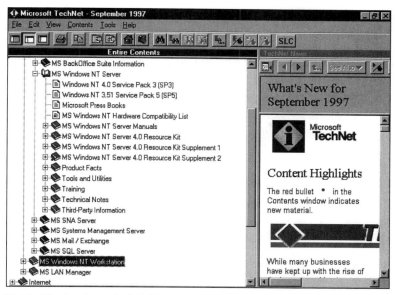

Figure 13.13. *The books included for NT Server in TechNet.*

Searching Within TechNet

One strength of any help information is the ability to search. In Figure 13.14, a search is being performed for DHCP near WINS. By default, near means within eight words. Options allow reducing the scope of the search, and to search only the title or the title and text.

Figure 13.14. *Starting a TechNet search.*

The results of the search are displayed in Figure 13.15. Two hundred and eight articles were found with DHCP within eight words of WINS. Note the second column indicates the book in which the article was located. If too many articles are displayed, a new query may be initiated within the last topics found.

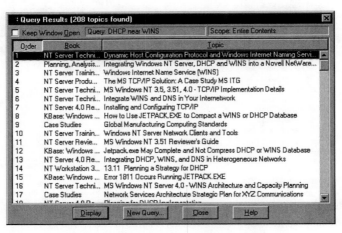

Figure 13.15. *Query results from a search for DHCP near WINS.*

## Chapter 14

UNIX Tools for Windows NT

- **MKS Toolkit**
  UNIX tools for UNIX administrators run on NT. Over 200 UNIX tools exist for the NT environment.

- **Case Study: V-Systems, Inc.**
  The MKS toolkit is used to allow one set of source code and development tools for UNIX and NT environments.

- **OpenNT**
  OpenNT is a replacement for the NT POSIX subsystem that has been accepted as a UNIX replacement by the U.S. Air Force.

- **Case Study: Appgen Business Software**
  Porting UNIX applications to NT is expensive. Run UNIX applications on NT instead.

MKS Toolkit

When UNIX administrators work on Windows NT, one of the first problems they face is the lack of command-line tools. The early versions of Windows NT had no scripting language other than the limited DOS batch language that is barren of the features UNIX administrators expect. The UNIX guru will also miss the commands that many non-UNIX people point out as the reason they consider UNIX arcane and cryptic. UNIX administrators and programmers have come to rely heavily on the feature-rich UNIX commands: grep, find, sed, vi, awk, and the shells such as Korn shell (ksh).

Fear not, UNIX administrators—the Mortice Kern Systems Toolkit, a.k.a. the *MKS Toolkit*, will save the day. The product literature advertises over 210 UNIX and Windows utilities. A handful of these utilities are discussed in the following sections.

vi

Feel like you can't venture into the world of Windows without vi? Figure 14.1 shows the MKS vi for Windows. Under the Options menu is control of Color, Buffer Size, Window Size, and the old familiar settings of Shift Width, Show Match, Beautify, Auto Indent, List, Number and so on. Just like vi on UNIX, but with a prettier face., vi for Windows still has all the power of UNIX vi.

> **Author's Note**
>
> *Those readers who are not familiar with vi may need to be reminded that vi is short for visual. Unlike several of my students' comments, it is not an acronym for virtually impossible.*

In Figure 14.1, I executed the statement in the lower box (the ex command area) on a list of file names. A nice feature is the drop-down box for commands executed in the bottom box.

> **Warning**
>
> *With the Windows backslash as a separator, you run into a problem because vi considers the backslash to be a metacharacter that removes special meaning from the following character. Without doubling the backslashes, the right side of the statement would read* e:BACKUP& *rather than* e:\BACKUP\<filename>.

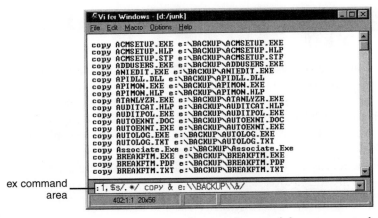

Figure 14.1. *A Windows vi session showing the use of the ex command area.*

grep

As a programmer, I found grep to be an indispensable tool. To be able to search text files for strings eases the search requirements of the programmer trying to find where a variable or database name appears in thousands of lines of code involving multiple files in subdirectories. The UNIX grep is limited in its ability to span multiple levels of subdirectories unless the user writes a script to enable traversing the file structure.

MKS has provided UltraGrep allowing descent into the lower regions of subdirectory structures. The Descend Directories options allow no descending—always descend—and a limit to the number of levels. Figure 14.2 illustrates the UltraGrep screen. The UNIX grep -v option is present in the Display Lines Not Matching Pattern check box. The grep -i option is present in the Ignore Case check box.

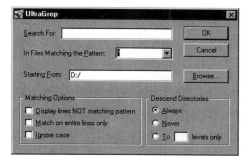

Figure 14.2. *UltraGrep can search for strings through multiple directory levels.*

If you do not care for the Windows method of displaying disk space, MKS has provided Display Free Space with a format like the UNIX df command. In Figure 14.3, the Complete Information option was selected as well as reporting in 1K blocks. Note that it also reports on connected shares, in this case \\Big_pc\UNIX_NT_BOOK.

Filesystem	Blocks	Used	Available	Capacity	Mounted on
C:/	16064	9728	6336	61%	C:
D:/	610438	441626	168812	73%	D:
E:/	104170	98304	5866	95%	E:
\\Big_pc\UNIX_NT_BOOK	1023824	522896	500928	52%	F:

Figure 14.3. *Display Free Space,* df, *reports on local and remote disks.*

Korn Shell Interface

Windows NT provides a command-line interface that is not an MS-DOS session, according to Microsoft. If not, why is the icon an MS-DOS symbol? The NT command line, whether DOS or not, is bereft of sophisticated programming and command-line capabilities. Instead, MKS provides a Korn Shell (sh) interface into NT.

Figure 14.4 illustrates the Korn Shell interface. One nice advantage for the UNIX administrator is the presence of the UNIX commands in ksh. The ls and lc commands work nicely while dir/w returns an error. The df command works properly, providing a character display of the data seen in Figure 14.3. In addition, sh provides the usual UNIX Korn Shell capabilities, such as command history and command-line editing.

The shell can be initiated by choosing Start, Programs, MKS Toolkit or from the Run option by entering **sh**. The shell can be used as a batch or interactive interface.

The UNIX commands do a good job of getting NT information. For instance an ls -l listing of a file may show the owner as Administrator and the group as <domainname>\DomainUsers.

```
MKS Korn Shell - C:/                                                    _ □ X
[C:/] df -P
Filesystem              512-blocks        Used  Available  Capacity Mounted on
C:/                        2037216     1057952     979264       52% C:
\\Cx47021-a\UNIX_NT        3684672      702528    2982144       20% E:
\\Cx47021-a\CX_D           3684672      702528    2982144       20% X:
\\Cx47021-a\CX_C           4120064     2505856    1614208       61% Y:
[C:/] lc
Directories:
COLLWIN           Excel            FOUND.000        NTRESKIT         PowerPoint
Program Files     TEMP             WINNT            WPDOCS           Word
collage           data             etc              examples         guide
mksnt             pipeplus         progdocs

Files:
23UNI04.PCX       23UNIX7.PCX      5955A-1.EXE      AUTOEXEC.BAT     CONFIG.SYS
F1PICTUR.EXE      Old Word Documents.lnk            environ.ksh      explore.bmp
pagefile.sys      profile.ksh      saver.zip        scousr.bmp       sh_histo
srvmgr.bmp        unattend.txt     users.txt        usrmgr.bmp

Read-Only+System Files:
boot.ini
[C:/] grep -i sos boot.ini
multi(0)disk(0)rdisk(0)partition(2)\WINNT="Windows NT Server Version 4.00 [VG
Aode]" /basevideo /sos
[C:/]
```

Figure 14.4. *The MKS Korn Shell illustrating the use of* df, lc, *and* grep. *Note that the normal backslash on the grep fails, while the UNIX style slash works correctly.*

The MKS Korn Shell moves on beyond the normal UNIX shell capabilities. With the Korn Shell, your UNIX ksh scripts are now portable to Windows NT, saving an enormous amount of work learning a new batch language and figuring how to make shell functions that work correctly in the NT environment. Be sure to test your scripts to make sure they work properly and that you are not accessing UNIX direcotries or files that may not reside on NT.

Windows NT is a graphical environment and MKS Korn Shell allows modifications to the shell script to create graphical input and output that Windows users expect. In place of a UNIX error message like:

```
echo "error from listit.ksh, File $1 is not found"
```

replace the text in the script with:

```
msgbox -fqb ok -i information listit.ksh "File $1 is not found"
```

In place of a character display error message, a message appears as shown in Figure 14.5. In addition to an error box, the `dlg` command allows display Windows dialog boxes for Yes/No/Cancel, the familiar Select a File dialog box that allows you to select your choice of drive and file types, and to navigate the file structure. Toolbars can also be added. In essence, the `msgbox` function provides a quick way to get your shell scripts running on NT and enhance them with a graphical interface.

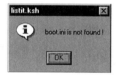

Figure 14.5. *Display graphical information and input boxes from MKS Korn Shell.*

The MKS Toolkit provides online help as well as a 200-page user guide and a 700-page reference guide. These guides should be considered an essential part of the UNIX guru's toolkit for working with NT.

Case Study: V-Systems, Inc.

V-Systems, Inc (VSI) is a software development company that produces VSI-Fax, a UNIX fax software package. VSI ported the VSI-Fax software to Windows NT and wanted to reduce the amount of work involved in maintaining source code. With nine UNIX platforms and NT to support, they needed a common platform for maintaining the code.

VSI switched from the SCCS (UNIX Source Code Control System) to MKS Source Integrity which runs on UNIX and NT. Rob Juergens of VSI said that it would have been impossible to do the port to NT and track the changes without the MKS tools. The same makefiles compile VSI-Fax whether on NT or UNIX.

The MKS Toolkit allows the same scripts that do much of the faxing to be ported to NT. Customized scripts on UNIX can be carried to NT without rewriting, saving customers time and money.

VSI is sold on the MKS Toolkit as a method of maintaining code on both UNIX and Windows NT.

OpenNT

Softway Systems' OpenNT allows UNIX software to run on Windows NT. The UNIX programs run in a UNIX subsystem without the requirement to reboot the system in UNIX. The U.S. Government has approved OpenNT and NT to be purchased as a replacement for UNIX in an Air Force contract that includes up to 37,000 workstations. The Air Force wanted NT, but their critical applications ran on UNIX. While most of the systems purchased under the contract will most likely be UNIX, some systems will run on the DEC Alpha chip with NT and OpenNT.

OpenNT essentially replaces the Windows NT POSIX subsystem. *POSIX* is the Portable Operating System Interface for Computing Environments standard. By running as a Windows NT subsystem directly accessing the kernel, performance is not adversely affected as it would be if OpenNT were an interpreter. Bypassing the Win32 interface allows UNIX programs to be recompiled on OpenNT and run without modifications.

OpenNT is useful for running UNIX and NT applications on the same computer. The reason for running both may be that UNIX and NT applications are required and one computer is desired as a means of porting software.

Softway Systems also has a product that combines Intergraph's NFS to provide UNIX with NFS capability on NT. This allows for OpenNT-to-UNIX file and print sharing via NFS. The combined product comes in a Workstation, Server and Gateway version.

OpenNT provides more than 200 UNIX and X11R5 (X Windows) commands and utilities. The three main UNIX shells— Bourne, Korn, and C shell— are included. UNIX scripting languages include awk, perl, sed, and Tcl/Tk. True UNIX file links and filename case sensitivity are part of OpenNT.

OpenNT includes a telnet daemon that installs as an NT service. Using the telnet daemon allows clients to log in to telnet sessions on the NT host, making NT multiuser. Figure 14.6 illustrates logging in as administrator to an NT system running OpenNT. Note the normal UNIX display from the ls command.

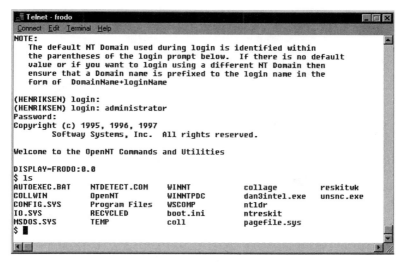

Figure 14.6. *A telnet session hosted by Open NT from another NT system.*

OpenNT is fully integrated with the NT security model and the NT file systems. X Windows support is provided through OpenNT's OpenNTIF, a Motif X11 window manager.

Tape drives on NT are referenced as /dev/tape*x* and /dev/ntape*x*, where *x* is 0 through 9. The /dev/ntape entry is a no-rewind version of the same device as /dev/tape. For true OpenNT-to-UNIX readability, the user will have to modify tape block sizes in the tape backup commands.

Figure 14.7 pictures an ls -l (long listing) of the files in an NT folder. Note that the Windows NT system files are listed as pipes; the first character of the line starts with the letter p. For this reason, you cannot use more or cat to see the boot.ini file, for instance. Boot.ini may be displayed with the type command at a DOS prompt, but more or cat will sit waiting for data in the pipe.

OpenNT is a real POSIX subsystem for Windows NT that may be useful for organizations needing to run UNIX and NT on the same platform simultaneously. It will also be useful for administrators needing to telnet into an NT system that requires access to a UNIX command line. It may be used as in the U.S. Air Force or Appgen examples (see the following case study) to run UNIX applications on NT as another UNIX operating system.

Figure 14.7. *An* ls -l *listing in OpenNT.*

Case Study: Appgen Business Software

Appgen Business Software is a leading UNIX software developer with over 30,000 installations on a variety of UNIX systems. Experiencing a demand for an NT version of Appgen software, the company explored different methods of providing NT support: using a porting tool for NT, rewriting for the Win32 interface, or using OpenNT.

After evaluating the first two methods, Appgen tried OpenNT. Because OpenNT supports UNIX system APIs, Appgen is able to maintain a single source code base for the applications for both UNIX and NT. OpenNT did not require retraining of the support or training staff.

Because OpenNT maintains support for character-based terminals, users would not have to go through expensive hardware upgrades.

The porting effort required three weeks to complete the conversion of all database management software, development tools and business applications. Appgen expects to continue selling a significant amount of UNIX software, but thinks NT will become a major part of its business.

Part **VI**

Appendixes

Appendix **A**

Products for File and Print Sharing

UNIX Products for File and Print Sharing

Advanced File and Print Server

Santa Cruz Operation
400 Encinal St.
P.O. Box 1900
Santa Cruz, CA 95061-1900
http://www.sco.com/products/Datasheets/afps.htm

Advanced File and Print Server is the SCO implementation of AT&T's
Advanced Server for UNIX, a port of Microsoft Windows NT remote file and
print services.

Advanced Server for UNIX

AT&T
http://www.att.com/unix_asu

Microsoft Windows NT code is ported to UNIX by AT&T, and is available
from the following UNIX vendors: NCR, Hewlett-Packard, SCO, Siemens-
Nixdorf, ICL, DEC, Bull, Olivetti and Data General.

FacetWin

FacetCorp
4031 West Plano Pkwy.
Plano, TX 75093
1-800-235-9901
http://www.facetwin.com

FacetWin offers file and print sharing plus drag-and-drop file copy over dial-up
connections.

POWERfusion95

April System Design AB
Vretenvagen 2
171 54 Solna
Sweden
http://www.april.se

SMB file and print sharing software for UNIX includes the AniTa terminal emulator.

SAMBA

Available from various sources, the original source for SAMBA is:

http://samba.anu.edu.au/samba/

SAMBA is included with Caldera Linux.

SunLink PC

Sun Microsystems, Inc.
2550 Garcia Ave.
Mountain View, CA 94043
http://www.sun.com/servers/ultra enterprise/sw/totalnet.html

An implementation of TotalNet Advanced Server, SunLink PC allows PC-to-UNIX integration with a heterogeneous Windows network.

TotalNet Advanced Server

Syntax, Inc.
840 South 333rd St.
Federal Way, WA 98003-6343
http://www.syntax.com

TotalNet Advanced Server is an SMB product for Sun Solaris, SGI Irix, Hewlett Packard HP-UX, and IBM AIX.

VisionFS

Santa Cruz Operation
400 Encinal St.
P.O. Box 1900
Santa Cruz, CA 95061-1900
http://www.vision.sco.com/products/visionfs

An SMB server for UNIX, VisionFS acts as an NT member server in a domain. VisionFS is available on SCO UNIX, SCO UnixWare, Hewlett-Packard HP-UX, Sun Solaris, IBM AIX and Digital UNIX.

Windows NT Products for File and Print Sharing

AccessNFS and AccessNFS Gateway

Intergraph Corporation
Huntsville, AL 35894-0001
`http://www.intergraph.com/nfs/default.asp`

Intergraph sells an NFS Client, Server and Gateway product.

Century Term and NFS Software

Century Software
5284 South Commerce Dr., Suite C-134
Salt Lake City, UT 84107
`http://www.censoft.com`

Century sells an NFS Client and Server and a terminal emulator.

Chameleon UNIXLink 97

NetManage, Inc.
10725 North De Anza Blvd.
Cupertino, CA 95014
`http://www.netmanage.com`

Chameleon's product line consists of NFS Client and Server, PC X server, terminal emulation, and TCP/IP utilities.

HyperACCESS

Hilgraeve
Genesis Center
111 Conant Ave., Suite A
Monroe, MI 48161

The official upgrade to the Hyperterminal program supplied with NT.

ICE.TCP

J. River, Inc.
125 N. First St.
Minneapolis, MN 55401
`http://www.jriver.com`

This Windows package includes terminal emulation, bi-directional printing, and file transfer.

MaestroNFS, Maestro NFS Server, MaestroNFS Gateway

Hummingbird Communications Ltd.
1 Sparks Ave.
North York
Ontario, M2H 2W1, Canada
http://www.hummingbird.com

Hummingbird sells both NFS and PC X Windows products for NT.

For free trial downloads:

http://www.hummingbird.com/freestuff.htm

MKS Toolkit

Mortice Kern Systems Inc. (MKS)
185 Columbia St. West
Waterloo, Ontario
Canada N2L 5Z5
http://www.mks.com/solution/tk/

The MKS Toolkit is a collection of more than 200 software tools for the administrator working on NT. Many UNIX tools are included.

OpenNT

Softway Systems, Inc.
185 Berry St., Suite 514
San Francisco, CA 94107
(415) 896-0708 phone
(415) 896-0709 fax
http://www.softway.com

A POSIX subsytem replacement, OpenNT provides a UNIX environment on NT.

For a 30 day evaluation copy:

http://www.opennt.com/info-request/InfoEval.html

Reflection

WRQ, Inc.
1500 Dexter Ave. North
Seattle, WA 98109
http://www.wrq.com

Reflection consists of an NFS suite for Windows NT with additional tools.

Solstice Network Client

Sun Microsystems, Inc.
901 San Antonio Rd.
Palo Alto, CA 94303
http://www.sun.com/solstice/net_client.html

Solstice Network Client is an advanced PC NFS for Windows NT and other Windows clients.

Slink and Slnet

Seattle Lab, Inc.
9606 NE 180th St
Bothell, WA 98011
http://www.seattlelab.com

Slnet is a telnet server for Windows NT. Slink turns NT into a server for serial devices and dumb terminals.

Tun Plus

Esker
222 Kearny, Suite 500
San Francisco, CA 94108
(415) 675-7777
http://www.esker.com

Esker also has offices in Canada and Europe.

Terminal emulation, ODBC, NFS, LPR/LPD printing, NIS resource browser.

Winsock Companion

Network Instruments LLC
Fourth Floor
8800 West Highway Seven
Minneapolis, MN 55426
http://www.netinst.com

Bidirectional LPR/LPD printing, FTP, Terminal emulation, NFS client, Ping, Trace-Route, R-Shell, and more.

Telnet and X Windows

Hummingbird Exceed

Hummingbird Communications Ltd.
1 Sparks Ave.
North York
Ontario, M2H 2W1, Canada
http://www.hummingbird.com

Exceed is an X Windows server for NT and Windows 95.

Multiview 2000

JSB Corporation
108 Whispering Pines Dr., Suite 115
Scotts Valley, CA 95066
http://www.jsb.com

Multiview 2000 is a terminal emulation package that provides facelifting of character-based screens.

SCO TermVision

TermVision is a telnet terminal emulation product that supports facelifting of applications.

SCO XVision

An X Windows server for NT and Windows 95.

Thin Servers

MicroNet Technology, Inc.

MicroNet Technology, Inc.
80 Technology Dr.
Irvine, CA 92618
(714) 453-6100 phone
(714) 453-6101 fax
http://www.micronet.com

Network Appliance

Network Appliance
2770 San Tomas Expressway
Santa Clara, CA 95051
(408) 367.3000 phone
(408) 367.3151 fax
http://www.netapp.com

Network Power & Light

Network Power & Light
Division of Mylex Corp.
34551 Ardenwood Blvd.
Fremont, CA 94555
(510) 608-2222 phone
(510) 608-2555 fax
http://www.npal.com

Application Brokers

Tarantella

Santa Cruz Operation
400 Encinal St.
P.O. Box 1900
Santa Cruz, CA 95061-1900
http://www.sco.com

Tarantella is described in Chapter 11, "Application Brokers."

Appendix **B**

References

Albitz, P. and Liu, C. *DNS and BIND*, Second Edition. Sebastopol, CA: O'Reilly & Associates, 1996.

Frisch, E. *Essential System Administration*, Second Edition. Sebastopol, CA: O'Reilly & Associates, 1995.

Fuller, D. and Shrock, B. *Browsing, WINS, and Active Directory*. Indianapolis, IN: Macmillan Technical Publishing, 1998.

Gilly, D. *UNIX in a Nutshell*, System V Edition. Sebastopol, CA: O'Reilly & Associates, 1992.

Heywood, D. *Networking with Microsoft TCP/IP*. Indianapolis, IN: New Riders, 1996.

Hunt, C. *Networking Personal Computers with TCP/IP*. Sebastopol, CA: O'Reilly & Associates, 1995.

Hunt, C. *TCP/IP Network Administration*, Second Edition. Sebastopol, CA: O'Reilly & Associates, 1997.

Microsoft course materials for Course # 688, TCP/IP

Microsoft NT Server Resource Kit

Microsoft NT Workstation Resource Kit

Minasi, M. *Mastering Windows NT Server 4*, Fifth Edition. Alameda, CA: Sybex, 1997.

Mohr, J. *SCO Companion: The Essential Guide for Users and System Administrators*. Upper Saddle River, NJ: Prentice Hall, 1997.

Pearce, E. *Windows NT in a Nutshell*. Sebastopol, CA: O'Reilly & Associates, 1997.

Stern, H. *Managing NFS and NIS*. Sebastopol, CA: O'Reilly & Associates, 1991.

Winsor, J. *Solaris Advanced System Administrator's Guide*, Second Edition. Indianapolis, IN: Macmillan Technical Publishing, 1998.

Winsor, J. *Solaris System Administration Guide*, Second Edition. Indianapolis, IN: Macmillan Technical Publishing, 1997.

Index

Symbols

\ (backslash), 210, 302
: (colon), 63
, (comma), 81
— (dash), 61
$ (dollar sign), 60
% (percent sign), 60
#(pound sign), 60, 80
-o raw option, 214
/? (slash, question mark), 105
3D demo (Exceed 3D), 274

A

Access Control List (ACL), 24
Access NFS Gateway, 313
accessing UNIX
    /etc/hosts/equiv file, 136-137
    .rhosts file, 137
    trusted hosts or users, 136
Account Information dialog box, 15
Account Locked Out option, 12
account policies (User Manager for
    Domains), 16-17
Account Policy dialog box, 16
accounts
    authorizations, adding, 70
    database, 10
    Global, 15
    Guest, 10
    Local, 15
    locking out, 17
    logins, maximum failed allowed, 17
    profiles, 12-13

of users, locating, 10
UNIX, administering, 176
ACL (Access Control List), 24
actions of permissions, 22
Active box (Master Printer Share), 242
Active Lease window, 102
adapters, 112
    bindings, 118
    multiple, installing, 116
Adapters tab (TCP/IP Properties
    window), 117
Adaptive Internet Protocol (AIP),
    259-260
Add Printer (Network Neighborhood
    window), 231
Add Printer Wizard, 235
Add Users and Groups dialog box, 23
address resolution protocol (ARP), 107
ADDUSERS (command-line tool), 296
administering users, 67-68, 70
administrations
    NetApp Filer, 200
    passwords, 12
    rights, assigning, 9
    user, 10
        Account Information option, 15
        Account Locked Out option, 12
        account profiles, 12-13
        Call Back option, 15
        Dialin permissions, 15-16
        logon hours restrictions, 13-14
        Password Never Expires
            option, 12
        policies, 16-19
        restricting logons to
            workstations, 14
        UNIX, 63-68, 70
        user properties, 11-12

M

T

X-Y-Z